A History of
Communication Technology

Philip A. Loubere

NEW YORK AND LONDON

First published 2021
by Routledge
52 Vanderbilt Avenue, New York, NY 10017
and by Routledge
2 Park Square, Milton Park, Abingdon, Oxon, OX14 4RN
Routledge is an imprint of the Taylor & Francis Group, an informa business

Library of Congress Cataloging-in-Publication Data
Names: Loubere, Philip A., author.
Title: A history of communication technology / Philip A. Loubere.
Description: New York, NY : Routledge, 2021. | Includes bibliographical references and index.
Identifiers: LCCN 2020043141 (print) | LCCN 2020043142 (ebook) | ISBN 9780367211493 (hardback) | ISBN 9780367211509 (paperback) | ISBN 9780429265723 (ebook)
Subjects: LCSH: Communication and technology--History. | Communication--Technological innovations--History. | Telecommunication--History. | Digital communications--History. | Current events--Psych
Classification: LCC P96.T42 L68 2021 (print) | LCC P96.T42 (ebook) | DDC 302.23--dc23
LC record available at https://lccn.loc.gov/2020043141
LC ebook record available at https://lccn.loc.gov/2020043142

ISBN: 978-0-367-21149-3 (hbk)
ISBN: 978-0-367-21150-9 (pbk)
ISBN: 978-0-429-26572-3 (ebk)

Publisher's Note
This book has been prepared from camera-ready copy provided by the author.
Typeset by the author in Libertinus Serif, PT Sans Narrow and Myriad Pro Condensed.
All graphics and illustrations are the work of the author unless otherwise noted.

Visit the companion website: **ComTechHistory.site**

Acknowledgments

This book is the result of a six-year endeavor facilitated by the support of my colleagues, family, and the educational institution that employs me.

Tackling such a broad topic has at times been challenging, and I am grateful for the encouragement and advice of my colleagues Drs. Katherine Foss and Sanjay Asthana, to the James E. Walker Library, which in addition to providing extensive resources also actively supports all faculty engaged in research, writing and publishing, and to Middle Tennessee State University, my workplace for the last twelve years as of this writing, which provides time and support to its faculty in their research and publication efforts. I'd also like to thank my wife Gladys for her tolerance of the many long days and late evenings it took to complete this book.

I am fortunate to have been raised by two scholars and authors, the late Drs. Joyce Loubere and Leo Loubere. Thanks to them, I was exposed at a young age to the value of reading, writing, and of educating oneself in a broad range of topics. Without that upbringing it is unlikely that I would have ever attempted this project.

—**Philip A. Loubere**

Contents

Introduction

At some point in the early 21st century, probably in 2017 or 2018 CE, the human race reached a milestone in communication technology: More than half of everyone on the planet, about 3.8 billion people, were now using the Internet. That was double the number from ten years earlier, and about nine times greater than at the turn of the century, when only about one out of every 17 people on the planet was on the Internet regularly.

This might seem slow for an almost 50-year-old platform—the Internet was born in 1969—but in the span of human history that counts as an almost overnight sensation. But it's not unprecedented. Television and radio also achieved widespread use rapidly after their invention, each within a few decades. In fact, many groundbreaking inventions in communication were quickly adopted: The telephone, the telegraph, even Gutenberg's 15th century press, which spread across Europe in a relatively few decades.

None of these inventions came out of the blue. Although the technology that makes the Internet possible might seem revolutionary, it is in fact built upon layers of previous inventions, in a direct line that can be traced over several centuries, and indirectly all the way back to the beginning of civilization.

If you're reading this on a digital device, that's only possible because of a succession of inventions and discoveries in a range of fields, the most central one being the discovery by two separate 19th century scientists that electric currents emit a magnetic field in waves whose length can be measured. Without that observation radio wouldn't have been invented, and without radio modern electronics wouldn't have come about. And that discovery only happened thanks to a string of researchers going back to the 18th century who were the first to understand the nature of electricity, and how to generate it and use it as an energy source.

Your smartphone works because of radio waves and electricity, and relies on a battery, the first one of which also goes back to the 1700s. The camera in your phone came about because of an early 19th century experiment using light-sensitive chemicals to make the first known photograph (after a day-long exposure). Digital photos and video owe their existence to earlier technology using celluloid film and then magnetic tape.

If you're reading this in a print book, that's only possible because of the invention of paper 2,000 years ago, followed by the first printing methods soon after that, then moveable type presses 500 years ago, and finally the automation of both paper making and printing in the 19th century during the Industrial Revolution, without which this book would be not just college textbook expensive but unaffordable to most.

Without this legacy, our modern digital world wouldn't exist, and all the ways that our culture and society have been transformed by digital media wouldn't have taken place. Before the moveable type press, literacy rates across the world were practically non-existent, but within a few centuries rose substantially, which led to changes in attitudes in politics and culture. Before electronic communication, news could take days or weeks to reach the public, leaving people at a remove from events outside of their immediate community, but radio and television helped connect people on national and global levels, which was further enhanced with the Internet. These communication platforms have caused cross-cultural

influences which manifest themselves in the media itself, in film and television and the art and music that have now been made accessible to audiences across the globe.

A study of the conditions under which new forms of communication are invented shows a common thread running throughout recorded history. Each new communication method was created to address the shortcomings of what existed at the time: Paper was more convenient and transportable than clay tablets or bamboo slips, and easier to make and more durable than papyrus. Printing presses made far more copies of documents than copying them by hand. The telegraph and telephone were much faster than the mail. Radio didn't need wires and could reach a broad audience, as could television. And the Internet was more personal, convenient, and offered easier access to much more content than broadcast media could provide.

In many cases new inventions were built on top of the technology developed by its predecessors, which becomes more apparent in the Industrial and Modern eras, as inventors improved on existing technology. First they found ways to automate processes previously done by hand, and then found ways to improve their efficiency. They discovered and put to use new forms of energy, first steam and then electricity, and then discovered that they could use electricity itself as a means of communication. In order to control electricity they invented devices such as vacuum tubes, and then improved on those with transistors, and then miniaturized those into integrated circuits, reducing the size of electronic devices from warehouse- to pocket-size.

By following the five-millenia-long timeline of all these developments, from Mesopotamian clay tablets to 21st century smartphones, we can see a common thread running throughout recorded history as people's ability to communicate and record information evolved into ever more efficient and far-reaching capabilities.

This book provides an overview of the emergence of the significant inventions that brought about new means of communication, particularly those capable of reaching a broad audience. It will explain and diagram in each case how the technology works, who invented it, and what effect it had on society and culture. In this way it will hopefully show a clear timeline across the whole of recorded history and explain how each new invention arose out of the methods and technology of its predecessors.

Although the theme is communication technology, some related and peripheral technologies must be covered as well, particularly when covering recent advances. For example, in order to understand everything from the telegraph to computers, some background in the physics of electromagnetism must be explained, and for digital media, how computers work. Fields such as chemistry and metallurgy are relevant to topics as far back as Gutenberg's press, and plastics becomes important in the 20th century.

So these topics will also be covered when necessary and when they are relevant.

The aim of this book is to avoid overly technical descriptions in an attempt to briefly and succinctly explain increasingly complicated technology by using layman terms and through the use of graphics. It is a very broad overview of over 5,000 years of human existence, and by necessity focuses on only those inventions that had significant impacts on the way people live and the cultures that surround them.

There are many interesting stories intertwined in this topic, of the triumphs and failures of inventors in competition with each other, of Phoenicians who sailed the length of the Mediterranean and into the Atlantic, in the process spreading the foundation of modern Western writing, of the ingenious methods of printing devised in both Asia and Europe and the industries they gave birth to, of the competition between Thomas Edison and Nikola Tesla to establish the modern power grid which transformed the world, of the remarkable prescience of those who first discovered electromagnetism and radio waves, and those who turned that discovery into a communication medium capable of reaching millions.

And that is the real theme of this topic, the two unique abilities that humans have: To communicate complex and abstract ideas, and to build remarkably intricate machines. In this regard, the story told here is a deeply human one, about the ways we've found to tell our stories to each other and to be connected to each other across the entire globe, for better or worse.

Overview

Human existence spans two broad periods: prehistory and recorded history. The first, for modern humans, started some 300,000 years ago; the second about 5,500 years ago.

Technological innovation began far earlier than recorded history and even before *Homo sapiens*: Early humans began using tools some three million years ago. The oldest artifacts that may have been attempts at expression are hundreds of thousands of years old, carved figurines. They would have required tools to create.

The origins of modern technology could be said to begin with metal casting 7,500 years ago. The time since then can be divided into three ages: pre-industrial, industrial-modern, and digital.

For technology that enables communication, there are several key transition points: Early writing media such as clay tablets and papyrus sheets beginning 5,500-5,000 years ago, the invention of paper about 2,000 years ago, the beginning of mass communication with the moveable-type press in the 15th century, the beginning of mass production and mechanization in the 19th century which automated paper production and printing, and in the 20th century the invention of electronics which enabled broadcast media, followed by the start of the digital age and the Internet.

Each of those historical points enabled greater levels of communication, allowing more and more people to have access to information. This in turn had profound effects on social structures and on how people lived their lives.

This book will provide an overview of the major inventions at each of those historical moments, and their social impacts.

Advances in communication

At key moments in the past, breakthroughs in communication had profound influences on how societies were structured and how people lived. These are the significant innovations:

Prehistoric period

Speech
Although its inception is unknown, our ancestors' use of sophisticated speech began at least 100,000 years ago if not much earlier.

Design
Early humans invented design by decorating utilitarian objects such as tools, clothing and pottery, and art by making objects for no purpose other than personal expression, including carved figurines, jewelry, and cave wall paintings. The earliest found artifacts are from 500,000 years ago.

Metallurgy
Mining of ores and smelting began with copper at least 7,500 years ago, probably about the time that writing was beginning, but there are no written records of the practice. Bronze, an alloy of copper and tin or arsenic, came into use about 6,000 years ago, and iron a little more than 3,000 years ago. Metal would become essential for communication technology in the current era, necessary for tools to carve woodblocks, for casting type slugs for printing presses, and for the manufacture of everything from printing presses to electronic devices following the Industrial Revolution.

Pre-industrial era

Writing
The invention of writing followed the start of agriculture and permanent human settlements about 12,000 years ago. The oldest written artifact discovered to date is about 5,400 years old, but writing is almost certainly older than that.

As written languages evolved in different parts of the world, clay tablets, papyrus sheets and bamboo or wood slips were the principal writing media for close to 3,500 years until the start of the current era.

Paper
Starting 1,900 years ago, paper gradually became the principal medium of communication up until the invention of electronics. First made in China, it was rapidly adopted across Eastern Asia, but didn't reach the Middle East, Northern Africa and Europe until about 800-900 years ago.

Printing
Block printing was invented in Eastern Asia, but printing didn't become a force for societal transformation until the invention of the moveable type press in the 1400s in Europe. The press introduced true mass communication for the first time in human history, as multiple copies of the same document could now be distributed and accessed by a large readership.

Industrial and Modern eras

Steam power and mechanization
This new power source enabled the invention of machines that started replacing manual labor. In the early 19th century paper making and printing became mechanized, greatly increasing production and making printed material more affordable and accessible to the general public.

Electricity
The 19th century saw the development of electricity into a reliable power source, one that could be accessed from great distances and that made new communication technology possible: At first the telegraph, telephone, and phonograph, followed by movies, radio and television, and eventually modern electronics, computers, smartphones and the Internet. It also made printing far more efficient, enabling the production of daily newspapers, periodicals, magazines and inexpensive books.

Photography
The process of capturing images on light-sensitive materials was first developed in the early 19th century, and refined over the course of the century into a practical medium. It also made movies possible, which first appeared at the end of the 19th century.

Broadcasting
Radio and television were both invented early in the 20th century.

Electronics
The transistor and integrated circuit boards made compact electronics possible, which led to a wide range of affordable consumer devices from TVs and audio systems to portable radios and music players.

Digital age

Digital devices
The transition from analog to digital media took place over the second half of the 20th century, culminating in personal computers, mobile phones and digital cameras.

The Internet
Close to the end of the 20th century the Internet became easily accessible to the public, starting a revolution in communication as computers evolved into media devices and became commonplace possessions in the industrialized world. In the early 21st century smartphones and tablets have become the primary source of information, entertainment and means of communication for a large part of the human population.

Prehistory timeline

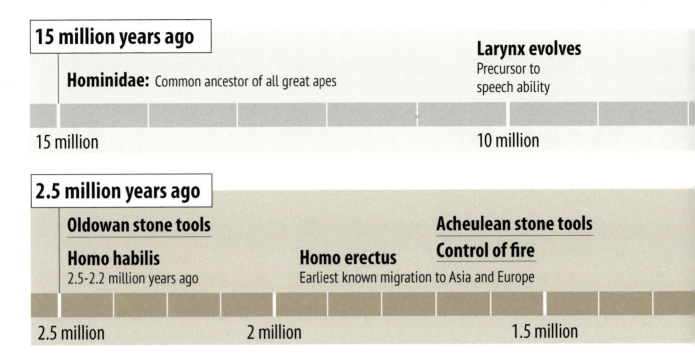

15 million years ago

Hominidae: Common ancestor of all great apes

Larynx evolves
Precursor to speech ability

15 million   10 million

2.5 million years ago

Oldowan stone tools

Homo habilis
2.5-2.2 million years ago

Homo erectus
Earliest known migration to Asia and Europe

Acheulean stone tools

Control of fire

2.5 million   2 million   1.5 million

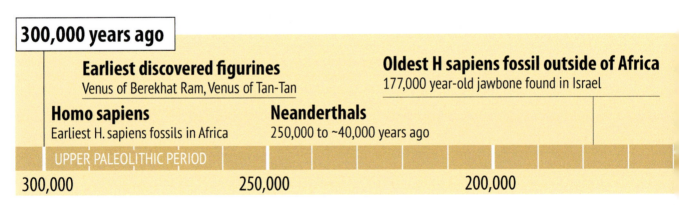

300,000 years ago

Earliest discovered figurines
Venus of Berekhat Ram, Venus of Tan-Tan

Oldest H sapiens fossil outside of Africa
177,000 year-old jawbone found in Israel

Homo sapiens
Earliest H. sapiens fossils in Africa

Neanderthals
250,000 to ~40,000 years ago

UPPER PALEOLITHIC PERIOD

300,000   250,000   200,000

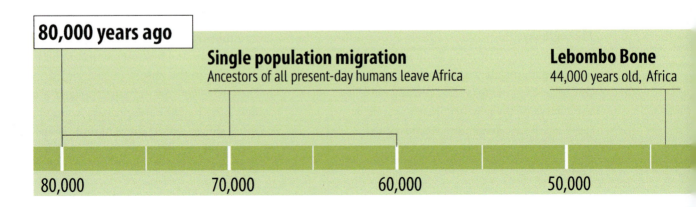

80,000 years ago

Single population migration
Ancestors of all present-day humans leave Africa

Lebombo Bone
44,000 years old, Africa

80,000   70,000   60,000   50,000

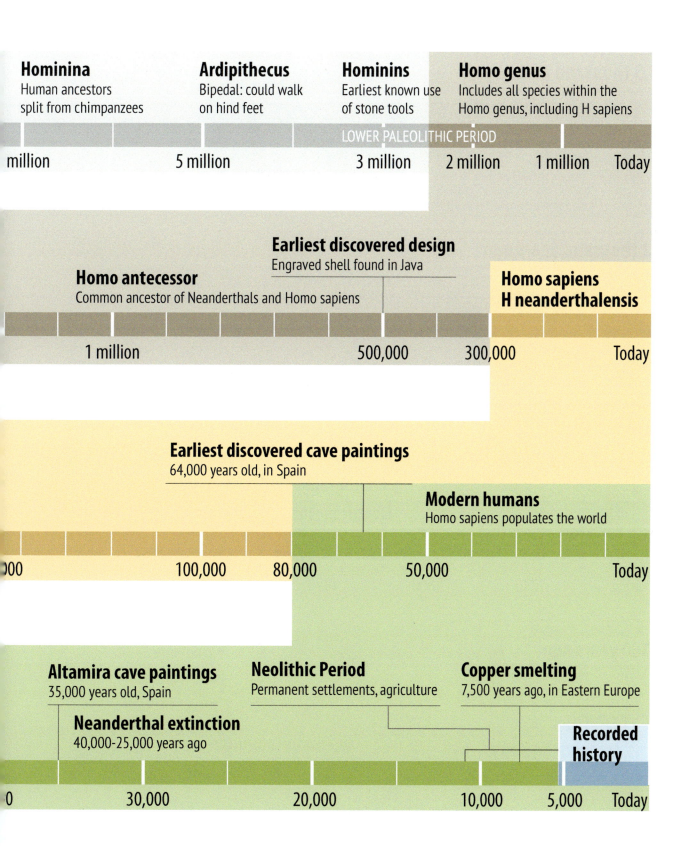

Hominina
Human ancestors split from chimpanzees

Ardipithecus
Bipedal: could walk on hind feet

Hominins
Earliest known use of stone tools

Homo genus
Includes all species within the Homo genus, including H sapiens

LOWER PALEOLITHIC PERIOD

million   5 million   3 million   2 million   1 million   Today

Earliest discovered design
Engraved shell found in Java

Homo antecessor
Common ancestor of Neanderthals and Homo sapiens

**Homo sapiens
H neanderthalensis**

1 million   500,000   300,000   Today

Earliest discovered cave paintings
64,000 years old, in Spain

Modern humans
Homo sapiens populates the world

000   100,000   80,000   50,000   Today

Altamira cave paintings
35,000 years old, Spain

Neolithic Period
Permanent settlements, agriculture

Copper smelting
7,500 years ago, in Eastern Europe

Neanderthal extinction
40,000-25,000 years ago

Recorded history

0   30,000   20,000   10,000   5,000   Today

Recorded history timeline

Dates on which the following innovations in communication first appeared.

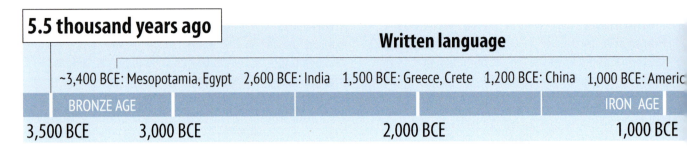

5.5 thousand years ago

Written language

~3,400 BCE: Mesopotamia, Egypt   2,600 BCE: India   1,500 BCE: Greece, Crete   1,200 BCE: China   1,000 BCE: Americ

BRONZE AGE   IRON AGE

3,500 BCE   3,000 BCE   2,000 BCE   1,000 BCE

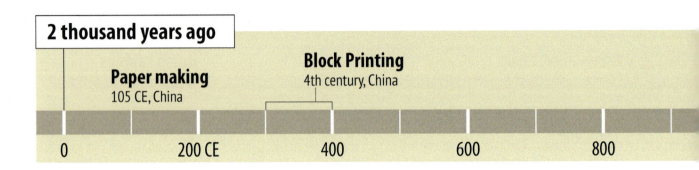

2 thousand years ago

Paper making
105 CE, China

Block Printing
4th century, China

0   200 CE   400   600   800

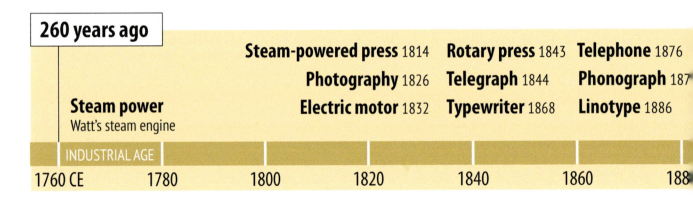

260 years ago

Steam-powered press 1814   **Rotary press** 1843   **Telephone** 1876
Photography 1826   **Telegraph** 1844   **Phonograph** 187
Steam power   **Electric motor** 1832   **Typewriter** 1868   **Linotype** 1886
Watt's steam engine

INDUSTRIAL AGE

1760 CE   1780   1800   1820   1840   1860   188

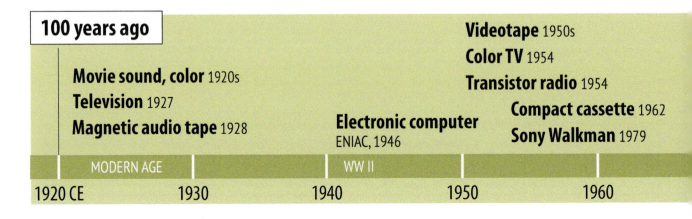

100 years ago

Videotape 1950s
Color TV 1954
Movie sound, color 1920s   **Transistor radio** 1954
Television 1927
Magnetic audio tape 1928   **Electronic computer**   **Compact cassette** 1962
ENIAC, 1946   **Sony Walkman** 1979

MODERN AGE   WW II

1920 CE   1930   1940   1950   1960

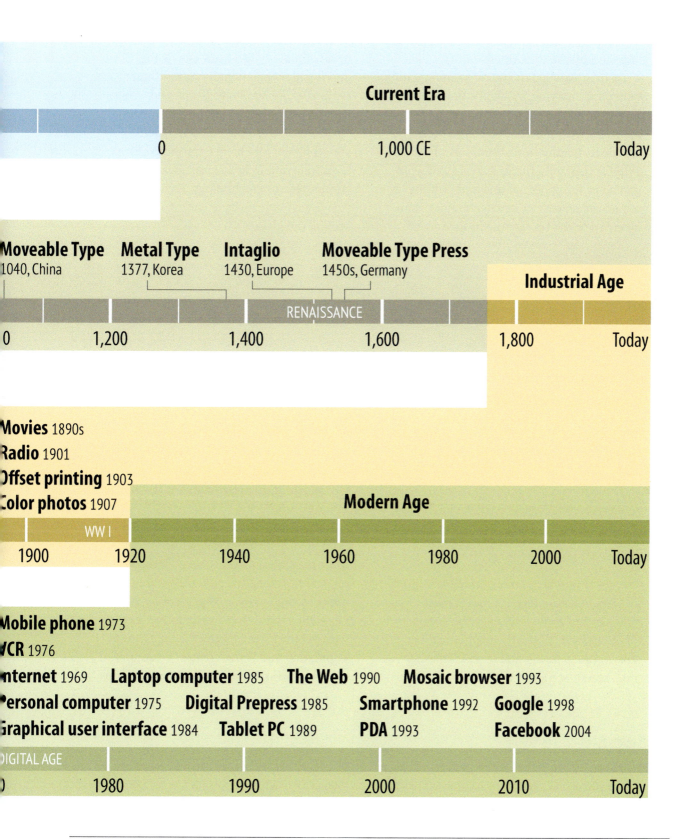

Current Era

0   1,000 CE   Today

Moveable Type
1040, China

Metal Type
1377, Korea

Intaglio
1430, Europe

Moveable Type Press
1450s, Germany

Industrial Age

RENAISSANCE

0   1,200   1,400   1,600   1,800   Today

Movies 1890s
Radio 1901
Offset printing 1903
Color photos 1907

Modern Age

WW I

1900   1920   1940   1960   1980   2000   Today

Mobile phone 1973
VCR 1976

Internet 1969   **Laptop computer** 1985   **The Web** 1990   **Mosaic browser** 1993
Personal computer 1975   **Digital Prepress** 1985   **Smartphone** 1992   **Google** 1998
Graphical user interface 1984   **Tablet PC** 1989   **PDA** 1993   **Facebook** 2004

DIGITAL AGE

1980   1990   2000   2010   Today

Innovation centers

Communication technology over the last two millennia emerged sequentially in three areas: first in East Asia, then in Europe, and most recently in the United States.

At first, Asia led the world in innovation with paper making, block printing and the first moveable type. Then Europe made advances with the moveable type press and photography, and at the start of the 19th century with the first steam-powered machines for paper making and printing. A remarkable streak of new technology then emerged in the US starting in the second half of the 19th century and extending through much of the 20th.

Since the later part of the 20th century new technology has been increasingly developed internationally rather than regionally. Japan, South Korea and China have become major producers of electronics, including computers and smartphones, and have contributed to their innovation. In a sense advances in communication technology, having moved steadily westward, have come full circle around the globe.

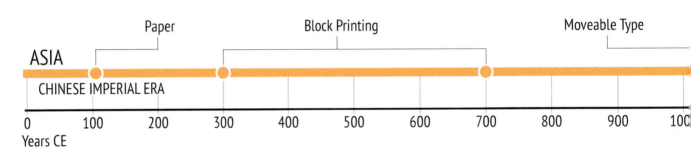

Global population growth

Human population numbers are less and less precise the further back we go in time. The human population 2,000 years ago has been estimated to have been anywhere between 200 million and 600 million, but the lower number is more widely accepted.

Data for more recent times is more reliable, and show that since the start of the Industrial Age the population has grown dramatically and at an increasing rate, reaching almost eight billion by 2020 CE, an eightfold increase in a little over two centuries.

One result of this is a dramatic rise in total media consumption, while at the same time literacy rates have increased on average globally—going from single digits in 1800 to over 80 percent by 2000 CE—which has also contributed to media usage. Today, Asia has by far the largest population and is the greatest consumer of media in print, broadcast and digital forms.

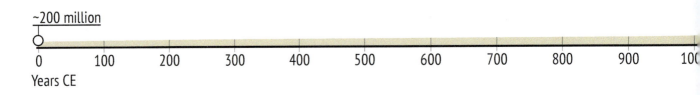

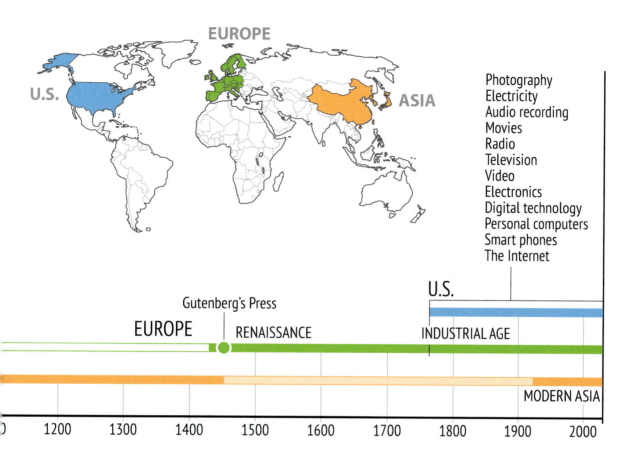

EUROPE

U.S.

ASIA

Photography
Electricity
Audio recording
Movies
Radio
Television
Video
Electronics
Digital technology
Personal computers
Smart phones
The Internet

U.S.

Gutenberg's Press

EUROPE · RENAISSANCE

INDUSTRIAL AGE

MODERN ASIA

| 1200 | 1300 | 1400 | 1500 | 1600 | 1700 | 1800 | 1900 | 2000 |

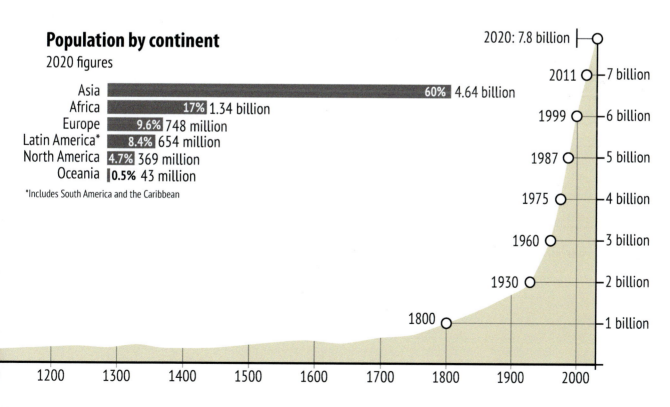

Population by continent

2020 figures

Asia — 60% 4.64 billion
Africa — 17% 1.34 billion
Europe — 9.6% 748 million
Latin America* — 8.4% 654 million
North America — 4.7% 369 million
Oceania — 0.5% 43 million

*Includes South America and the Caribbean

2020: 7.8 billion
2011 — 7 billion
1999 — 6 billion
1987 — 5 billion
1975 — 4 billion
1960 — 3 billion
1930 — 2 billion
1800 — 1 billion

| 1200 | 1300 | 1400 | 1500 | 1600 | 1700 | 1800 | 1900 | 2000 |

Prehistory to Early History

Although most of modern humans' existence has preceded recorded history, we have evidence of or can infer several innovations from that time period. First there was the development of speech, and then the earliest purposeful designs, including sculpted objects and paintings on cave walls, which might be the earliest records of story telling. Also, there were technological advances such as metal casting and ceramics, and the invention of counting systems.

Speech

The earliest form of human communication is spoken language. Its origins are unknown and the subject of much debate. There are several competing hypotheses as to whether it evolved over a long period of time or appeared relatively recently and quickly.

The linguist Noam Chomsky has proposed that a genetic variation roughly 100,000 years ago enabled humans to rapidly develop complex languages. In an opposing proposal, biologist Oren Kolodny and psychologist Shimon Edelman argue that complex language began about 1.6 million years ago, at the same time that humans developed more complex toolmaking skills involving more than one step. The cognitive ability to plan a process involving several steps could have also been applied to language, increasing its complexity.

In yet another hypothesis, author Yuval Noah Harari proposes in his book *Sapiens, a Brief History of Mankind* that language gained complexity due to gossip. Among tribal groups, it became important to evaluate the skills and reliability of others in the group, and so more conceptual and nuanced phrases evolved for that purpose. The fact that contemporary twitter feeds are composed most often of critical observations about others lends credence to Dr. Harari's hypothesis.

But short of finding complete human genomes from the past, or time travel, it's unlikely that we'll ever know the answer to how language came about.

However it evolved, humans have the most complex speech of

any animal, which has enabled the cooperation necessary for us to advance technologically and culturally.

Of course, there are many different spoken languages, which implies that complex languages evolved separately in different parts of the world. And languages are constantly changing and evolving. Whatever tongues prehistoric people spoke eventually evolved into the 20,000-30,000 languages estimated to have existed in all of human history. There are more than 7,000 in use in the world today. But what they have in common is that they all have fairly common structures, words for certain purposes and grammatical rules, and the capacity to convey almost all thoughts, emotions, observations and collective knowledge to others. Because of this, it is possible to translate one language to another.

Design

Humans have been making tools for at least two and a half million years, at first for hunting, then much more recently for agriculture and shelter. At some point they started using tools to create objects for what appear to be purely artistic reasons: sculptures, engraved bones and shells, and cave paintings. The pictures they drew are thought to have evolved into symbols that formed the basis for counting and writing systems, at which point recorded history began.

The oldest evidence of purposeful design made by humans discovered so far is more than 500,000 years old: A pattern carved into a shell discovered in the 1890s in Indonesia.

More recent findings include two small figurines, one found in the Golan Heights in 1981, known as the **Venus**

Venus of Berekhat Ram

of Berekhat Ram, and the other in Morocco in 1999, the **Venus of Tan-Tan**, that are likely 250,000-300,000 years old, although possibly much older. While the Indonesian shell markings appear to be abstract, these figurines seem to be attempts at human representation, possibly female fertility symbols. All these objects would have been created by members of *Homo erectus*, ancestors of *Homo sapiens*.

Counting

The earliest forms of record keeping were counting systems, which are much older than written language. They usually involved notches cut into a stick or a bone, known as tally sticks. One, known as the **Lebombo Bone**, is about 44,000 years old and was found in southern Africa. 29 notches in its side seem likely to have been used for counting, possibly of lunar phases. There are other notched bones as old as 80,000 years, but it is unclear if they were for counting purposes.

It should be noted that counting, as with spoken language, is not unique to humans. Numerous experiments with animals, surprisingly including some fish and bee species, have revealed innate abilities to distinguish the relative size of groups, to count small numbers of things, and to even perform some math calculations. So

it may be a reasonable assumption that our human ancestors have always had the ability to count.

Story telling

A recent discovery of cave paintings in Spain has been reliably dated to be at least 64,000 years old, at a time when only Neanderthals lived in Europe. More recent cave paintings date from up to 35,000 years ago, and are found in Indonesia, Europe, Africa and South America. Some of the older artwork in Europe, particularly in Altamira, Spain, was possibly also created by Neanderthals.

Many of the scenes depict human figures hunting animals. This artwork is evidence of using stylized images to record observations about the world, and possibly narratives of events. If the latter, these would be the earliest known attempts at story telling.

Interestingly, the animals are often depicted with remarkable realism while the humans are more often iconic or abstract. This might be how the first pictographic writing began, as increasingly stylized depictions of various things such as people evolved into symbols. But if so, it was a long evolution. The first evidence of written language didn't appear until 60,000 years after the earliest known cave paintings.

Lebombo bone

Museo de Altamira y D. Rodríguez

Bison painting in Altamira, Spain. Some of the cave's artwork could be as old as 35,600 years.

Peter80 / Creative Commons

Drawing of a person, bird and bison in the Lascaux caves in France from 19,000 years ago.

Prehistoric cave art

New discoveries of ever older cave art keep emerging. Here are some of the oldest around the world, and how many years ago they were painted. The recent discoveries in Spain, dated to over 64 thousand years ago, would have been done by Neanderthals, as they predate the arrival of modern humans.

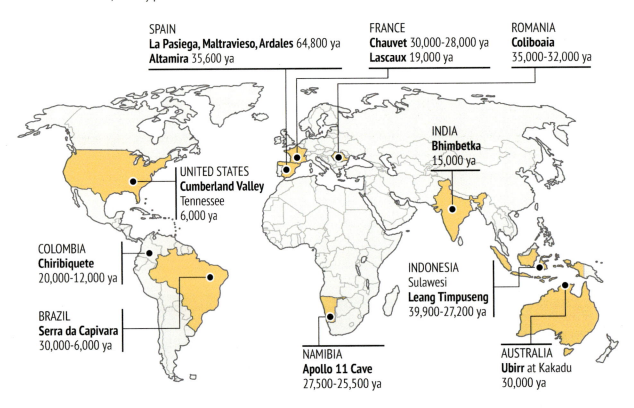

SPAIN
La Pasiega, Maltravieso, Ardales 64,800 ya
Altamira 35,600 ya

FRANCE
Chauvet 30,000-28,000 ya
Lascaux 19,000 ya

ROMANIA
Coliboaia
35,000-32,000 ya

INDIA
Bhimbetka
15,000 ya

UNITED STATES
Cumberland Valley
Tennessee
6,000 ya

COLOMBIA
Chiribiquete
20,000-12,000 ya

BRAZIL
Serra da Capivara
30,000-6,000 ya

INDONESIA
Sulawesi
Leang Timpuseng
39,900-27,200 ya

NAMIBIA
Apollo 11 Cave
27,500-25,500 ya

AUSTRALIA
Ubirr at Kakadu
30,000 ya

Modern human migration

Based on current evidence, these are the approximate years ago that the direct ancestors of contemporary humans migrated to different parts of the world, and the likely routes they took.

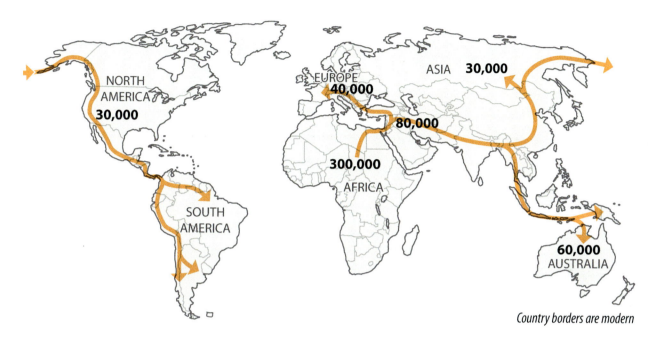

Country borders are modern

Migration

New discoveries and DNA analysis have provided a more accurate assessment of when and where prehistoric humans lived, but the picture is still very incomplete, and likely to change.

Our early ancestors, *Homo erectus*, had left Africa and migrated into Europe and Asia as early as two million years ago. More advanced hominids, such as *Homo heidelbergensis*, followed them about 600,000 years ago, and Neanderthals populated Europe and parts of Asia starting 230,000 years ago.

Modern humans, *Homo sapiens*, appeared 300,000 years ago in Africa and various groups migrated to Europe and Asia in several different waves. The direct ancestors of everyone who lives outside of

Africa today, according to several genetic studies, left Africa sometime between 80,000 and 60,000 years ago, moving first into the Middle East, then into Asia and Europe, and eventually to the Americas and to every habitable corner of the planet. Their population grew to several million individuals and they may have absorbed the older groups, the last of whom, Neanderthals, had disappeared by 28,000 years ago.

For tens of thousands of years humans lived nomadic lives in small tribal groups, and likely had oral histories passed from one generation to the next, which, as far as we know, was their only form of communication and record keeping.

The first civilizations

NORTH AMERICA

● **Olmecs**

MEXICO

ATLANTIC OCEAN

SOUTH AMERICA

First settlements

About 12,000 years ago people began farming and herding cattle, leading to a profound change in lifestyle. Agriculture made permanent settlements possible, which eventually attained city size, leading to complex societies with class structures, regional governments with codified laws, and trade.

The first cities were usually in river valleys which offered irrigation and fertile soil as well as transportation by boat, and it was generally along great rivers that the largest populations grew: the Tigris and Euphrates in Mesopotamia, the Nile in Egypt, the Indus in India, the Yellow in China.

These are the principal locations where the first permanent settlements evolved into cities and states with complex societies and governments. It is also where the first writing systems appeared, marking the beginning of recorded history.

Country names and borders are modern.

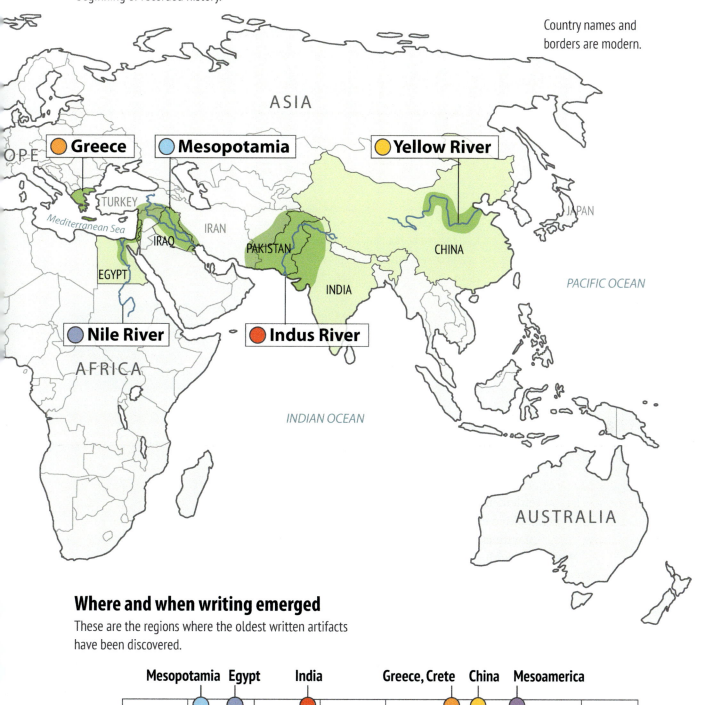

Where and when writing emerged

These are the regions where the oldest written artifacts have been discovered.

| Mesopotamia | Egypt | India | Greece, Crete | China | Mesoamerica |

| Years ago: | 5,500 | 5,000 | 4,500 | 4,000 | 3,500 | 3,000 | 2,500 | 2,000 |

First cities and states

There is no consensus on which is the oldest city in history, or even what defines a city. The earliest ones would have rarely had populations over 10,000 and typically under 5,000. Often they were walled, and had buildings for purposes other than housing, such as temples. Usually as they grew they established political control over the surrounding region, forming the first states.

Population centers first started attaining city status roughly 7,000 years ago, a few thousand years after they were first settled: Uruk and Eridu in Mesopotamia, Argos and Athens in Greece, Harappa and Mohenjo-Daro in the Indus River valley, Banpo and Jiangzhai in the Yellow River valley.

Most states followed a pattern of rise and fall of successive empires or dynasties.

The Fertile Crescent

The Fertile Crescent extends from the Nile River valley to the Persian Gulf in a broad arc, encompassing some of the earliest land farmed by humans. The term 'fertile' is misleading: Most of the region was and is arid desert, but its rivers provide irrigation and fertile soil.

Country borders and names are modern.
Cities in gray are modern.

Mesopotamia

In what is now Iraq and parts of neighboring countries, Mesopotamia was the site of the earliest known civilizations with regional governmental structures and laws, and a writing system. Its history is not of a single nation but of a series of successive empires and cultures, including the Assyrians, Sumerians, Akkadians and Babylonians.

The geography of the region was a key factor in its growth. The area, in particular the southern half of the Tigris and Euphrates river valley, is too arid for stable farming. Requiring irrigation, a system of canals and waterways was built, which greatly increased farm production and led to larger and denser population centers, eventually becoming cities.

Several cities in Mesopotamia are certainly among the oldest, including Uruk and Eridu, which were first settled as early as 11,000 years ago. 4,900 years ago Uruk was likely the largest city in the world, with a population between 50,000 and 80,000.

Babylon was first settled around 4,300 years ago and became the center of the Babylonian Empire a few hundred years later under the reign of its most famous king Hammurabi, who is best known for establishing the Code of Hammurabi, one of the earliest codified judicial systems. At its height about 2,500 years ago Babylon had a population of 200,000.

Egypt

Egypt was first unified 5,200 years ago and went through a 3,200-year succession of thirty dynasties until its conquest by Rome in 30 BCE. Its first major city, Memphis, was founded at the time of unification.

Greece

Successive cultures dominated Greece, first the Minoan, then the Mycenaean and after that the Hellenic, but the region was never unified into a single state. Instead it consisted of over 1,000 independent city-states such as Athens, Sparta and Corinth, each being composed of a city center and varying amounts of surrounding territory. But they shared a common culture and language.

India

The Indus civilization occupied a large region along the Indus River in present-day Pakistan and India, and thrived from 4,600 to 3,900 years ago. At its height it was the world's largest urban development with a regional population of around a million people.

China

China is considered the oldest continuous civilization in history, although it wasn't called China until the 16th century CE. The Romans and Greeks called it Seres, 'the land of silk'. Marco Polo in the 13th century CE called it Cathay. In Mandarin Chinese, it is 'Zhongguo', meaning 'Middle Empire'.

As in Egypt, China was dominated by a series of imperial dynasties, the first of which was the Xia 4,000 years ago in the Yellow River valley, and the last the Qing, which ended in 1912 CE with the founding of the Republic of China. At times the country was divided into several kingdoms, at other times it was unified.

Americas

In the Americas, the earliest farming communities appear to have started 7,100 years ago in present-day Mexico, eventually becoming the Olmec civilization, whose most prominent city San Lorenzo Tenochtitlán reached its peak about 3,400 years ago. The Olmecs thrived for the next thousand years. They are considered the first major civilization in the Americas.

Cities also appeared in other locations around the world: Çatalhöyük, Turkey 9,500 years ago and Caral, Peru 4,400 years ago, to name two. But the ones discussed here are where we find the earliest evidence of writing systems and record keeping.

Earliest cities and writing

In each region where civilizations first developed, the earliest written artifacts found so far are more recent than the establishment of the first cities. The beginning of writing appears to only have happened following permanent settlements.

○ First cities   ■ Earliest writing found

Mesopotamia	○ Eridu SUMERIA ○ U
Egypt	PRE-DYNASTIC PERIOD
Indus River	○ Harappa ○ Mohenjo-Daro
Greece, Crete	○ Argos
Yellow River	○ Banpo, Jiangzhai
Mesoamerica	

YEARS AGO: 8,000   7,000   6,000

Cities and writing

The settling of the first cities in history precedes the oldest written artifacts found to date, which seems to indicate that writing only began after permanent communities were established. Regional and global trade and systems of government with established laws would have required written records, which likely spurred the evolution of writing systems. Cities appear to have been the necessary foundation for all the things that make writing systems both possible and necessary.

Cities also provided the resources and level of cooperation necessary for technological development. As technology became increasingly complex it required advances in several fields in order to work, from metallurgy to chemistry to new energy sources, and that level of cooperation is only possible in stable, established societies.

The social orders in our world today, and to some degree the political structures and divisions, have their roots in the first civilizations that had their nascence 12,000 years ago on the banks of the world's great rivers.

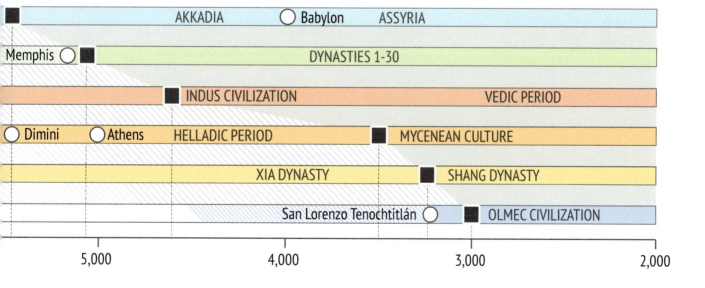

AKKADIA   Babylon   ASSYRIA

Memphis   DYNASTIES 1-30

INDUS CIVILIZATION   VEDIC PERIOD

Dimini   Athens   HELLADIC PERIOD   MYCENEAN CULTURE

XIA DYNASTY   SHANG DYNASTY

San Lorenzo Tenochtitlán   OLMEC CIVILIZATION

5,000   4,000   3,000   2,000

Writing

People had been drawing pictures long before the earliest evidence of writing—the oldest cave paintings are from 64,000 years ago. It's reasonable to assume, given the pictographic nature of the earliest writing systems, that this is how writing evolved, that simple pictures started being used to represent ideas.

A fully developed writing system, however, requires standardized characters and syntax—rules about how to arrange those characters—that all those using it agree on and understand. And such systems don't appear to have emerged until after the first permanent human settlements evolved into cities, beginning around 6,000 or 7,000 years ago.

A writing system is different than a language, and most systems are used for multiple languages. For example, the Latin alphabet is used for many Western languages including English, Spanish and German, with minor modifications in each, such as accents or variations on letter forms. So there are many more languages than writing systems.

The oldest systems were logosyllabic, pictographic or logographic, in which each character represents, respectively, a syllable, a word, or a phrase. Many of the systems were combinations of these. The earliest versions of characters were essentially stylized drawings, which, as they evolved, tended to become more abstract to the point of no longer being recognizable. These systems also tended to have hundreds of characters and complicated rules for writing.

Alphabet systems, using far less characters, evolved a little later, and eventually became widely adopted across most of the world geographically. Writing systems today are largely alphabetic except in eastern Asia, where logosyllabic systems are used, principally in China and Japan.

Archaic writing systems

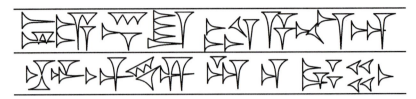

Cuneiform

The oldest known fully developed writing system is attributed to the Sumerians, who dominated Mesopotamia from 5,500 to 5,000 years ago. The system remained in use through a succession of empires including the Akkadians, Babylonians, Hittites and Assyrians up until the first century CE, marking a 3,500-year stretch, the longest period that any writing system has been in use.

The system at first consisted of pictographic characters, which over time evolved to become combinations of wedge-shaped marks due to the most common medium of the region: impressions in clay tablets made with a sharpened reed.

There are at least half a million cuneiform tablets that have been discovered (the British Museum alone has 130,000), evidence of their once wide-spread use. They have been discovered in virtually every excavation site in that region, including those of common residences, although it's possible that they were merely used as construction materials. Most were used for a single purpose and then discarded, much as modern people might use a scratch pad. Many of the recovered tablets had been used by students for writing practice.

The tablets were used for daily affairs and correspondence: Private communication was even sealed in clay envelopes. They were also used for poetry, literature and story telling.

Originally there were over a thousand characters, but eventually the number was reduced to a few hundred. The characters are phonograms representing spoken syllables, and logograms representing complete words, along with determinatives, which indicate a word's category. At first texts were written vertically top to bottom, but later changed to left to right rows.

Cuneiform evolution

Change in the symbol for ox, from 5,400 years ago to 2,600 years ago, demonstrates how it evolved from a simple drawing to an abstract character.

The last two characters are shown as they would appear as sets of impressions done with a reed in a clay tablet.

Years ago: **5,400**   **5,000**   **3,800**   **2,600**

Hieroglyphics and hieratics

In Egypt, a hieroglyphic writing system appeared soon after Mesopotamian cuneiform, about 5,200 years ago, and was in use for the entire Dynastic period up and into the first century of the current era, a period of 3,300 years.

The common image when we think of hieroglyphics is of the detailed characters carved into or painted on temple walls, but there were two other scripts in use.

One, called **hieratic**, appeared about the same time as hieroglyphics but was used for more common, daily purposes such as record keeping and writing letters. It is a cursive script consisting of simplified versions of the hieroglyphic characters. Most papyrus documents were written with hieratic script. Interestingly, while hieroglyphics were most often read right to left (but sometimes left to right: You could tell by which way the animal characters were facing), hieratic was read left to right.

A later script, **demotic**, came into use about 2,700 years ago and remained up until the 5th century CE before falling into disuse. It was essentially a simplified version of the hieratic script.

In the hieroglyphic system, there are about a thousand characters. Among those there are four kinds: phonetic representing a single sound, syllabic in which several characters make a word, logograms for complete words, and determinative, which provides context or additonal meaning to another character, a little like adjectives or adverbs.

The literacy rate in Egypt was likely very low, less than one percent of the population. An intellectual scribe class appeared around 4,000 years ago, when written records became more common. As in Mesopotamia, records were for administrative and business purposes, but there were also literary works including obituaries, private letters, hymns and poems.

Some examples of hieroglyphic characters and their hieratic equivalents.

Meaning	Hieroglyph	Hieratic
Owl		
Man or person		
Woman		
Boat		
Eye, or to see		

Hans Hillewaert / Creative Commons

The Rosetta Stone

Discovered in the Egyptian port city of Rosetta in 1799 CE by soldiers in Napoleon's army, this fragment of a stone stele has most of a royal Egyptian decree from 196 BCE engraved into its surface in three versions: hieroglyphs, demotic script and ancient Greek. This made it possible to begin to translate hieroglyphics and demotic script, knowledge of which had been lost since the fall of the Roman empire.

A french artist, Nicolas-Jacques Conté, devised a method to make prints from the stone surface, allowing copies of the text to be distributed to various scholars who over time were able to decipher it.

The stone, kept in the British Museum, is 44 inches in height.

Other archaic systems

Greece

The oldest Greek written artifacts, from about 3,500 years ago, used two logosyllabic scripts called **Linear A** and **Linear B**. These were used by two early Greek civilizations, the Minoan on the island of Crete, which is considered the first advanced culture in Europe, and the Mycenaean, the first advanced culture in mainland Greece and which dominated the region until 3,000 years ago. The Trojan War, described in the Iliad and the Odyssey, took place during this time, 3,250 years ago.

These scripts fell into disuse during a 400-year dark period between the collapse of the Mycenaean culture and the emergence of Classical Greece in the 6th century BCE.

India

In present-day India and Pakistan, the earliest artifacts with symbols on them date to 5,500 years ago, while a fully developed writing system, called the **Indus** or **Harappan** script, dates to 4,600 years ago. The script, which is pictographic, is still untranslated.

The Indus people engaged in extensive trade as far as the Middle East, in fact, artifacts with Indus symbols have been found in Mesopotamia. This raises the possibility that the two cultures influenced each other's writing systems, but there is no conclusive evidence of that.

The Indus civilization declined about 3,800 years ago and the practice of writing in India was lost for the next thousand years, along with the Indus Script.

Americas

The oldest written artifacts in the Americas have been found in the Southeastern region of Mexico where the Olmecs lived, including the discovery of a 3,000-year-old stone slab in the state of Veracruz, although some dispute its age and authenticity. If true, it is evidence of a complete writing system from that time.

Regardless of its age, the Olmecs did have a writing system, evidence for which includes other artifacts besides the Veracruz stone. The system was pictographic, but has not been deciphered.

Modern writing systems

Alphabetic systems

From Hieroglyphs to Latin

About 3,800 years ago a group of Middle Eastern people had a revolutionary idea. Instead of having to learn all thousand Egyptian or Mesopotamian characters and their complicated usage rules, why not only use a couple dozen, and have each one only represent a speech sound? That way, you could write a string of characters that when pronounced, sounded out words.

These people were the Canaanites, a Semitic group living in the areas between Egypt and Mesopotamia, from the Sinai Peninsula to present-day Lebanon. And as far as we know they were the inventors of the first completely alphabetic writing system, called the **Proto-Sinaitic** or **Proto-Canaanite** script, one that formed the basis for many alphabet systems used today.

In the first version of this script the character shapes were derived from

Writing systems today

Predominant systems in use today by country and region.

- Latin
- Cyrillic
- Indic
- Arabic
- Ethiopic
- Hebrew
- Greek
- Georgian
- Armenian
- Chinese
- Japanese
- Korean

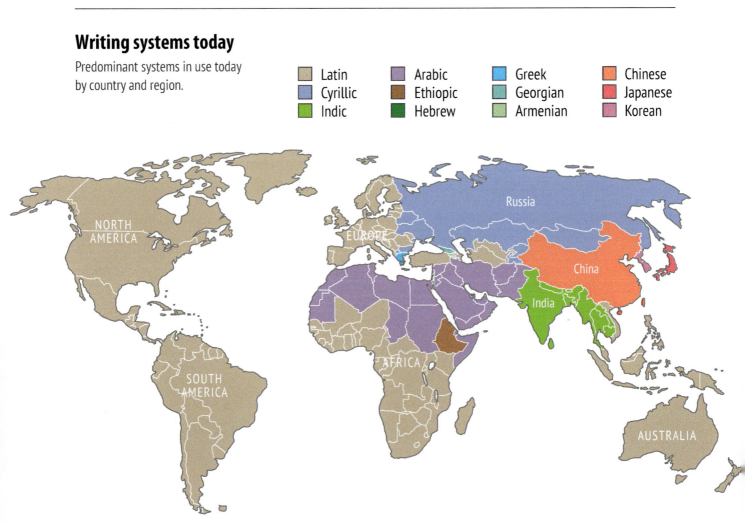

Egyptian hieroglyphs and had the appearance of being pictorial, but didn't carry meaning beyond representing a single sound.

The Canaanites engaged in sea trade across the Mediterranean, putting them in contact with other cultures. The Greeks called them Phoenicians, after a Greek word for a reddish-purple dye these traders were known for, and this became the more common name for the people and region.

By about 3,000 years ago a modified version of the script had evolved, known as the **Phoenician** alphabet, which consisted of 22 consonants and no vowels (they were implied). This was in turn adopted by the Greeks about 2,700 years ago, who modified it into the classical Greek alphabet with 24 letters (now including vowels), known as the **Euclidean** alphabet.

The Etruscans, early inhabitants of present-day Italy, learned the alphabet from the Greeks, and the Romans got it from them, who in turn modified it into the **Latin** alphabet, consisting at first of 23 letters.

At its height the Roman Empire occupied most of Europe and parts of western Asia, bringing the Latin alphabet into widespread use across the western world. Subsequently the Romance languages, with their roots in Latin, and the Germanic languages of northern Europe came to use the Latin alphabet.

Evolution of alphabet writing systems

Three of the most widely used writing systems today, Latin, Arabic and Cyrillic, all have their roots in the Proto-Sinaitic and Phoenician scripts, as do Euclidean (present-day Greek) and Hebrew alphabets.

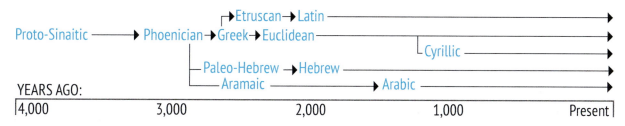

Latin alphabet evolution

This chart shows how characters evolved from one writing system to the next, from Proto-Sinaitic script about 3,800 years ago to the 23-character Latin alphabet as used in Rome about 2,000 years ago. The Proto-Sinaitic characters were copied from Hieroglyphic ones, some of whose original meanings are shown, but they were now instead used to represent speech sounds.

Roman writing was in all capital letters. Lower case versions were created in the 8th century CE, possibly by monks who were making copies of manuscripts.

The Latin characters U and W were added some time between the 5th and 10th centuries CE in order to distinguish between the Roman use of the letter V as either a consonant or a vowel. The letter J was added in the 14th century CE for the same reason, to distinguish between Roman use of the letter I as either a consonant or vowel.

The archaic Greek alphabet shown here is just one of many variations used in different regions of pre-Euclidean Greece. The Euclidean alphabet, adopted in either 403 or 402 BCE (by democratic vote in Athens), became the standard and is still the one used in Greece today.

Original meaning	Proto-Sinaitic	Phoenician	Archaic Greek	Euclidean Greek	Latin Roman
Ox	(ox head)	(sym)	A	A	A
House	(house)	(sym)	B	B	B
Throwstick	(sym)	(sym)	Γ	Γ	C
Door	(sym)	(sym)	Δ	Δ	D
Cheering	(figure)	(sym)	E	E	E
Hook or Peg	(sym)	Y	F	F	F
Question	=	I	I	Z	G
Fence	III	(sym)	H	H	H
Village		⊗	⊕	Θ	
Arm or Hand	(sym)	(sym)	(sym)	I	I
Palm of hand	(sym)	(sym)	K	K	K
Shepherd's crook	(sym)	C	L	Λ	L
Water	(sym)	(sym)	M	M	M
Snake	(sym)	(sym)	N	N	N
		‡	‡	Ξ	
Eye	(eye)	O	O	O	O
		Ɔ	Γ	Π	P
	(sym)	(sym)			
Monkey	8	Φ			Q
Head	(sym)	(sym)	P	P	R
	ω	W	M	Σ	S
Break or divide	†	X	T	T	T
			Υ	Υ	V
				Φ	
				X	X
				Ψ	Y
				Ω	Z

Arabic

Arabic is the third most used writing system in the world today, after Latin and Chinese. It is used across a wide swath of western and central Asia, the Middle East and North Africa, for a variety of languages from Persian to Urdu and Pashto.

Arabic descends from Aramaic, a group of languages spoken by a Semitic group in Mesopotamia. About 3,000 years ago during the neo-Assyrian period Aramaic was widely spoken across the entire Mesopotamian region. Aramaic was first written using the Phoenician alphabet, eventually evolving into its own alphabet.

A semi-nomadic group known as the Nabataeans, who lived in the Mediterranean lands of the Middle East, further modified the Aramaic script starting about 100 BCE, and it became the Arabic system between 400 and 700 CE.

The system consists of 18 characters that can be modified by diacritical marks to express 28 different phonetic sounds. There are no upper or lower case letters. It is read right to left.

The Arabic alphabet:

Cyrillic

The Cyrillic alphabet was named for a Greek monk named Cyril, who either invented it or a precursor to it in the 9th century CE in present-day Bulgaria. It is derived from the Greek alphabet and is now in use in numerous central Asian and Eurasian countries for over fifty different languages, including Russian, Bulgarian, Serbian and Ukrainanian. The script varies depending on the language, and overall has more than 100 letters, although Russian only uses 33. It is read left to right.

An early version of the Cyrillic alphabet:

А Б В Г Д Е Ж Ѕ Ꙁ И І К Л
М Н О П Р С Т ОУ Ф Х Ѡ
Ц Ч Ш Щ Ъ Ы Ь Ѣ Ꙗ Ю
Ѫ Ѭ Ѧ Ѩ Ѯ Ѱ Ѳ Ѵ Ҁ

The modern Russian alphabet:

А Б В Г Д Е Ё Ж З И Й К Л
М Н О П Р С Т У Ф Х Ц Ч
Ш Щ Ъ Ы Ь Э Ю Я

Hebrew

The Paleo-Hebrew alphabet started as a variation of the Phoenician script about 2,800 years ago in the kingdoms of Israel and Judah. It was influenced by the square characters in the Aramaic script and is sometimes called the Square Hebrew alphabet.

The Jewish people suffered a series of displacements and exiles known as the diaspora, first under Assyrian and Babylonian rule beginning in the 8th century BCE, then followed by the Roman destruction of Jerusalem in 70 CE. As a result Hebrew writing remained largely limited to scholarly use until recently with the re-establishment of Israel and the resurgence of Hebrew as a spoken language.

The script is read right to left.

The Hebrew alphabet:

י ט ח ז ו ה ד ג ב ב א
ע ס ן נ מ ם ל ך ד כ כ
ת ת ש ש ר ק ץ פ ף פ פ

Indic

Indic or Indo-Aryan languages make up the principal language family of South Asia, including India, Bangladesh, Nepal, Pakistan and Sri Lanka. In modern India the most common language is Hindi, and the predominant writing system is called **Devanagari**, which has been in use since the 7th century CE. It is both syllabary, in which a character represents a syllable, and alphabetic. It has a standard set of characters with 35 consonants and 11 vowels.

Language in the Indian subcontinent and surrounding areas is complicated. There are 22 semi-official languages in India alone, and many more in Southeast Asia. Many of these evolved from Vedic Sanskrit, a language from about 2,000 years ago. Most use some variant of Brahmic writing which preceded Devanagari in India.

Devanagari is read left to right.

Example of Devenagari writing:

श्रियं सरस्वतीं गौरीं गणेशं
स्कन्दमीश्वरम् ।
ब्रह्माणं वह्निमिन्द्रादीन्वासुदेवं
नमाम्यहम् ॥
नैमिषे हरिमीजाना ऋषयः
शौनकादयः ।
तीर्थयात्राप्रसङ्गेन स्वागतं
सूतमब्रुवन् ॥

Logosyllabic systems

Chinese

The earliest written Chinese artifacts are 3,200 years old, from the Shang dynasty, which followed the Xia. Writing appears to have first been used on oracle bones, a divination practice of the time which involved carving a message on a bone, heating it till it cracked, then interpreting the results. This was practiced at all levels of society.

Chinese writing has evolved through several versions, the earliest of which, called **Jiaguwen**, was pictographic, meaning that each character represents a single object or concept. The common one in use today, called **Xiaozhuan** or Lesser Seal script, came into use 2,700 years ago, making it the oldest writing system still in use today.

The characters, of which there are thousands, are generally logosyllabic, with each one representing a spoken syllable. There is little punctuation, it is left to the reader to identify sentence and phrase endings based on context.

There are two versions, simplified and traditional. There have been simplified versions of characters since the 3rd century BCE, but it wasn't until the 20th century CE that a simplified character set was officially adopted in mainland China. Singapore, Taiwan and Hong Kong still use traditional characters.

In the past Chinese was written in vertical columns which were read in right to left order. Today it is written in horizontal rows from left to right.

Japanese

The origins of the Japanese language are unknown, the only major modern language with that distinction. The spoken language is not similar to Chinese or to any other. Japan is the only country in which it is the primary language.

Japanese writing, however, is very similar to Chinese writing. It uses many of the same characters as Chinese, and to those unfamiliar with either language it is difficult to tell the two apart. Many of the characters have the same meaning in both languages, although the pronunciations are different.

In addition to the Chinese characters, which are called **Kanji**, Japanese has its own unique characters called **Kana**, which are simpler in form. There are, as in Chinese, thousands of characters, and to be literate requires knowing at least 2,000 of them, although there are over 50,000 Kanji characters. The system is primarily logographic, meaning that each character represents a word or phrase.

Japanese writing is relatively recent: The oldest known artifact is from 712 CE, a Shinto text called the *Kojiki*.

As in Chinese, Japanese writing was traditionally written in vertical columns read right to left, but modern Japanese is written in horizontal rows read left to right.

Below is the following phrase: "Japanese writing uses many of the same characters as traditional Chinese.", first in Chinese and then in Japanese:

日文寫作使用許多與繁體中文相同的字符。

日本語の文章は、繁体字中国語と同じ文字の多くを使用します。

Korean

Unlike its two closest neighbors China and Japan (in fact its only two neighbors), Korea has its own unique system, using an alphabet rather than logosyllabics.

Up until the 15th century CE Koreans used Chinese characters for writing. Then in the 1440s a Korean king by the name of Sejong oversaw the creation of an alphabet system, with the intention of promoting literacy by being easier to learn. It is called **Hangul**, and is the system in use in both North and South Korea today, surviving opposition following its introduction and even being banned for a short time by a later king.

Originally it had 28 letters but currently has 24 letters with 14 consonants and 10 vowels.

Unlike Western alphabet systems where each letter is written separately, Korean letters are combined into blocks to form syllables, with several characters combined either side by side or above and below each other into what appears to be a more complex character.

The Korean alphabet. The top row shows the consonants and the bottom row the vowels:

ㄱ ㄴ ㄷ ㄹ ㅁ ㅂ ㅅ ㅇ ㅈ ㅊ ㅋ ㅌ ㅍ ㅎ
ㅏ ㅑ ㅓ ㅕ ㅗ ㅛ ㅜ ㅠ ㅡ ㅣ

Here is the phrase "Korean writing" written with blocks of characters:

한국어 작문

Other systems

There are several regional systems that are unique, including Ethiopic, Georgian and Armenian.

Ethiopic

Known as Ge'ez, this writing system is used for several languages in Ethiopia and Eritrea. It is what's known as an abugida system, in which characters are combinations of consonants and vowels. It evolved from Arabic writing, making it part of the Proto-Siniatic group of writing systems. Its earliest known use dates to the 4th century of the current era.

There are 26 consonants which are modified into syllables by attaching a vowel marker. It is written left to right.

Georgian

Known as the Mkhedruli alphabet, it is used in the Caucasus region between the Black and Caspian seas in central Asia, including Georgia and parts of neighboring countries. There are actually three writing systems used for the Georgian language. Their origins are in dispute, but appear to have emerged some time around the 5th century of the current era.

Depending on the language, there are 33 to 36 letters used, some corresponding to Greek equivalents. It is written left to right.

Armenian

The Armenian alphabet was developed in the early 5th century CE, and is used principally in the south Caucasus region around present-day Armenia. As with Georgian, some of the characters have equivalents with Greek ones. There are 38 letters, and it is written left to right.

Media

Mesopotamia

Clay

Clay was the most common writing surface in Mesopotamia. It was plentiful in the Tigris and Euphrates river valleys due to the slow flow of the river waters across relatively flat land, leaving heavy sediment deposits on the river banks. Clay was used for many purposes, from pottery to bricks for construction, and for writing tablets for thousands of years.

Clay tablets—The original note pads

The method was simple: A cut and sharpened reed was used to impress characters into a slab of wet clay, which was then left to dry.

Most of the tablets were small, roughly palm-sized, both rectangular and round.

They appear to have been used most often for daily business and correspondence in much the same way as pen and paper are used in modern times, but also for literature, poetry and story telling.

The Flood Tablet in the British Museum.

BabelStone / Creative Commons

The Epic of Gilgamesh

Considered the earliest work of notable literature, this Sumerian epic tells of a series of adventures by king and demigod Gilgamesh and his friend Enkidu, who fight monsters and visit the underworld in a search for immortality. The earliest version of the story is thought to be about 4,000 years old.

Shown above is the 11th tablet from an Akkadian version written about 2,700 years ago. Known as the 'Flood Tablet', this part of the epic is the earliest known version of the story of the Great Flood, predating the Christian Bible version by about 1,500 years.

The first tablets of the Epic were discovered in 1853 CE. English scholar George Smith was the first to decipher it, publishing an English translation in the 1870s.

The Flood Tablet is six inches in height.

The first reproductions

The earliest known method of making multiple copies of text and images was through the use of seals and stamps. Their use began in Mesopotamia at least 6,000 years ago.

Mesopotamian seals and stamps were used to make impressions in wet clay. Stamps were also commonly used in Egypt and China, but with ink.

Cylinder seals

These appeared in Mesopotamia at about the same time as clay writing tablets, around 5,500 years ago. They were small stone or ceramic cylinders, 3-4 inches long, engraved with imagery or patterns, that were rolled on top of wet clay tablets to leave an impression. They were used as a form of signature or notation and for administrative purposes.
The cylinder seal shown here depicts scenes from the Epic of Gilgamesh.

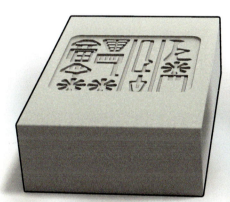

Brick stamps

Mud and clay bricks used for construction sometimes had an impression made with a stamp, itself made of clay or stone. This practice is at least 4,300 years old. Prior to that bricks were sometimes inscribed by hand. Brick stamping was common in Mesopotamia, Egypt, and later in Rome.

Stamp seals

These small stamps were typically less than an inch in width, and were similarly used to make impressions in wet clay. They came into use more than 6,000 years ago, preceding cylinder seals, after which their use became less common. They were typically used as a form of signature, and prominent citizens usually had their own unique seal design.
Besides sealing documents they were also used to seal containers of goods such as jars or boxes by shaping clay over the lid and stamping it.

Egypt

Papyrus

The papyrus plant is a wetland plant once common to, among other places, the Nile River delta. In Egypt it was used to make not only writing material but a variety of products including mats, rope, footwear and even reed boats.

The earliest written papyrus artifact is about 4,500 years old, discovered in an Egyptian port city on the Red Sea. Its use was common in Egypt throughout the dynastic period, and was also common throughout the Mediterranean region by the time of the Roman Empire, and later in Europe until the 11th century CE.

Papyrus sheets had an advantage over clay tablets in that they could be rolled up. Sheets were often sewn together to make scrolls, the most common book form in the ancient world.

They were, however, more prone to damage from moisture and wear and tear. As a result there are fewer papyrus artifacts in existence, and those that have been discovered are usually damaged.

Front and back of a papyrus document known as the Heqanakht letter, which was written some time between 1,961 and 1,917 BCE. Heqanakht was a high court official during the 12th Egyptian dynasty. The contents of the letter, written in hieratic script, are instructions to his family to send two servants to rent land in a place called Perhaa. This document was discovered along with others in the early 1920s CE in a tomb site near the temples at Deir el-Bahri, outside of the city of Luxor.

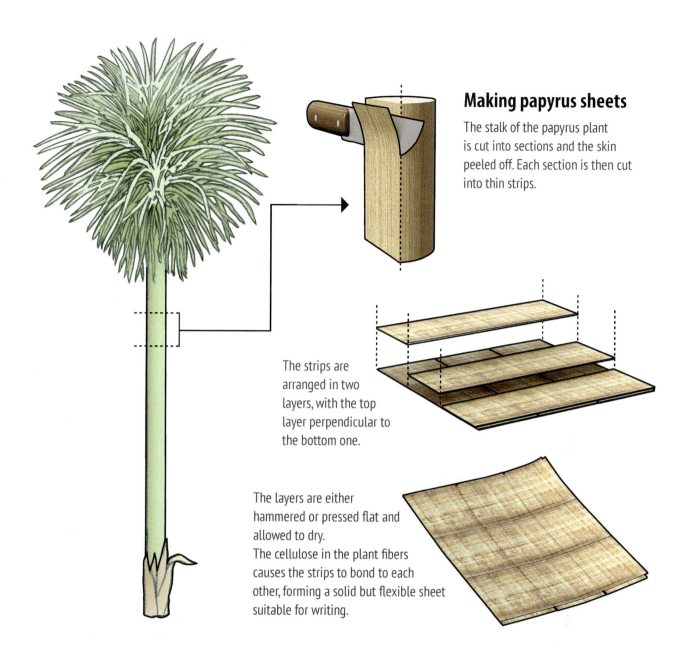

Making papyrus sheets

The stalk of the papyrus plant is cut into sections and the skin peeled off. Each section is then cut into thin strips.

The strips are arranged in two layers, with the top layer perpendicular to the bottom one.

The layers are either hammered or pressed flat and allowed to dry.
The cellulose in the plant fibers causes the strips to bond to each other, forming a solid but flexible sheet suitable for writing.

Parchment and vellum

Parchment is typically made from calf, goat or sheep skin. **Vellum** is more specifically made from calf skin. Both are made by soaking the skin in lime, scraping it clean and stretching it on a frame to dry.

By the start of the current era, the use of parchment and vellum was becoming more common in place of papyrus, although the latter was still less expensive to manufacture. The material was more durable and smoother as a writing surface. It also could be folded, which was another weakness of papyrus, which tended to crack. As codices—books made of separate pages as is common today—gained popularity over scrolls, parchment and vellum were preferred.

In 1455 CE Gutenberg printed some of the copies of his 42-line bible on vellum, but the rest on paper.

China

Bamboo

In Asia, strips of bamboo or other wood, known as slips, were bound together to make scrolls on which characters were written in ink. There is evidence of these dating back as early as 3,250 years ago.

In the past Chinese was written vertically top to bottom, and the columns were read in sequence from right to left.

This medium had the advantage of being editable: A character could be scraped off with a knife. The disadvantage was weight: A collection of scrolls amounting to a book was heavy and hard to transport, often requiring a cart.

Ink and colors

In Egypt and China, ink used for writing and illustration had a full range of colors.

Ink is essentially just thin paint. Both consist of a pigment suspended in a liquid, usually water, and a binder that helps the pigment stay suspended in the liquid and stick to the writing surface. Egyptians commonly used gum from acacia plants as a binder.

Pigments

Black is made with carbon, obtained from burning plant material, bones or oil.

Reds and oranges can be made with iron oxide, found naturally in earth deposits. Orange can also be made with realgar, an arsenic sulfide mineral.

Yellows were made with orpiment, also an arsenic sulfide mineral similar to realgar. Both are toxic, but nevertheless were widely used throughout the Middle East until the 19th century CE.

The Egyptians made what is believed to be the first artificial pigment, Egyptian Blue, by cooking a number of materials together including quartz, copper and calcium oxide. Different blues can also be made from a range of minerals such as manganese and cobalt.

Greens can be made with copper minerals such as malachite, or chromium oxide, arsenic and a number of other chemicals.

Black and red were the two most often used ink colors in Egyptian documents, red to highlight introductory and important sections, and black for the rest of the text. The other colors were more commonly used for paintings and illustrations.

An Egyptian scribe's ink palette, with wells for black and red ink. Thin reeds with crushed tips were used as writing implements.

Egyptian pens made from reed stalks. The Chinese made similar ones from bamboo.

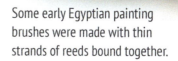

Some early Egyptian painting brushes were made with thin strands of reeds bound together.

Writing's social impact

We know little about prehistoric societies except that human lifestyles changed significantly starting about 12,000 years ago, with the beginning of agriculture. Farming appears to have started in multiple locations about roughly the same time, give or take a few millennia, from the Americas to China.

Farming led to permanent settlements, which over time grew into the first cities. These cities tended to share similar characteristics, most notably closely packed buildings surrounded by walls. From those walls we can infer why people chose to live in cities: They provided protection. There is evidence that prehistoric life was violent—most of the human remains that we've discovered have signs of violent injury. It's estimated that about a quarter of all prehistoric deaths were the result of violence inflicted by other humans.

To be clear, most people during this time and throughout most of history didn't live in cities, since almost everyone worked in agriculture. But cities became centers of trade and commerce and exerted political control in their regions, and served as refuges from outside threats.

This new urban lifestyle brought about several major societal changes:

• **Government**. Laws had to be codified in order for larger populations to co-exist in a crowded space. Most systems were autocratic, but there were occasional experiments in democracy such as in Hellenic Athens and in Rome before Caesar, when there was a senate (although only native-born males were eligible).

• **Commerce**. Wide-scale trading began to take place, along with the manufacture of goods, often across broad regions. The Phoenicians traded across the entire Mediterranean and even into the Atlantic, and Indus artifacts have been found in Mesopotamia, evidence of trade between two regions more than 1,200 miles apart.

Over the course of this period of history methods of payment changed from a barter system to money, but it appears to have been gradual. It probably started with metals being used as payment, which eventually led to the first true coins being minted. The earliest ones we know of were made in cities in present-day Turkey in the 7th century BCE.

• **Technology.** The increase in commerce likely spurred development of better production methods. Large temples started to appear in major cities, which would have required improved building methods, and ships capable of carrying goods to distant ports would have required better shipwright skills.

And the use of metal to make tools, weapons and other objects also began during this period: copper smelting about 7,500 years ago, bronze (a mixture of copper and tin or arsenic) about 6,000 years ago, and iron about 3,200 years ago.

• **Diversification of labor**. No longer did everybody do the same thing, namely, hunting and gathering. Now there were farmers, cattle herders, stone masons, brick makers, sailors, shop keepers and craftspeople making pottery, fabrics, clothing, tools and weapons along with a wide range of other consumer goods, and builders, architects and shipwrights. And in some cases professional soldiers, as city-states organized armies, and clerical government jobs.

- **Social classes.** Societies became stratified into upper and lower classes, largely based on wealth and profession. And social position became attached to families, with status passed on to succeeding generations, creating ruling classes and royal lineages.

Slavery also became a widespread practice in virtually all societies across the world, a form of endemic violence that has sadly persisted to this day, although it has not been as prevalent in the last two centuries compared to the past.

- **Organized religion.** Most early cities had temples, some of the first permanent structures that served a purpose other than habitation. Along with them came a priest class and the establishment of state orthodoxies, which usually tied government and religion together.

With writing, the first historical records appeared, along with the earliest literature and poetry, the first books, and records of every kind of human knowledge and activity. It enabled governments to function and for orderly commerce to take place.

It's feasible that commerce was the catalyst that enabled the development of writing systems. Counting systems predate the founding of agriculture and cities by tens of thousands of years, but with the growth of manufacture and trading, it would have become necessary to keep more accurate records of inventory and transactions. Likely the first written characters were simple drawings depicting things: symbols for cattle and baskets of grain, for example. Over time the system would evolve to more fully represent all that could be expressed through spoken language. Eventually it would become possible to document the full range of speech and thought, and to record in detail events both real and fictional.

The technology used for writing varied by region, and was usually whatever material was locally abundant: clay in Mesopotamia, papyrus in Egypt, bamboo in China. The material of choice influenced the design of characters: Cuneiform evolved into patterns of triangular indentations due to the use of sharpened reeds pressed into wet clay, while Egyptian hieratics took on shapes easier to write with ink on papyrus using a simple stylus, as did Chinese characters written on a narrow strip of bamboo with ink and brush.

In most societies during this era literacy rates were very low, possibly less than one percent of the population, and limited to a professional scribe class, a state of affairs that has largely persisted up until very recent times: Just 500 years ago the worldwide literacy rate among adults was practically zero, in 1900 CE it had risen to about 20 percent, and not until 2000 CE had the rate risen to over 80 percent. For most of recorded history reading and writing has been the privilege of an elite class.

The complexity of the earliest systems such as cuneiform and hieroglyphics might have contributed to low literacy rates during their eras. More likely it was a result of social class structure. But whatever the explanation, a net result was that the government and the elite classes controlled information, a situation that persisted until well into the Enlightenment era of a few centuries ago.

This 10,000-year time period is when human civilization as we know it came into existence. As we next examine the current era over the last 2,000 years, we will see how new developments in communication technology increased access to information and ideas, and the effect that had on human societies.

Paper

The date traditionally assigned to the invention of paper is 105 CE, and is credited to Ts'ai (or Cai) Lun, a court official in the Eastern Han dynasty of China. However, several paper fragments predating this time have been discovered, the oldest dating to as early as 179 BCE, so it's unknown when paper was first made.

The problem with making paper is not so much technical—it's a fairly simple process—as the amount of effort involved. In this way it was similar to papyrus or vellum, both of which required considerable time and labor to produce, making each sheet precious. For paper, the biggest problem is preparation: It's made from the fibers of cellulose plant material, and requires a method of shredding the material and separating the individual fibers, which is labor and time intensive.

Also, the problem is cost of materials. The earliest paper fragments were made from expensive materials such as silk. It's likely that what Ts'ai Lun is credited with was a practical and economical method of making paper from cost-effective materials such as common vegetation and old rags.

Paper was first adopted for a number of uses besides writing, particularly as wrapping material and padding. Its use as toilet paper began in the 6th century CE, and as teabags in the 7th. Paper money was first printed in China in the 10th century during the Tang dynasty.

But its use as writing material also spread rapidly as it replaced bound bundles of bamboo slips, which were bulky and heavy. Books could now be contained in a single scroll, easily hand carried (the slip bundles for even a single book required a cart).

The result was an increase in the spread of literature and of literacy in Chinese society, with many more individuals owning copies of books. By the 4th century CE, Chinese library collections were several times larger than those in Europe.

The spread of paper

The earliest paper

Although Ts'ai Lun is traditionally credited with the invention of paper in 105 CE, at least one artifact has been found that is one or two centuries older than him, shown below. So the origins of paper are still unclear.

There have been several discoveries of paper from the first centuries CE. A collection of letters written about 150 CE was found in the Great Wall of China. And in Turkestan, a region between China and India, papers have been found that were made between the 2nd and 8th centuries CE. They were made of mulberry bark, hemp and other natural fibers, some of which had previously been cloth. These provide evidence of the spread of paper beyond China.

In eastern Asia, paper manufacture spread from China to Japan and Korea by the 6th century CE. Going west, paper was exported along the Silk Road, the trade route between China and the West that passed through central Asia. Chinese silk was the most sought after Asian product in the West, and it was transported by land along with other goods such as tea, rice and spices starting as early as the 2nd century BCE when the Han Dynasty opened its borders to trade with the

Creative Commons

This is the oldest piece of paper yet discovered, a fragment of a map drawn with black ink, found in a 2,100-year-old tomb in Fangmatan, in the Gansu province of north-central China. The fragment is a little over two inches wide.

Roman Empire. In time trade articles came to include porcelain and gunpowder, and paper as its manufacture began, acquainting the West with it.

Samarkand

The spread of paper making outside of China to the West may have been initiated by a singular event, a battle in 751 CE between the Arab Caliphate and the Tang Dynasty near the border of present-day Kazakhstan and Kyrgyzstan in central Asia. The Arabs were victorious and the Chinese forced to retreat, leaving the region under Arab control for the next several centuries.

According to some accounts, among the Chinese who were taken prisoner were two papermakers, who were compelled to reveal the secrets of their trade to their captors. Soon paper making started in the city of Samarkand in modern-day Uzbekistan, where there was plentiful hemp, flax and clean water.

Regardless of the truth of this story, paper making did in fact start in Samarkand in the 8th century CE,

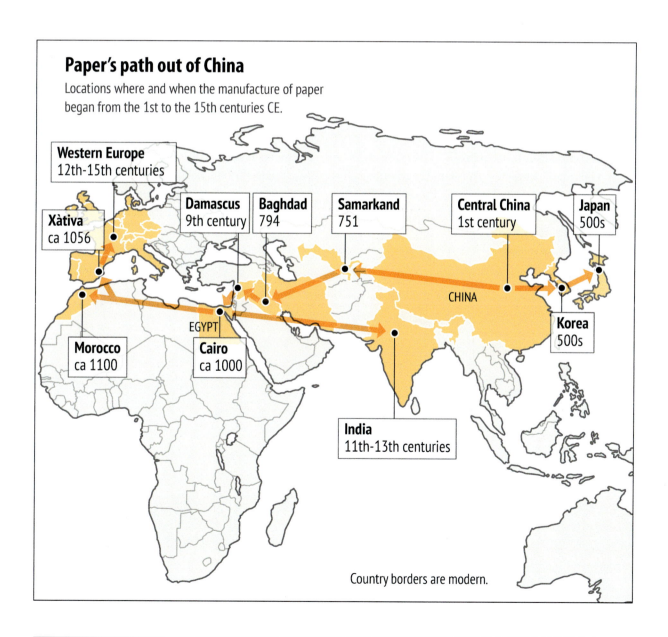

Paper's path out of China

Locations where and when the manufacture of paper began from the 1st to the 15th centuries CE.

Western Europe 12th-15th centuries

Xàtiva ca 1056

Damascus 9th century

Baghdad 794

Samarkand 751

Central China 1st century

Japan 500s

CHINA

Korea 500s

EGYPT

Morocco ca 1100

Cairo ca 1000

India 11th-13th centuries

Country borders are modern.

and the quality of the product gained a high reputation throughout the Arab world, becoming known as the *Paper of Samarkand*. But more importantly, the process of paper making was now known outside of Eastern Asia, and over time spread to the West.

Arabic paper

Paper production began in Baghdad in 794 CE, and then in Damascus, which became the main supplier of paper to Europe for the next several centuries, where it was known as *Charta Damascena*.

The industry came to Cairo in the early 11th century CE. The Islamic world occupied all of Northern Africa and parts of Spain at that time, and paper production advanced along that route. The earliest known paper mill in Europe was in the city of Xàtiva, in Arab-occupied Spain, in the mid-11th century. The oldest known European document on paper made in Europe is the 1080 CE *Missal of Silos*, probably using paper made in Islamic Spain.

In India, Chinese paper was being imported as early as the 7th century, but was not widely used. The common writing media were tree bark in northern India and palm leaves in the south. A growing presence of Islam brought paper making to southeast India in the 11th century, and paper usage gradually increased over the next two centuries as paper mills came into operation in the rest of the country.

Into Europe

From Spain paper mills started appearing across Europe, one in France by 1190 and one in Italy by 1276, in Fabriano. It spread into Holland and Germany in the 14th century, to the rest of Continental Europe in the 15th, and to Britain by the 16th.

With paper made affordable by domestic production, it rapidly displaced other media such as parchment, first in the Arab world and then in Europe, facilitating advancements in printmaking, in particular the development of moveable type in the 15th century in Germany.

Paper making

Paper can be made from any fibrous cellulose material: cotton, rice, hemp, flax, bamboo or tree bark, and also from rags, rope and fishing nets—any material that can be shredded into individual fibers. Cellulose, a natural plant substance, works well for making paper because when wet the fibers stick together and then remain stuck after drying, resulting in strong but flexible paper sheets.

Making paper by hand

1 Materials such as cotton, tree bark or rags are shredded to separate their fibers.

The shredding process makes pulp, which is a collection of loose fibers.

2 The pulp is stirred into a basin of water.

A frame with a fine mesh screen, called a **mold**, is used to gather the pulp fibers into a sheet. Another frame called a **deckle** fits over the top of the mold to contain the pulp and provide an even edge to the sheets.

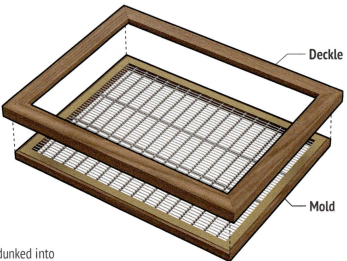

Deckle

Mold

3 The mold and deckle assembly is dunked into the water basin and lifted back out, collecting a layer of pulp.

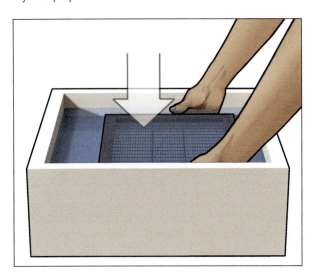

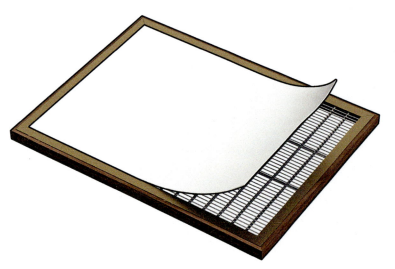

4 The deckle is removed and the newly formed paper sheet is pulled from the mold. It is then pressed, typically between sheets of felt, and hung to dry.

Making pulp manually

Separating plant and rag fibers to produce pulp is the most labor-intensive part of the paper-making process. It was typically done by soaking or boiling the raw materials in water, followed by beating or stamping with devices designed for that purpose.

The first step was usually to soak or boil the material after it had been cut into small pieces.

After soaking, the material was pounded to produce pulp. The device shown here is a mortar and pestle, similar to what T'sai Lun may have used.

Over time a variety of devices were invented to more efficiently produce pulp. These are called stampers.

Ink and calligraphy

The technique of writing with an ink brush has long been respected as an art form in China and Japan, and was facilitated by the invention of paper.

A high-quality ink was developed for this purpose by using soot from the burning of oil or pine chips, called lampblack, which is mixed with a binder made from fish or animal hides.

The earliest evidence for this type of ink dates to 256 BCE. In English it is called India Ink in spite of its Chinese origins. In French it is *Encre de Chine*, or Chinese Ink. In Chinese it is called *Ch'i*.

This ink has excellent archival qualities. It doesn't fade with time, as ancient documents demonstrate.

Carbon burner

Carbon to make black ink is produced by capturing soot from burning oil or pine chips. The device collects soot inside a dome above an oil lamp.

The soot is mixed with a gum or gluten binder and placed in molds to make solid ink sticks.

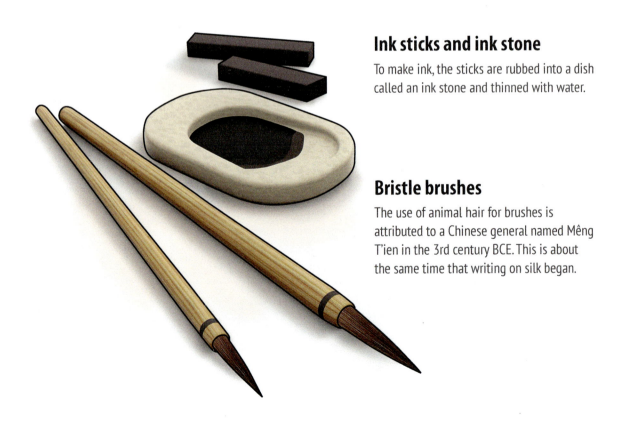

Ink sticks and ink stone

To make ink, the sticks are rubbed into a dish called an ink stone and thinned with water.

Bristle brushes

The use of animal hair for brushes is attributed to a Chinese general named Mêng T'ien in the 3rd century BCE. This is about the same time that writing on silk began.

Calligraphy

This is a copy of a page written by Wang Xianzhi in the 4th century CE during the Eastern Jin dynasty in China. Xianzhi was a renowned calligrapher, part of a family of respected calligraphers which included his father and siblings. The writing is a recipe for traditional medicine. The copy is in the Taitō City Calligraphy Museum in Tokyo, Japan.

Pulp machines

Stampers

The water wheel was the first invention to use a source of energy other than human or animal power. Evidence for them goes back at least as early as the 3rd century BCE. They were most often used for irrigation and to grind grain. Water-driven grain mills appeared in both China and Europe in the 2nd century BCE.

So the technology was already established when it was applied to the production of pulp. The earliest concrete evidence for a water-powered stamper is in 1282 CE in Xàtiva, Spain, already the site of the first paper making in Europe since 1052. The first one in Northern Europe was in Nuremberg, Germany in 1390.

The typical design uses the same principle as earlier foot-powered stampers, raising and dropping hammers onto pulp material.

The largest such mills had several pulp basins, each with up to four hammers.

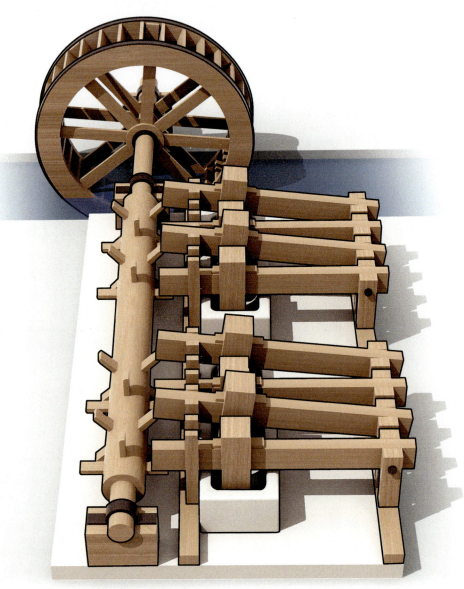

Water wheel stamper

The water wheel turns an axle with spokes, which alternately raise and drop heavy wooden hammers in a basin filled with pulp material.

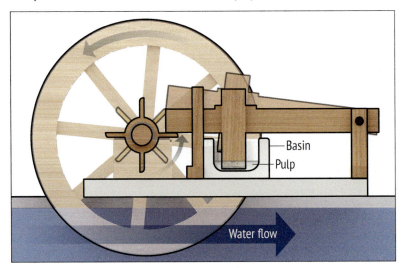

Basin
Pulp
Water flow

Hollander beater

Devices of this sort were invented in Holland in the 16th century CE, and proved to be more efficient at producing pulp than stampers. They could be powered by water, wind or animal labor.

They did not make as good a quality of pulp, as the process tended to result in shorter fibers, which made weaker paper. Nevertheless, beaters came into widespread use due to their greater productivity.

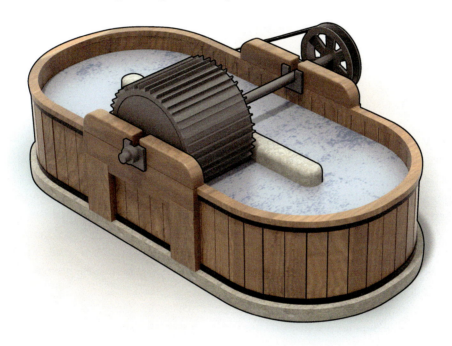

Pulp material is added to the water tank, where it is ground up by the rotating wheel.

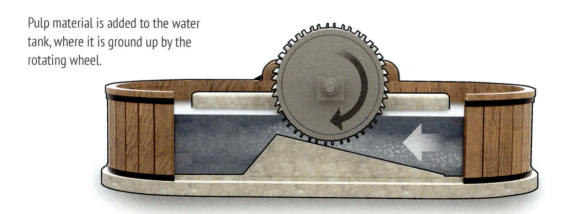

The paper industry

High-quality paper was being made at established mills in China and the Middle East at the time that paper making started appearing in the West. As new mills appeared across Europe and paper came into more common use, technology and methods improved incrementally over the centuries leading up to the Industrial Age, but the basic process remained essentially the same, with each sheet being gathered by hand with a screen dunked into a basin.

We have few records of the precise methods used by different mills. China had kept its methods a state secret until they were revealed at Samarkand, and similarly each mill in the rest of the world carefully guarded its techniques. As long as it was made by hand, it remained more of an art than a standardized process.

There are a number of factors that influence paper quality. These include:

• **Fiber quality.** The pulping process needs to create fibers of sufficient consistency and length to give pages durability and strength. This will depend not just on the raw material used but on the method with which the fibers are separated.

• **Color.** To make white or light-colored paper requires removing dark fibers or chemically altering their color. Bleaches weren't used until the 19th century, so quality depended on the raw material and water free of debris or silt. The highest quality white paper was made from light colored rags of good material; lower quality paper tended to be brown or gray.

• **Water quality.** Mineral content in the water, or other impurities, also affects paper color and quality. For this reason, paper mills were most often located next to streams and rivers, which also provided the power to run the pulp stampers.

• **Absorbency.** This depends on what the paper will be used for. In Asia prior to the modern era, where it was most commonly used for hand-written calligraphy with a brush, the paper needed a soft surface and greater absorbency. Later with the invention of printing presses, a harder surface was needed that was less absorbent, so that characters would keep a crisp and even edge.

Different materials called sizing make the paper surface less absorbent. Rosin can be added to the pulp prior to forming the pages, or the finished pages can be coated with starch-based compounds. Also pressing the paper during drying will make a harder, less-absorbent surface.

• **Longevity.** Paper made from highly acidic materials such as wood chips turns yellow and crumbles with time. Paper made from more acid-neutral materials such as cotton or flax lasts a lot longer. There are books printed centuries ago that are still in near perfect condition due to the quality of the paper. In contrast, most books printed in the last century, when wood pulp came into widespread use, become brittle and crumble in a few decades.

Also, resistence to insects and mold is a consideration. Certain chemicals can be added to the paper for this purpose.

Books

Virtually all books as we know them today are **codexes**, which means they are made of sheets folded and bound together at one edge.

The codex's origin precedes the current era. In the first and second centuries BCE the Romans had been using a precursor, a set of double-sided, wax-covered wooden tablets bound at one edge, for note-taking purposes. In time, the wood was replaced with parchment, vellum or papyrus. By the first century CE, the codex was replacing the older format of scrolls in the West, and within a few centuries it was the standard format for virtually all books.

In medieval times, each book was not only hand-written but was hand-built as a unique object, with no two being alike. Many had highly decorated and even jewel- and precious metal-encrusted covers, and were treated as treasured objects.

As paper making spread across the world and with the introduction of printing presses, book-making methods became somewhat standardized. In time paper sizes within regions became standardized as well, but there weren't, and still aren't, globally accepted sizes: Standard book sizes are different in the US than in Europe or Japan.

As long as paper was handmade, page sizes were restricted by the size of the mold used to make it, which was generally no wider than a person's spread arms, three feet at the most but usually about two feet.

With printing presses, the method was to print several pages on each sheet of paper, which was then folded and cut. So, a single sheet would make either four pages or a multiple of that. A sheet folded once, making four pages, was called a *folio*, with two folds making eight pages a *quarto*, with three folds making sixteen pages an *octavo*, and so on to yet smaller sizes.

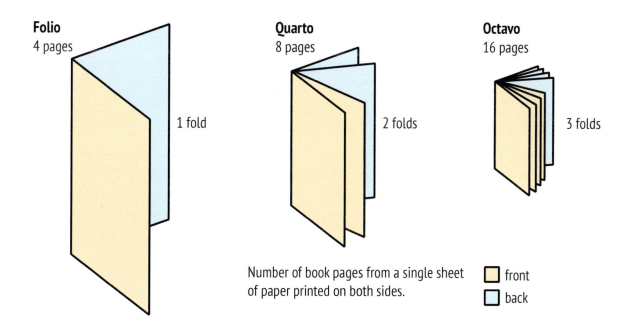

Folio
4 pages

1 fold

Quarto
8 pages

2 folds

Octavo
16 pages

3 folds

Number of book pages from a single sheet of paper printed on both sides.

□ front
□ back

Codex books were more practical than scrolls. They held more content in an easier to access format, and were easier to store. One could bookmark relevant pages. By numbering the pages, it became easier to find a specific passage through the use of a table of contents and an index. In short, it was a better way to organize content.

As printing presses increased the number of copies, the practice of making books became an industry, and binderies came into existence to fill this new industry need. But until the Industrial Age it remained a skilled craft trade, with each book being assembled and bound by hand. Until machines took over that task, printed books remained expensive and collected only by the well-to-do and the upper classes, whose members were also the most likely to be literate.

Book making

A sheet is folded and cut to make leaves, with a page on each side.
The collection of leaves is called a gathering.

The gatherings for the entire book are brought together and bound at the spine side.

The bound leaves are enclosed with a cover, usually by gluing at the spine.
Covers were typically made of hard paper board, and themselves covered with leather or similar material.

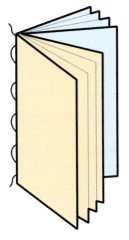

The leaves are sewn together at the fold.

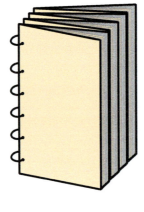

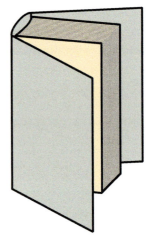

Paper's impact on the world

It took the better part of a millenium from the time paper was invented to its eventual availability across all of the Old World, from Japan to Great Britain. And it took 1,500 years from its inception in China to its manufacture in most of Europe, with a mill finally opening in Great Britain in the 1500s. In that time it gradually replaced earlier media for writing, illustrating and printing.

And it provided a ready and affordable material for use in block printing in eastern Asia, facilitating the first mass distribution of printed text, and then in printing presses in Europe in the 15th century, making possible the mass production of books.

Paper was at first more expensive and less durable than parchment, limiting its use in medieval Europe. Until mills were established in the West, all paper had to be imported, at first by the Silk Road from China, and then from Damascus. Generally goods from the Silk Road were expensive and considered luxury items given the cost of transport.

But by the 15th century it became the foundation of mass communication, and remained so through the 20th century when broadcast and electronic media started to compete with it. In spite of that, its use has grown every year and continues to do so, as printing technology has improved and lowered costs, and as worldwide population growth has increased demand for printed products. Whether that growth will be sustained as digital media becomes universal remains to be seen.

Creative Commons

This is the earliest known representation of paper making in Europe, in a 1568 German woodcut by Jost Amman in *The Little Book of Trades*.
A watermill stamper and a printing press are depicted in the background.

Printing

Printing as we think of it, lines of text impressed in ink on paper, probably began in China some time in or before the 7th century CE. The oldest known printed document of this kind is from the early 8th century, a small dharani woodblock print discovered in 1966 at a temple in Korea.

Printing patterns on fabric precedes printing on paper, starting some time in the 2nd century in China. And various other methods of making copies of text and images are also older, including stone rubbings, stencils and stamps. As discussed in the chapter on writing, stamps and cylinder seals were used in the Middle East thousands of years earlier, principally to make impressions in clay, and the use of stamps and seals was common in many parts of the world.

But none of those earlier methods of reproduction were of much use in making multiple copies of written text or drawn images. Making copies from stone inscriptions or by using stencils took a long time for each copy, and stamps had size limitations.

Woodblock printing was the first technology that allowed copies to be made more efficiently, and which led to the first mass distributions of printed material.

Next came the concept of moveable type, with each character on its own block. The earliest known use of this method was in the 11th century in China, but it didn't gain widespread use.

Gutenberg's moveable type press was built in the mid-15th century in Germany. This was the innovation that is often cited as revolutionizing communication, as similar presses appeared across Europe and eventually the world over the next several centuries, making all manner of printed material available to broad audiences.

Printing predecessors

Two of the oldest methods of making reproductions are seals and stone rubbings, and both are thought to have led to the concept of woodcut printing, and later moveable type. They work by similar principles.

In the case of seals, parts of the design not intended to print are cut away, leaving raised areas that are inked. In the case of stone rubbings, the characters to be printed are cut into the stone, making them the only parts not inked, in the process making a reverse image with white text on a black background.

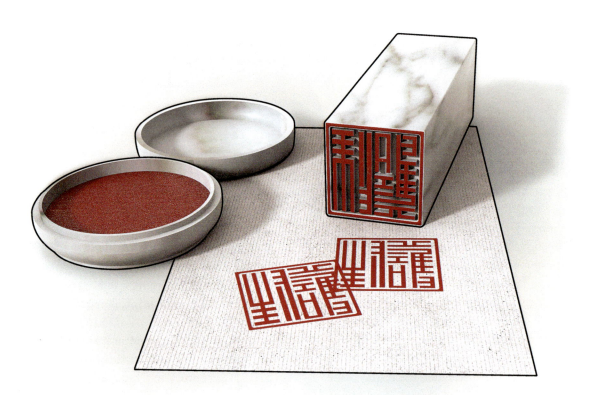

Seals and stamps

Interestingly, the Chinese word *yin* means both print and seal. Seals came into use under emperor Ts'in Shih Huang in the 3rd century BCE, primarily for certifying contracts. Previously this was done by breaking a piece of bamboo or jade, with each party retaining a piece.

Seals were carved out of jade, metals such as gold, silver or copper, or from ivory or rhino horn. At first as in the Middle East, they were used to make impressions in clay. But in the T'ang Dynasty during the 5th and 6th centuries CE, they started being used with red ink, thus becoming stamps.

Stamps later came into use for creating copies of charms on paper. Charms are symbols or text with various meanings or intended to bring good fortune.

Stone rubbings

Rubbings made from stone tablets began in China during the Han dynasty, probably during the first or second centuries CE.

The process was simple but time consuming. Text, most often of a religious passage, was carved into a slab of stone. Copies were done by laying a sheet of felt on the stone and a sheet of paper on top of that, which was then moistened, hammered and rubbed with a brush to push the paper into the indentations in the stone. When dry, the paper's surface was inked with a pad stuffed with cotton or silk, leaving only the indented parts of the paper blank.

Notice that the text in the stone tablet is not reversed, since the side of the paper that got inked was the top and not the side facing the stone.

Although not an efficient method of reproducing text, stone rubbings are still done to this day. As with stamps, they were precursors of woodblock printing.

Woodblock printing

The oldest existing document made from a woodblock was created in the 8th century CE in Korea. Printed on a small sheet of mulberry paper, it is called the *Pure Light Dharani-sutra*, a Buddhist scroll.

Woodblock printing is believed to have started a century earlier, in the 7th, in China during the T'ang Dynasty.

Variously called woodcut, woodblock, block, xylographic or relief printing, the method is to cut away all the parts of a board's surface that will not be printed, leaving the print areas elevated. This process was quicker than stone carving, more portable, and allowed for a larger print area than stamps.

The use of woodblocks spread to Japan and Korea, and eventually the same method came into use in Europe with the production of low-cost but also low-quality illustrated books for sale to the public in the 15th century.

The woodblock printing process

1 Cutting

The design is drawn or transferred to the woodblock's surface, in reverse. All non-printing areas are cut away with chisels.

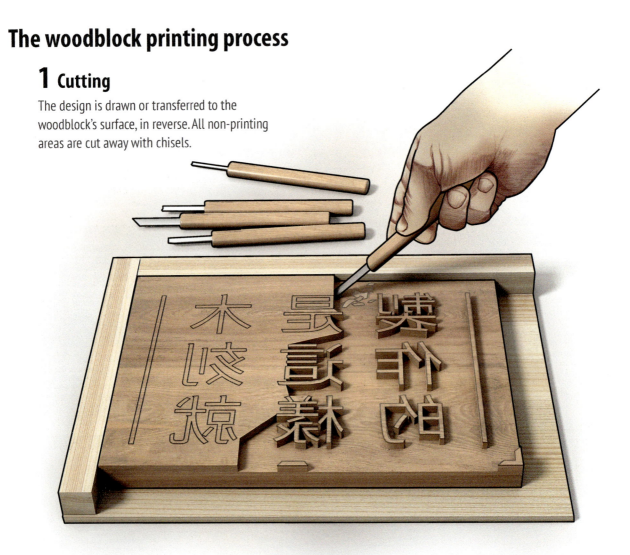

2 Inking

Raised surfaces are inked with a brush.

3 Printing

A sheet of paper is placed on the block, lined up with corner and side marks. The paper is then pressed with a baren.

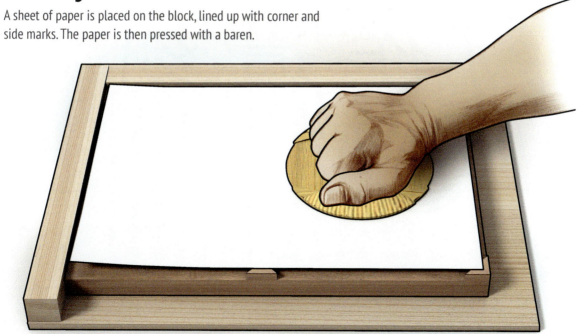

4 Finished print

The paper is removed to dry, and the block is re-inked for each additional copy.

The characters in the print are now facing in the right direction. The print below is written as Chinese was in the 8th century, in vertical columns read in order from right to left. The text says "This is how woodcuts are made" in traditional Chinese.

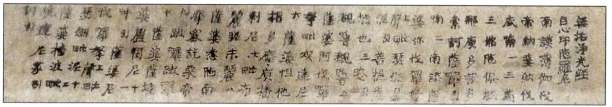

One of the woodblock prints from the Million Pagoda project.

First mass printing

The earliest known large-scale printing of single documents happened in Japan in the 8th century CE. In 764 Empress Shōtoku ordered the construction of one million miniature wooden pagodas, each about 4½ inches in height, with each to contain a woodblock printed scroll of a Buddhist passage from the *Vimala-nirbhasa-sutra*, a Sanskrit work that was translated into Chinese characters for this purpose.

The project was completed in 770, and the pagodas distributed to temples across Japan.

The prints consisted of four different charms, and were about 18 inches long and two inches in height, each with 30 columns of five characters each.

The four charms each told a different short story. One was similar to a modern chain letter, claiming that making 77 copies of it and placing them in 77 clay pagodas would cure illness and ensure a long life. This might have been the Empress' motivation in ordering the project, but it didn't work: She died of illness as the pagodas were being distributed.

Woodcuts became a respected art form in Japan from this time on, and became the most common printing method in eastern Asia up to and into industrialized times. It is still practiced as an art form not only in Japan but in much of the world.

British Library

One of the million wooden pagodas. They were originally painted white. This one is part of the British Museum collection.

First block prints

The oldest complete blockprint book discovered so far is the *Diamond Sūtra*, printed in China in 868 CE. A copy was discovered in 1900 in a cave in present-day Gansu Province, in northwestern China, in a location along the original Silk Road. It is a Buddhist manuscript consisting of a 16.5-foot long scroll, made from individual block prints sewn together.

The high quality of the print along with the fineness of the illlustrations indicates that the art of blockprinting was already well developed by the 9th century, and was likely an established industry.

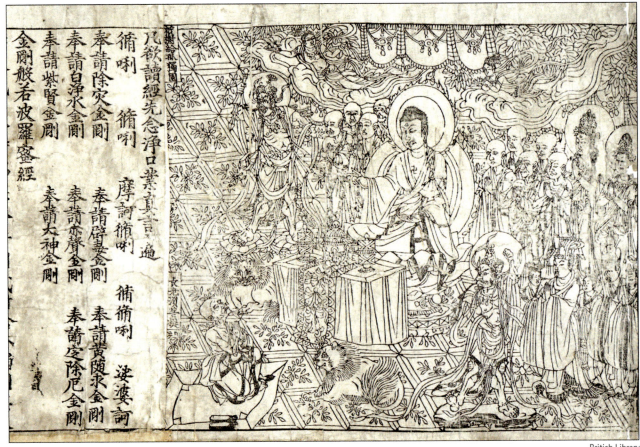

Frontispiece of the *Diamond Sūtra*, depicting Buddha addressing disciples in a tree grove.

European block books

Books made from single woodblocks appeared in Europe about the same time as Gutenberg's press in the mid-15th century. They typically consisted of illustrations with little text, depicting religious scenes. Often the text, if any, was added by hand after printing, and also hand colored if in color.

They were usually only made up of a few pages, printed on one side of the paper with the blank sides glued together, folded and sewn into a codex.

They were probably marketed as inexpensive alternatives to emerging moveable type books, which were expensive.

In this scene, a dying man is tempted by demons with crowns, an allegory for pride and earthly possessions. In the background Christ and Mary look on disapprovingly.

A page from the Biblia Pauperum or "Bible of the Poor". It was hand colored after printing.

Intaglio

Intaglio printing is the opposite of woodblock in that instead of raised surfaces being inked, depressions in the surface are inked.

Many print illustrations prior to the development of photography were done as engravings and etchings, the two most common forms of intaglio.

Engraving

Engraving, the practice of cutting grooves into a surface, began as a decorative art form far back in prehistory. As metallurgy developed it became a way to decorate items such as jewelry.

It may have become a print medium when jewelry engravers in the Middle Ages began making records of their designs on paper. In the 1430s in Germany it emerged as a method of making paper prints of artwork, and the practice was soon taken up across the continent.

A number of Northern European artists produced remarkably intricate and sophisticated illustrations using this method; of particular note were Albrecht Dürer and Lucas van Leiden.

Etching

Engraving is a skill requiring practiced precision. Etching is somewhat easier, as it employs acid to do the cutting. As with engraving, etching started as a method of decorating metal surfaces, particularly of armor. A German craftsman, Daniel Hopfer, is credited with extending the practice to printing plates in the early 16th century.

Being easier to both learn and execute, etching soon gained popularity over engraving, although the two methods can be used together. Dürer also did etchings, as did Rembrandt.

Melancholia I, an engraving done by German artist Albrecht Dürer in 1514 CE. The print is 12 inches in height.

Intaglio printing

Both engraving and etching aim for the same result, a plate with grooves cut into its surface. Engraving achieves it by directly cutting the grooves with a tool called a burin. Etching does it with acid: The plate surface is coated with wax, into which the design is scratched with a needle. The plate is then doused in an acid bath, which cuts into the surface where the wax has been scratched away.

Engraving can be done on wood or metal; etching requires a metal that can be dissolved by acid. Copper is often used in both processes.

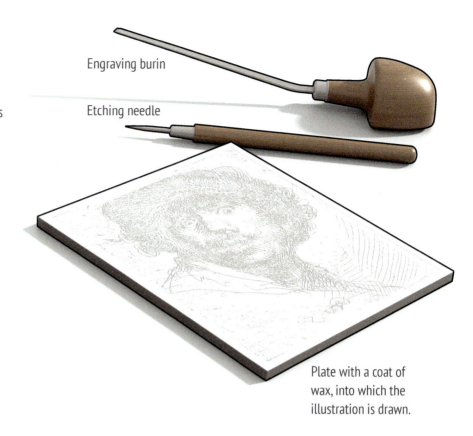

Engraving burin

Etching needle

Plate with a coat of wax, into which the illustration is drawn.

Once the plate has been engraved or etched—with the wax surface removed in the case of etching—the surface is inked and then wiped clean, leaving ink only in the grooves. A sheet of paper is then pressed on the plate to make a print. Presses were developed for this specific purpose.

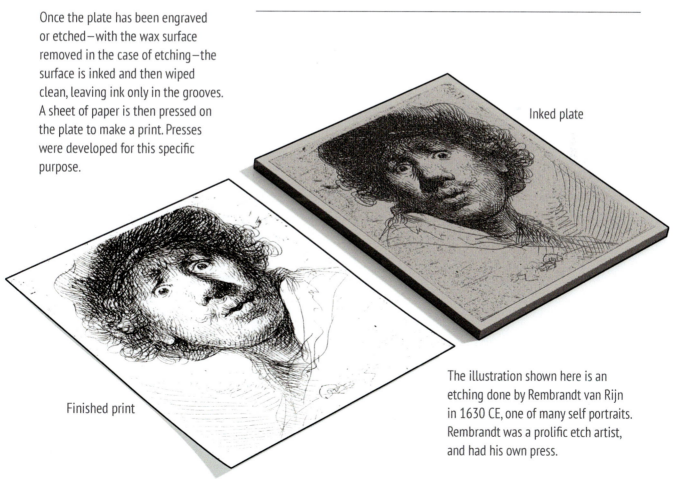

Inked plate

Finished print

The illustration shown here is an etching done by Rembrandt van Rijn in 1630 CE, one of many self portraits. Rembrandt was a prolific etch artist, and had his own press.

First moveable type

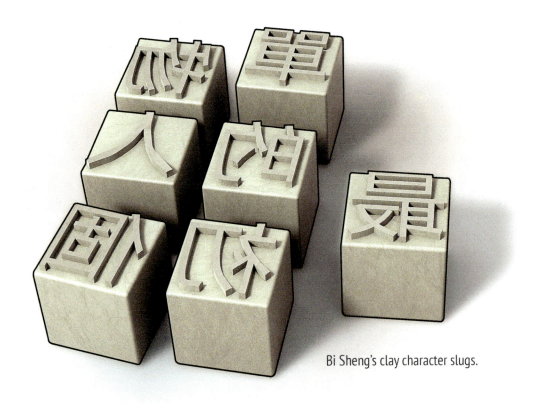

Bi Sheng's clay character slugs.

The first use of characters on individual blocks is attributed to a Chinese woodblock printer named Bi Sheng in the 11th century CE. He first carved blocks out of wood, but found that they became uneven after getting soaked in ink, so he changed to clay, carving each block with a single character and then baking them hard. He then typeset them on a heated iron plate and cemented the whole form together with pine resin and wax, pressing the blocks down with a board to make the tops even. From this he could print as one would from a woodblock.

Individually carved wooden slugs were subsequently used for several other printings in China, including a book discovered in Ningxia in 1991 titled *Auspicious Tantra of All-Reaching Union*, that was likely printed in the mid-12th century, and 100 copies of a record book in the Chinese province of Anhui in 1298 by an official by the name of Wang Zhen. But wood remained problematic and wore down quickly, requiring new slugs to be carved.

First copies of moveable type

Some time between the 12th and 14th centuries a method of casting copies of typeslugs was invented, by pressing a clay or wooden slug into sand and pouring molten metal—copper, bronze, iron or tin—into the cavity. This was the first time that multiple copies of the same slug could be made.

There is some evidence of paper money being printed in China from metal moveable type in the 12th century CE.

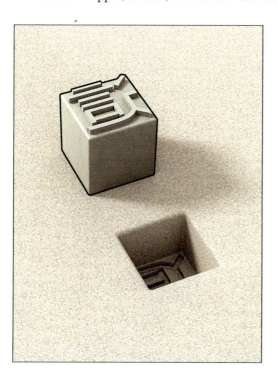

Bronze slugs arranged into a form.

Early moveable type books

The first set of books to be printed with moveable metal type is generally recognized to be the *Jikji Simche Yojeol*, printed in Korea in 1377 CE. Its full title is *Anthology of Great Buddhist Priests' Zen Teachings*, and was printed during the Goryeo Dynasty. It was a set of two books, but unfortunately only one copy survives, of the second volume. it is kept in the National Library of France.

But moveable type did not come into widespread use in either China or Korea, likely because of the thousands of characters used in Chinese writing, which was also what was used in Korea up to the 15th century. Woodblock printing was still the simplest and most efficient way to reproduce an entire page of text due to that circumstance. The same was true in Japan.

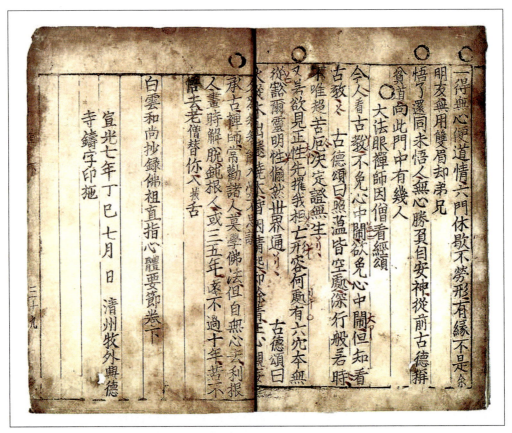

Pages from the Korean *Jikji*, the first book to be printed using moveable metal type. The only existing copy is in the National Library of France.

Gutenberg's press

His moveable-type press, which went into operation in 1450, is generally credited with revolutionizing printing and transforming Western civilization. In order to make it work, he had to solve several technological challenges.

First, he had to devise a method to produce large quantities of identical type slugs, and second, he had to design and build the press in which the slugs could be arranged. In addition, a different composition of ink was needed, one that would stick evenly to the metal slugs, as well as paper that had the right level of absorbency and texture.

The next pages will show how we think he made his slugs and how his press worked.

Johannes Gutenberg ~1400-1468

Not much is known about Gutenberg, or how he arrived at his concept of a moveable type press. It's not even clear if he was the first innovator. A Dutchman named Laurens Janszoon Coster (or Koster) is claimed by some to have built such a press in Haarlem in the 1420s, but there is insufficient evidence, perhaps because the city was destroyed by fire in 1426 while under seige. The story continues that one of Coster's assistants, a letter cutter named Johann Foust (or Fust), stole the presses and type on Coster's death and took them to Mainz in Germany to start his own printing company. Again, there is no conclusive evidence to support these claims.

What is known of Gutenberg is that he was born in Mainz sometime around 1400, but the precise year is unknown. His father was a merchant and his family was considered upper class. He worked in blacksmithing and goldsmithing, and engaged in various enterprises with limited success.

Over a period of time in the 1440s, he developed his idea for a moveable type press, and had it in operation by 1450, when it was used to print a German poem, possibly his first printing job. The press was subsequently used to print various texts such as Latin grammars, but its most lucrative jobs were the printing of thousands of indulgences for the church. Many of these that survive are dated 1454-1455.

Gutenberg took on several investors, including the afore-mentioned Johann Foust, to fund what would become his best known project, the printing of a bible, which began in 1452. In 1455, he printed his 42-line bible, making 180 copies, some on vellum and some on paper.

In 1456 he was sued by Foust for failure to repay his loans. Foust won in court and took possession of the press and half the bibles, leaving Gutenberg destitute. Gutenberg appears to have been involved in several printing projects in the following years, including another bible, but there are no firm records. Gutenberg died in 1468. His grave is lost.

Type slugs

The first problem that Gutenberg faced was how to make multiple copies of slugs for each character. Think of how many letter e's, for example, there are in a single page, and how many in a book: There could be thousands. The solution was to make a mold that could be used to repeatedly and quickly cast multiple copies of each character slug.

And Gutenberg needed lots of molds: The typeface he used for his 42-line bible had at least 270 characters, as he wanted various widths of each letter to facilitate making justified lines of type.

Not all experts agree on how Gutenberg did this, but a likely solution was to make a reusable mold that would open up to remove the slug after it was cast, and to have an interchangeable character form so that the same mold could be used to cast any character.

The following illustrations show how slugs were made by hand in foundries in the centuries following Gutenberg and up to the Industrial Revolution, when new technologies automated the process.

The punch and matrix

The **matrix** is a flat metal bar with the impression of a single character, which is inserted into a slot in the mold in order to cast a slug of that character. In order to make the impression, a **punch** is first made with the character carved into its end. The punch is then hammered into the surface of the matrix. Here are the steps:

1 The characters are designed and drawn. Gutenberg's Bible used an ornate design belonging to a group of typefaces called Blackletter, which emulated hand-written texts of the time.

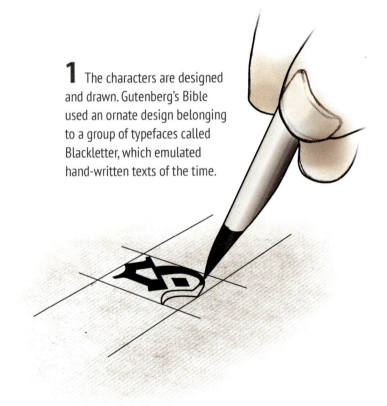

2 The design is then transferred to the tip of a metal bar which will be used as the punch. This might have been done by rubbing a charcoal or grease pencil drawing onto the tip of the punch.

Note that the letter shape is reversed.

3 The tip of the punch is then carved with fine files until the character is left as a raised shape. When done, the punch is hardened and tempered.

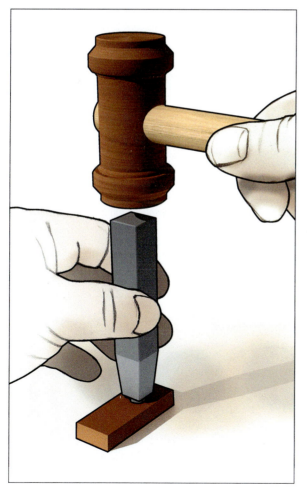

4 The punch is then hammered into the surface of the matrix, leaving an impression. The matrix is made from a soft metal such as copper.

The finished matrix.

The type mold

Its two interconnecting parts form a cavity in which to cast the slug.

1 The matrix is inserted into a slot in the bottom.

2 A molten mixture of lead, tin and antimony is poured into the mold. These metals have low melting points and cool quickly.

3 The mold is then pulled apart to remove the type slug.

Note: We don't know what Gutenberg's type molds looked like, or precisely how they functioned. These illustrations are roughly based on existing type molds.

The finished type slug.

Setting the type

After the slugs are cast, they are arranged in rows to make the lines of text for each printed page. The typesetters who did this job used a device called a **composing stick** to facilitate the task.

Gutenberg and his assistants likely used wooden composing sticks, although of unknown design. Later ones were made of metal and had clamping mechanisms to hold the slugs in place.

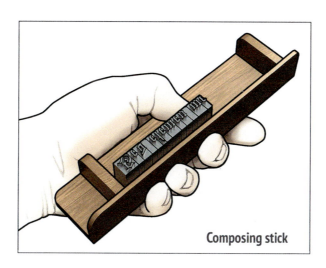

Composing stick

After a line of slugs is arranged in the composing stick, it is transferred to a frame that will be used to print an entire page.

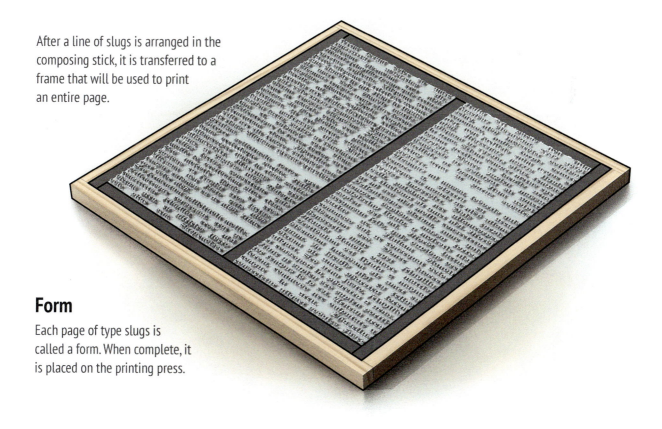

Form

Each page of type slugs is called a form. When complete, it is placed on the printing press.

The most time-consuming step in the type slug process was the carving of the letter form into the end of the punch. It required an expert craftsman, probably a jewelry maker. It might take an entire day to complete a single punch. This meant that creating the 270-character set for Gutenberg's Bible project, likely all done by the same artisan, would have taken the better part of a year.

Once the punches were created though, mass producing type slugs would have been a rapid process, which would have been essential for casting the approximately 100,000 slugs needed for the entire book. And that is the most innovative aspect of this invention: It allowed for the rapid reproduction of large numbers of identical characters.

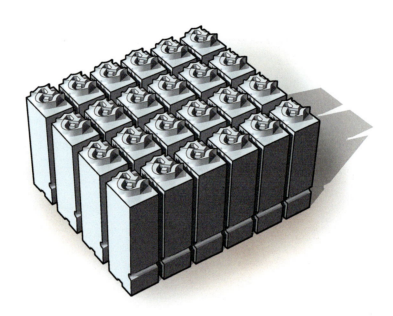

Moveable type press

Gutenberg's press probably looked something like this illustration. It would have been made almost entirely of wood, including the screw, except for a few pieces of metal hardware and, of course, the type slugs.

This illustration is loosely based on a functional press made for a 2008 BBC documentary, 'The Machine that Made Us.' It was built by Professor Alan May at the University of Reading in England. It stands about 5½ to 6 feet tall.

The technical problem of the press was how to provide even pressure across a sheet of paper in a single action so that pages could be printed quickly and efficiently. Also, the sheets of paper had to be consistently placed in the correct position, then flipped over to print the other side with the same margins.

Inspiration was likely found in agricultural presses that were common at the time, which used screws to exert downward pressure. The screw is at the heart of the press: It pushes down a solid board called a platen, hung from strings beneath the screw, which in turn applies even pressure to the paper beneath it.

Press parts

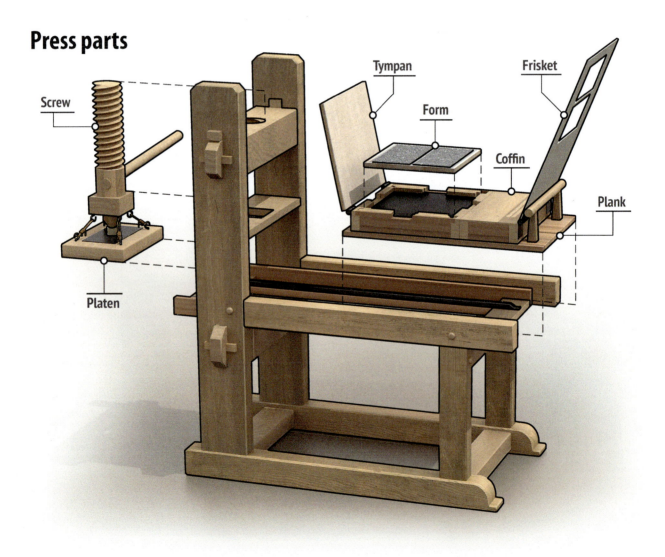

Screw

Platen

Tympan

Form

Coffin

Frisket

Plank

Ink

A press with metal slugs needs a different composition of ink than woodcuts or brushwork. The ink needs to stick evenly to the metal surface of the slugs, so it can't be water-based. Gutenberg used a mixture of lampblack, varnish and egg white for his ink.

The paper also needs to be denser and less absorbent, so that the ink doesn't bleed.

Ink balls

These devices were used to apply ink to the type slugs. Their bottoms are covered with leather stuffed with wool or cotton padding.

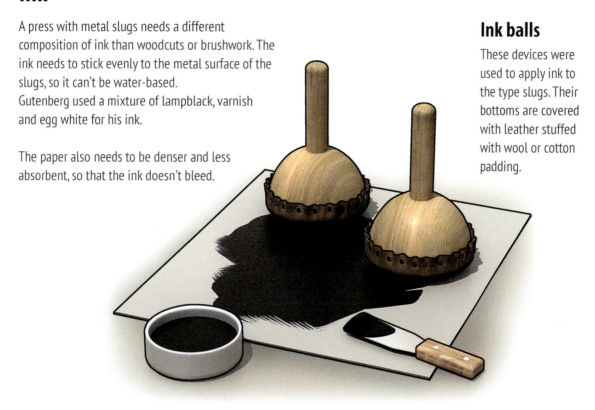

Operating the press

After a page is typeset, the form that holds it is placed on the press and inked. Then a sheet of paper is placed on it, the assembly that holds the form and paper is slid under the screw assembly, and the page is pressed. The steps:

1 The inkballs are used to coat the tops of the typeslugs with ink. A good quality print requires a thin, even coat of ink.

2 The frisket is folded down on top of the form, and a sheet of paper is placed on top of it. The frisket provides the paper a flat surface to rest on that is even with the tops of the type slugs.

3 Next the tympan is folded down on top of the paper, and the plank and coffin assembly is pushed under the screw assembly. The tympan helps in providing even pressure across the page.

4 The bar that turns the screw is pulled, pushing the platen down and pressing the paper onto the type slugs. The page is printed.

5 The plank and coffin assembly is pulled back to remove the printed page. The frisket is raised again in order to re-ink the slugs, and the operation is repeated for every page printed.

The Nuremberg Chronicle

The *Liber chronicarum*, as it was called in Latin, is a German book published in 1493. It is a remarkable example of technical innovation, combining the moveable type press with the most print illustrations of any 15th century publication. It has 1,804 illustrations, which are often described as woodcuts but are more likely wood engravings. A history of the Christian world, it is the work of Hartmann Schedel, with the artwork commissioned from several illustrators, and printed in the shop of Anton Koberger, the largest print shop in Germany at the time.

Previously book illustrations were most often added by hand following the printing of the text. In this book the illustrations were printed along with the text, although they were hand colored afterwards. This was likely more economical than making and printing additional plates for each color, since runs were typically in the hundreds of books. As a result, the amount and quality of color between copies varied considerably.

There were about 1,500 copies of the book made in Latin and somewhere between 700 and 1,000 copies in German. About 400 of the Latin and 300 of the German copies are still in existence.

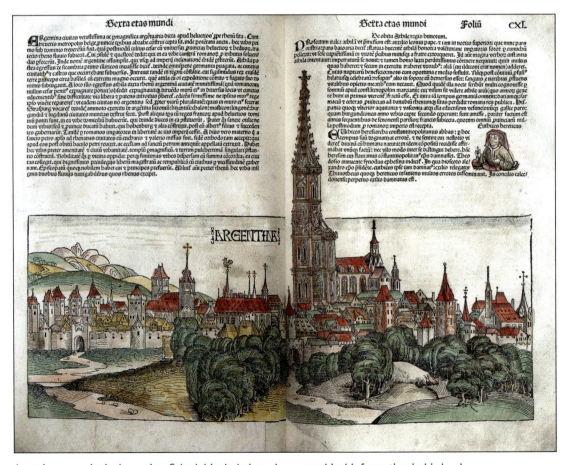

A section on a city in Argentina. Schedel included much geographical information in his book.

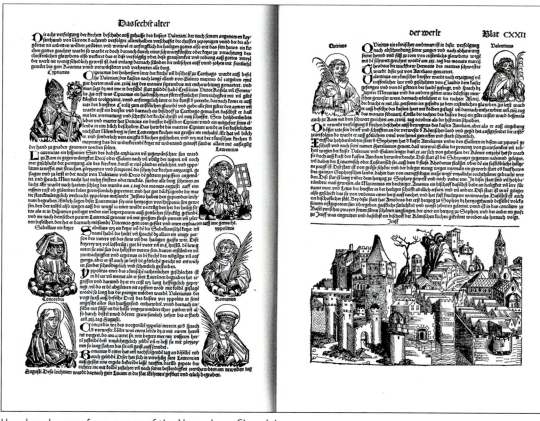

Uncolored pages from a copy of the Nuremberg Chronicle.

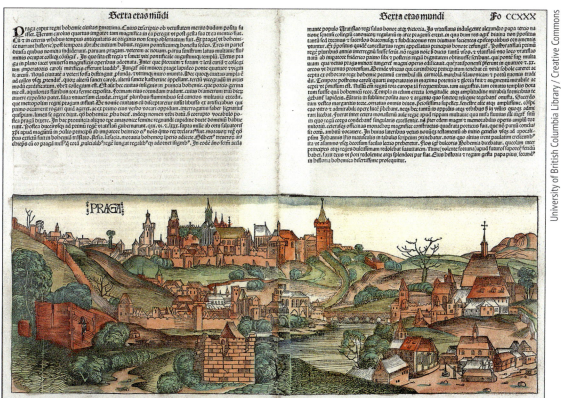

A section describing the city of Prague.

Typography

The standardized appearance of print characters didn't really begin until the invention of the moveable type press. Before that, when books were hand written, and even with block printing, the appearance of text varied depending on the individual creating it, even if there were established writing styles.

Gutenberg's type slugs emulated the common way that texts at the time were written, in ornate Gothic characters, a style that came to be known as Blackletter. Perhaps because of their complexity, which would have made them harder to create, and perhaps because it was harder to read, a simpler style was soon adopted, known as Roman in its imitation of classical Roman characters with serifs.

The majority of all typefaces from the 16th to the 20th centuries were in the Roman group of typeface design, and still are. This group can be broadly divided into three subgroups: Old Style, which were the first designs in the 16th century, Transitional, 17th to 19th century, and Modern.

Sans Serif typefaces only came into wide use in the 19th century, primarily for advertising. They were called 'Grotesque', somewhat derogatorily. It wasn't until the 1920s, with the rise of the Bauhaus school of simplified and blocky design, that their reputation improved. Helvetica, perhaps the most recognizable sans serif typeface, was created in 1957 by Swiss designer Max Miedinger.

The availability of different typefaces was limited in the metal type era because a print house had to own the complete set of type slugs at each specific font size, which was expensive. A font set, called a series, typically consists of more than a hundred characters, and multiple copies of each character are needed to set type.

The Digital Age has dramatically altered this. Computers make it much easier to both create and select different typefaces, which can be set at any font size. As a result there has been a wide proliferation of typefaces in all categories, particularly for specialized purposes.

Type terminology

Typographers refer to a font as, for example, 'Garamond bold 12/16'. This specifies the typeface, style, point size (12) and leading (16), which is the distance between lines of type.

It's called leading because on a Gutenberg press the lines of type slugs were separated by strips of lead.

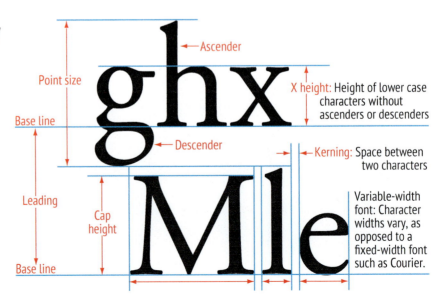

Type categories

The terms typeface and font are often used interchangeably in common parlance, but technically they are not the same. Typeface, or family, is the design, whereas font is more specific and includes style and point size.

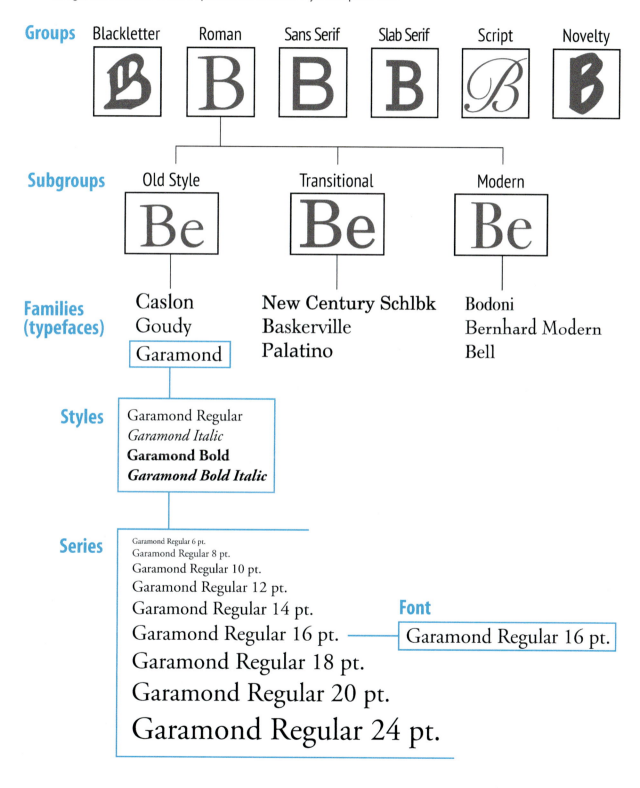

Groups Blackletter Roman Sans Serif Slab Serif Script Novelty

Subgroups Old Style Transitional Modern

Families (typefaces)
Caslon
Goudy
Garamond

New Century Schlbk
Baskerville
Palatino

Bodoni
Bernhard Modern
Bell

Styles
Garamond Regular
Garamond Italic
Garamond Bold
Garamond Bold Italic

Series
Garamond Regular 6 pt.
Garamond Regular 8 pt.
Garamond Regular 10 pt.
Garamond Regular 12 pt.
Garamond Regular 14 pt.
Garamond Regular 16 pt.
Garamond Regular 18 pt.
Garamond Regular 20 pt.
Garamond Regular 24 pt.

Font
Garamond Regular 16 pt.

Printing's impact

Gutenberg's press is commonly cited as one of the most transformational inventions in human history. But as we've seen, printing started in China long before he built his press and cast his slugs. Yet, even though the first distributions of printed text and images happened in Asia centuries earlier, there is little evidence that those earlier publications had significant impact on societies and culture of the time.

The majority of early printed artifacts that have been discovered in Asia were of a religious nature, mostly Buddhist. The Japanese Million Pagodas woodblock prints were of Buddhist scripture, as was the Diamond Sutra woodblock scroll, both printed in the 8th and 9th centuries CE. And the first metal moveable type book, the Korean *Jikji* printed in the 14th century, was a compilation of Buddhist teachings.

In China Buddhism was controversial at different times. There was a series of episodes of Buddhist persecution between the 5th and 10th centuries, during which Buddhist property was confiscated or destroyed, including woodblocks and prints. One of those episodes, in 845 CE during the Tang Dynasty, came after a couple of centuries of progressivism and acceptance, in which not only was Buddhism tolerated but so were Christianity and Judaism, and the arts were encouraged. It was during this time that woodblock printing became fully developed. But the crackdown ended that tolerance, and both religious and artistic expression were repressed.

Later, in the 15th century, an imperial eunuch by the name of Zheng He led seven extensive and large maritime expeditions that reached as far as India, Arabia and Africa, establishing trade routes and outposts along the way. Had China continued this expansion it might have become the colonizer of foreign lands that Europeans eventually became, and in the process it would have spread its culture and technology across the world. But instead in the early 16th century the royal court, which had shifted to Confucianism and away from Buddhism, ordered all foreign voyages to cease and the expedition ships burned. China became isolationist, a stance it maintained into modern times.

As a result, Chinese literature and texts did not spread widely outside of the country. And if printed material had any influence within China, it would have been in promoting Buddhism, which did spread to some degree, but there is little evidence of substantial changes to culture or social structures as a result of printing in China or in other east Asian countries.

The logographic nature of Asian languages was also a likely impediment. Needing separate slugs for thousands of characters would have made moveable type printing less practical than with alphabetic languages.

The impact of printing in the West was quite different. Gutenberg's 15th-century printing system started a new industry that spread rapidly, with press houses and type foundries opening across Europe within decades. His system became the standard until the Industrial Revolution more than three centuries later.

And the print industry fundamentally transformed not only communication but ultimately societal and economic structures in Europe and eventually

Double press

This press is capable of printing two pages
in one pull. It is representative of how
moveable type presses evolved in the
centuries following Gutenberg.
This illustration is based on an existing
press at the Crandall Historical Printing
Museum in Alpine, Utah.

the World. Publication efficiency was multiplied by several factors over the hand copying of individual texts. By 1700 CE a book could be produced nearly 25 times faster than in 1450. Multiple copies of books and documents could now be economically printed and distributed, leading to increased literacy and access to information by a broader segment of the population. According to the English Short Title Catalogue, by the year 1700 there were approximately 2,000 new English-language books being published per decade compared to a couple hundred per decade a century earlier; by 1800 the number had jumped to close to 8,000.

There is little data on literacy rates during this time. Several studies of the number of people who could sign important documents such as marriage registers or court papers give us some indication. Based on this, it appears that literacy rates in northern Europe and the British colonies, including North America, increased substantially between the 16th and 18th centuries to a point where more than half the male population could read. Unfortunately rates for women were lower, and it took another century for them to catch up.

The first effect of printing in the West was to challenge religious orthodoxy. It didn't take long for the distribution of printed documents to form cracks in the foundations of church and state authority. Martin Luther used leaflets to distribute his radical criticisms of the Roman Catholic church, eventually leading to a schism and the start of multiple protestant sects during the period known as the Protestant Reformation. He was by 1520 CE the most published author in Europe, with about 160 documents printed in 828 editions.

Several significant publications over the next few centuries had profound effects in many fields from science and medicine to economics and politics, including Andreas Vesalius' anatomy book *De Humani Corporis Fabrica* published in 1543, Copernicus' *De Revolutionibus Orbium Coelestium* ("On the Revolutions of the Celestial Orbs") also published in 1543 and which informed Galileo's works on astronomy, Adam Smith's 1776 *The Wealth of Nations*, and Thomas Paine's 1791 *The Rights of Man*. Each of these became foundational texts in their respective fields, raised public awareness of their topics and changed perceptions about their topics.

Increased literacy among average citizens also contributed to the growth of an economic middle class, which would gradually gain political power, challenging the central authority of royal houses.

Printing was one of the forces that advanced progressive social changes, from the Renaissance to the Enlightenment and the Scientific Revolution that began in the 17th and 18th centuries. And it paved the way for the Industrial Revolution, which will be discussed in the next section.

Literacy rates in England, 1625-1925

There is little data for literacy rates in England prior to
1800, and almost none prior to 1500, but it's likely that
before Gutenberg's press the rates were extremely low,
as it was worldwide. In his book *A Farewell to Alms*,
Gregory Clark compiled several studies of the number
of people at the time who could sign marriage registers
or court documents, which gives us some of the data
for the chart below.

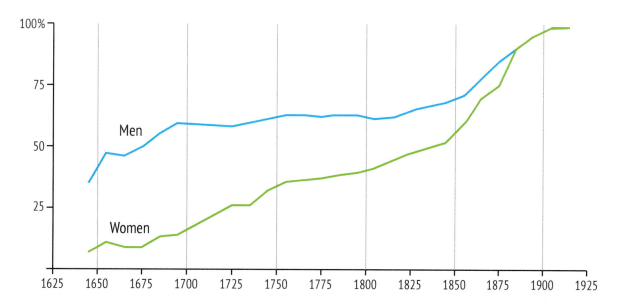

Source: Gregory Clark, *A Farewell to Alms*, p. 192

The Industrial Revolution and the Modern Era

Power, steel and plastics

The Industrial Revolution, beginning in the 1700s and extending into the late 1800s, and the Modern Era of the 1900s were both times of dramatic change in technology, which led to equally dramatic changes in how people live.

There have in fact been several industrial revolutions according to many historians. The first began about 1760 CE with the introduction of new manufacturing methods and with a new power source, steam. It came to an end between 1820 and 1840 when societal advantages of increased wages and productivity stalled.

The second industrial revolution began around 1870 with a new round of inventions, improved mass production and steel manufacturing methods, and with another new power source, electricity.

Communication technology made dramatic improvements beginning in the 1800s, with machines for paper making and printing that greatly improved production, and then during the second revolution with the emergence of entirely new media: audio recordings, photography, movies, the telegraph and telephone.

The 1900s saw the emergence of electronic media, including radio and television, as electricity became available to most households. Within a few decades movies gained sound and television color. Improved methods of recording and distributing electronic media became available by mid-century, such as audio and video tape. Integrated circuits using transistors made electronic devices cheap and portable.

Following World War II plastics manufacturing provided an inexpensive and easily molded material with which to manufacture a wide range of products including electronic devices.

It was during these two centuries, the 19th and 20th, that communication technology was transformed. By the 1970s and on the threshhold of the Digital Age, people in most parts of the world had access to an unprecedented amount of news and information through print, film, broadcast and recorded media.

Key developments

The industrial and modern eras experienced a succession of dramatic developments in communication technology. The key events:

Print media

Paper making
In the first half of the 19th century paper making became mechanized and no longer hand made. In the second half of the century wood pulp largely replaced rags, cotton and other plant materials, making paper significantly less expensive while increasing supply.

Presses
Mechanical, steam-powered presses also appeared early in the 19th century. Incremental improvements in their design gradually replaced all manual tasks. Near the end of the century typesetting became mechanized.

Offset lithography
This more economical printing method gradually replaced letterpress in the 20th century for most large-scale commercial printing. Phototypesetting made traditional typesetting obsolete while greatly improving printing efficiency.

Color printing
Lithography made printing with multiple ink colors more practical and affordable.

Photography

Print photography
Incremental improvements in the 19th century led to photographs replacing etchings and engravings in print media in the modern era.

Electronic media

Sound recording
Although the first audio recordings were mechanical, audio media became increasingly popular with the help of electronics, and became a medium capable of communicating through spoken language to a mass audience.

Broadcast media
Radio and television transformed the media landscape, providing new platforms of communication to broad audiences other than print. These media also had profound impacts on society and culture.

Magnetic tape
Tape for audio and video provided quicker and more affordable ways of creating and distributing content.

Transistors and integrated circuits
Increasingly smaller components made radios and TVs more compact and affordable, starting in the 1960s. This new technology also set the stage for computers and digital technology, which began to reach mainstream audiences in the 1980s, marking the transition from the Modern Era to the Digital Age.

Movies
Moving pictures are, as the name implies, based on photography. Movies became a new form of visual communication in the 20th century.

Energy production

Steam

James Watt built a steam engine that was capable of driving industrial machinery in 1776. This power source enabled the start of factory production in numerous industries, including printing presses in the 1800s.

Electricity

It took the better part of the 1800s and the work of numerous inventors to turn electricity into a practical power source. In the 1830s the first electric motor was built. Starting in the 1840s telegraph lines began to encircle the Earth. In 1879 Thomas Edison succeeded in his quest to make a long-lasting lightbulb. The first electric street lights came into use, and the first power company began to sell electricity, marking the beginning of the modern electric grid. In 1884 Nikola Tesla's electric alternator produced AC power, which became the standard way to generate electricity. From then on electric grids gradually spread across the country and then the world, making it possible to access a power source hundreds or even thousands of miles away for lighting and to run machinery. Electricity was also what made all the advances in 20th century communication possible through electronic media.

Construction materials

Steel and metals

Improved steel making methods were essential to the first two industrial revolutions. Steel is an alloy of iron, superior in strength and flexibility to cast iron, but prior to the 18th century difficult to make and not widely available. In 1740 Benjamin Huntsman, an Englishman, developed a method of making cast steel in clay crucibles, resulting in a harder and higher quality steel. In 1855 Henry Bessemer, also an English inventor, developed a process to make the manufacture of steel less expensive. The availability of high-quality and cost-effective steel is often cited as one of the factors leading to the second industrial revolution.

Plastics

Synthetic polymer was invented in 1869, the first material that didn't come from a natural source such as wood or metal ore, and that could be molded into any shape. Plastic made from petroleum was developed in the 20th century. World War II spurred a big expansion of plastic manufacturing and development, and its use became commonplace. Its availability made communication devices lightweight and affordable. Synthetic rubber also made insulation for electric wires more affordable.

Steam power

Unlike water power which required proximity to a river, the steam engine provided a source of power at any location. As long as there was coal or wood to burn, it provided consistent and dependable mechanical energy.

The first steam engines were built early in the 1700s but were inefficient and limited in power, and found use only in pumping water out of coal mines. In 1776 **James Watt**, an Englishman, is credited with improving the design to create a practical engine that could run industrial machinery. Its earliest implementations were in textile, flour and iron mills, as well as for transportation, powering trains and ships.

Steam-powered printing

Steam power came to serve the print industry in two ways, by powering presses and paper-making machines, and by improving the speed and precision of lathes used in the manufacture of metal machine parts, which made it possible to build more complex printing equipment.

The first steam-powered presses began operation in England in 1814, eventually replacing the hand-pulled presses that were descendants of Gutenberg's design. Over the next few decades, increasingly complex presses powered by steam greatly increased production rates and efficiency, making large-run daily newspapers possible as well as the printing of inexpensive books and magazines.

And steam power made possible the invention of mechanical systems to make paper out of wood pulp, meeting the increased demand of the ever expanding print industry.

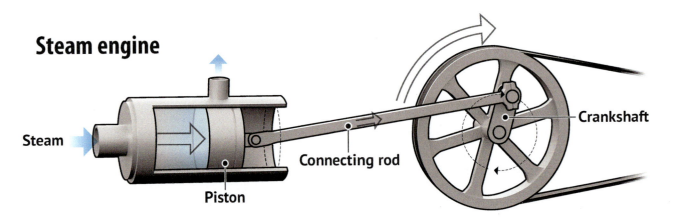

Steam engine

Steam · **Piston** · **Connecting rod** · **Crankshaft**

This simplified diagram of a steam engine shows its basic parts and operation. Steam, produced by boiling water with a wood or coal fire, enters the cylinder through an intake valve, pushing the piston forward, which in turn pushes the connecting rod and turns the crankshaft.

When the piston reaches its furthest point of travel an exhaust valve is opened and releases the steam pressure, allowing the piston to return to its starting point, and for the cycle to start over. For each forward and back motion of the piston the crankshaft makes one complete rotation.

Electricity

The existence of electricity has been known since ancient times, often referred to as a "mysterious force." The unraveling of its mystery, which came to fruition in the 19th century, took the work of many researchers and inventors.

A 4,700-year-old Egyptian text describes electric fish in the Nile River, the earliest known description of electricity. The phenomenon of static electricity, from, say, rubbing an animal's fur, was also known to ancient cultures, but was of no practical use.

In the early 1700s Englishman **Stephen Gray** discovered that certain materials conducted electricity, and Frenchman **Charles Francois du Fay** found that it came in two forms, which he called resinous and vitreous but that we now call negative and positive.

In 1745 two different men, Dutchman **Pieter van Musschenbroek** and German **Ewald Christian Von Kleist**, coincidentally invented a method of storing electricity and releasing it on demand, which came to be known as the **Leyden jar**, named after the German city of Leyden where Von Kleist lived. The Leyden jar was the first battery.

Electricity basics

Electricity is a phenomenon that occurs in an element whose atoms have weak attraction between electrons and the nucleus, allowing some electrons to jump from one atom to the next if a stronger force pulls them along. When this happens heat and light are released, and if properly harnessed, this flow can be converted to mechanical energy.

Certain metals easily lose their electrons and make good conductors. Silver is the most conductive, followed by copper, gold and aluminum.

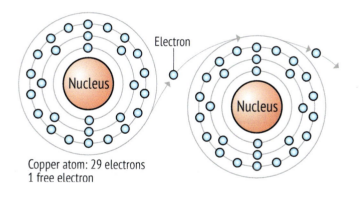

Copper atom: 29 electrons
1 free electron

How electricity is measured:

The challenge here is in gauging how many electrons are moving from one atom to the next and at what speed.

An analogy to water is imperfect but useful: Think of an electric wire as a water pipe. The amount of water that can pass through the pipe will depend on two things: the diameter of the pipe and the amount of water pressure. In electricity the equivalent of water pressure is **volts**, which is the difference in charge between each end of a circuit. For pipe diameter, what is actually being measured is the pipe's maximum capacity, that is, how much water it can hold. For electricity, it's how many electrons can flow through the wire. That's measured in **amperes**, which is the number of electrons passing a point on the wire in one second.

Electric power is measured in **watts**. A watt is a charge of one volt flowing at a rate of one ampere. **Ohms** measures how resistant a material is to electricity flowing through it. The higher the ohms, the less conductive the material is.

There is some dispute as to whether **Ben Franklin**'s iconic 1752 kite experiment ever actually took place. The only record of it was written by an acquaintance, English chemist Joseph Priestley, 15 years after the supposed event. But another experiment inspired by Franklin did take place in May 1752 in Marly-la-Ville, France, a month earlier than Franklin's supposed kite flight. **Thomas-Francois Dalibard** erected a tall metal pole sitting on top of some wine bottles and waited for lightning to strike it, which eventually happened, resulting in observable electric sparks.

This was the first observable evidence that lightning was electricity, confirming Franklin's hypothesis. Shortly after Dalibard's report the experiment was reproduced by a number of other researchers in Europe. Franklin's subsequent invention of lightning rods, based on this discovery, could be considered the first practical application in the control of electric currents.

A number of electricity terms which we now use are derived from the names of researchers of the late 1700s and early 1800s: **Luigi Galvani**, **Charles-Augustin de Coulomb**, **Alessandro Volta**, **Andre-Marie Ampere**, **Georg Ohm**, **Michael Faraday**, **James Prescott Joule**. They all contributed to methods of measuring and controlling the flow of electricity in a conductive material, and thanks to their work the nature of electricity was better understood, but its practical application was still lacking.

Practical applications

In 1800 **Alessandro Volta**, for whom volts are named, demonstrated that electricity could be generated chemically when he created the first electric pile, the precursor of modern batteries. The pile consisted of a stack of alternating disks of

Motors and generators

Electric motors and generators are essentially the same, but act in opposite ways: A motor creates mechanical energy from electricity, while a generator makes electricity from mechanical energy.

Electric motor

A current running through the coil creates a magnetic field that is repelled by the magnets surrounding it, causing the coil and the shaft to spin.

Electric generator

The shaft and coil are rotated through mechanical force, such as a steam or hydro turbine. As the coil rotates through the magnetic field, an electric current is generated.

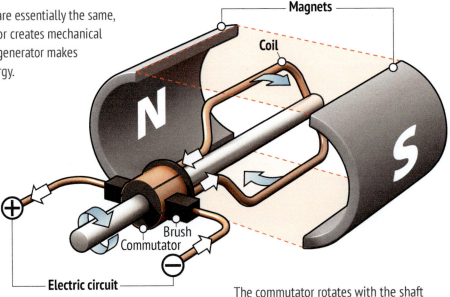

The commutator rotates with the shaft while the brushes are stationary, allowing the electric current to flow uninterrupted.

copper and zinc separated by an electrolyte such as saltwater brine, which allows free electrons to flow from one disk to the next when its two terminals are connected.

Michael Faraday, **Joseph Henry** and **William Sturgeon** separately demonstrated that magnets and electricity were of the same phenomenon, from which comes the term electromagnetic energy. Henry found that wrapping electric wires around a magnet increased the power of the magnet. On this basis Faraday in 1821 demonstrated the principle of the electric motor, making a wire carrying a current spin in a magnetic field. Ten years later he also demonstrated the reverse process by sliding a magnet back and forth inside a coil of copper wires, which generated electricity. But practical electric motors and generators wouldn't arrive for a few more years.

Numerous inventors across the world theorized or demonstrated electric motors of various designs, but the first one capable of operating machinery is generally credited to **William Sturgeon**, in England in 1832. **Thomas Davenport**, a Vermont blacksmith, received the first US patent in 1837 for a motor that could run machine tools and a printing press.

But lacking a source of electricity beyond batteries, which were expensive and still rudimentary, these motors would not be of much practical use until power grids were built, which wouldn't begin to happen until the 1880s.

In 1878 Englishman **Joseph Swan** invented the first lightbulb, but it burned out quickly. In 1880 **Thomas Edison** succeeded in making a bulb that would last about 1,200 hours.

AC vs DC

Following the success of his lightbulb, Edison's next plan was to start a commercial enterprise of power generators

Electric motor

This diagram shows the essential inner parts of a simple motor. When the circuit is closed, electricity flows through the coils, creating a magnetic field that is repelled by the magnets surrounding the coils, causing the coils and shaft to rotate.

The coils are wrapped around the armatures, which are attached to the shaft.

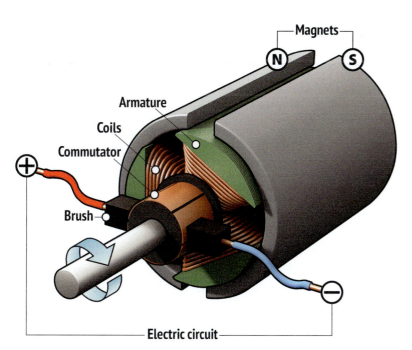

Magnets

N   S

Armature

Coils

Commutator

Brush

Electric circuit

with which to electrify entire city blocks. In 1882 he opened his first plant at Holborn Viaduct in London, which could power 3,000 lights, and then the Pearl Street station in New York City, which powered 5,000 lights.

Edison's generators produced DC, or direct current, electricity, which had several advantages: It didn't require high voltage to illuminate lightbulbs, and motors at that time could only run on DC current. But it had a significant drawback: It lost power rapidly over distance. Customers would have to be within a mile of the generator, which meant that to power a city, there would have to be a generator in every square mile.

Nikola Tesla, a Serbian immigrant, had worked briefly as an engineer in Edison's lab upon arriving to the US in 1884, but quit over what Tesla claimed was a withheld bonus. Based on his work on a motor that could run on AC power, he was hired by the Western Union Company, where he designed a practical system to generate AC, or alternating current.

AC differs from DC in that in the latter, the electron flow is constant in one direction, from the negative terminal to the positive one, but in AC, the flow direction is constantly and rapidly reversed, back and forth. AC has the major advantage that it can be transmitted over great distances without significant loss of power, unlike DC's one-mile range.

AC's disadvantage is that it requires higher voltage, which makes it more dangerous to the public. Edison tried to use that to discredit Tesla's system, even engaging in a publicity campaign to instill fear in the public of the AC system.

In 1888 Tesla found financial backing for his system from George Westinghouse, who was in competition with Edison. Tesla licensed his plans to Westinghouse for cash and royalties.

Following much litigation, Westinghouse's corporation ultimately defeated Edison, and AC became the industry standard, which it is to this day. As a result, power plants can now transmit electricity over hundreds and even thousands of miles, and to rural and sparsely populated regions, something Edison's system would not have been capable of.

Electrification of the world

Through this series of incremental discoveries (there are many more contributors than have been mentioned here), electricity became a practical power source. In the next few decades grids were installed in cities around the world and large generators powered by steam from burning coal or gas or by hydro power started producing enough electricity to energize entire regions.

It's hardly possible to overstate the impact of electricity on the world. The ability to easily and instantaneously draw power from a central generator enabled all kinds of new inventions. And electric light increased productive hours and changed the way people lived.

And it transformed communication, first with the telegraph and telephone, and then by powering the entire printing process and increasing its efficiency, and then by making entirely new communication methods possible, from broadcast radio and television to audio and video recording to portable electronics to computers, smartphones and the Internet.

Thomas Alva Edison   1847-1931

Easily one of the most recognizable names in US history, Edison is credited with numerous significant inventions, including a practical lightbulb, the phonograph, a movie camera and projecting system, and an electricity-generating system.

He grew up in Port Huron, Michigan. He worked briefly as a telegraph operator while still a teenager, and at age 19 for the Associated Press news wire.

At age 22 he obtained his first patent, an electric vote recorder for state legislatures. After moving to New York City he invented the quadruplex telegraph, which could send four separate messages at the same time on a single wire, and sold it to Western Union for $10,000 (more than $200,000 today). It was his first financial success.

With that money Edison established his Menlo Park laboratory in 1876. Within a year his lab had developed the first phonograph. In 1880 he was granted a patent for the first long-lasting lightbulb. In the same year he began his electricity-generating business, but eventually lost out to Westinghouse's AC generators.

In the 1890s his lab made one of the first movie cameras, the Kinetograph, and a viewing device, the Kinetoscope, which enjoyed commercial success for close to a decade. Edison's movie operations produced close to 1,200 films, most of them less than a minute long.

Edison accumulated 1,093 single and joint patents in the US, and 512 patents in other countries.

He died in West Orange, New Jersey from complications of diabetes, at the age of 84.

Edison and his phonograph, c. 1878

National Portrait Gallery

Nikola Tesla 1856-1943

Tesla was born and grew up in what is now Croatia, and emigrated to the US in 1884, becoming a naturalized citizen. Although he studied engineering in his youth he never received a degree.

Upon arriving in the US, Edison hired him based on a letter of recommendation. But it was a short tenure. According to Tesla, Edison offered him $50,000 if he could improve Edison's DC generators. Tesla did so within a few months, but Edison refused to pay. There is reason to doubt at least the specifics: that sum of money would be equivalent to a million dollars today. It would have been remarkable for Edison to offer such a reward.

Nevertheless, Tesla quit and pursued his own inventions. He had already worked out how to build an AC-powered motor, which remained one of the biggest drawbacks to an AC power system. Western Union hired him, where he designed AC systems.

Tesla patented his AC system and motor, and licensed them to George Westinghouse. The royalty portion of the deal would have made Tesla billions over time, but the cost of litigation against Edison had nearly ruined Westinghouse. Tesla agreed to tear up the contract.

His next interest was in wireless transmissions, leading to his invention of a coil capable of generating high levels of voltage and radio frequencies, making radio transmissions possible. He patented that invention in 1897, narrowly beating Marconi to it.

Tesla envisioned wireless communication and even predicted cell phones in the future. He managed to get financial backing from JP Morgan in the amount of $150,000 to build a wireless transmission tower, which became known as Wardenclyffe Tower on Long Island. But money ran out before its completion and Morgan declined further investment, bankrupting the project. At the

Nikola Tesla c. 1890   Photo by Napoleon Sarony

same time Marconi successfully demonstrated his radio in 1901, drawing investors and leaving Tesla defeated both financially and emotionally.

Tesla sued Marconi, claiming infringement on 17 of his patents, but lost in court (his rights were eventually restored, but not until shortly after his death).

Tesla began to exhibit obsessive-compulsive behavior and withdrew socially. He became obsessed with the number three and patterned his activities on it. He also became obsessed with pigeons, in particular a white one for which he professed his love.

The last chapter of his life was spent living in the New Yorker Hotel, room and board paid for by Westinghouse, as Tesla was now destitute. He died in debt at the age of 86.

Metallurgy

Improvements in steel and metal production were essential for the Industrial Revolution. Up through the 18th century wood was still the most often used construction material, even for machines. But for the increasingly complex machinery that made industrialization possible in the 19th century, precisely machined steel parts were necessary. And of course, conductive metals were essential to make machines powered by electricity and for electronic devices.

First use of metals

Metals as a general term refers to items made from single elements, such as copper or tin. Their use goes back to the beginnings of civilization. The first metals used were those that could be shaped in their natural form, such as gold and copper, without the need to melt them. They were used for tools and ornaments. The oldest copper artifact is a 10,700-year-old ornament, found in present-day Iraq. One of the oldest tools discovered is a copper axe found with the frozen corpse of a 5,400-year-old man, known as Ötzi, discovered in the Alps in 1991. 4,700-year-old copper water pipes were found in the Egyptian pyramids. What is commonly called the Copper Age or Chalcolithic Period, distinguishing it from the earlier Neolithic, or Stone Age, is usually dated from 6,500 to 5,500 years ago.

The process of melting and casting metal ores in molds appears to have also begun during this time period.

The Bronze Age began with the discovery about 6,000 years ago that mixing tin or arsenic with copper made bronze, a harder and more durable alloy than either metal alone. The Copper and Bronze Ages overlap because each began and ended at different times in different parts of the world.

Iron and steel

The oldest iron artifacts discovered are 3,800 years old, found in present-day Turkey. By about 3,000 years ago iron production had appeared in the Mideast and China.

Iron ore is harder to purify and melt than copper or tin, but it makes a more durable object. As the process became better developed, iron replaced bronze in much of the world, and remained the primary material used for weapons, tools and machinery up to the industrial age.

Iron is the fourth most common element on Earth, comprising five percent of the planet's crust. But unlike copper or gold, it isn't found in its pure form. It is mined as ore from which it has to be extracted, and then melted to form a solid, a process called smelting. It requires higher temperatues than copper and bronze, and a more controlled environment. Pure iron, like other elements, is soft and easily reshaped, but doesn't have sufficient hardness for practical use.

Steel is an alloy made by combining iron with carbon and sometimes other elements, which makes iron harder. At sufficiently high temperatures molten iron starts absorbing carbon. More carbon makes for harder steel, but it also becomes more brittle. Objects have to be cast in the desired shape since it's difficult to rework. This was the impediment to using steel for anything larger than what could practically be cast in a mold.

Two improvements made steel more practical. The first was in the 1740s, by Englishman **Benjamin Huntsman**, who invented a process of melting iron at a higher temperature in a crucible, resulting in a higher quality steel with which more precise machine parts could be made. This was one of the inventions that sparked the beginning of the first industrial revolution.

The second improvement, patented in 1856, had the greatest economic impact. The inventor was Englishman **Henry Bessemer**, after whom the process is named. His method was to blow oxygen through the molten iron, which both raised its temperature and allowed greater control over the amount of carbon it absorbed, making it easier to make different grades

Periodic table

Progress in technology has been dependent on elements such as iron and copper, as well as semiconductors such as silicon. As scientists strove to better understand the nature of these elements, they began to classify them according to their characteristics. The earliest table was by **Antoine Lavoisier** in 1789, listing 33 elements. The current form of the periodic table was first published in 1928 by US chemist **Horace Deming**.

As the table shows, most elements are metallic, and are malleable, meaning they can be reshaped without breaking. They conduct electricity and heat to varying degrees. The most conductive are number 47 silver, 29 copper and 79 gold, which are all in the same column near the middle. Aluminum, number 13, is also very conductive.

The numbers are the atomic numbers of each element, which indicate the number of protons in each atom's nucleus. If an atom has as many electrons as protons, it will have no charge. The metals are conductive because they have at least one loosely attached electron that can be passed on to another atom, resulting in the atom having a positive or negative charge.

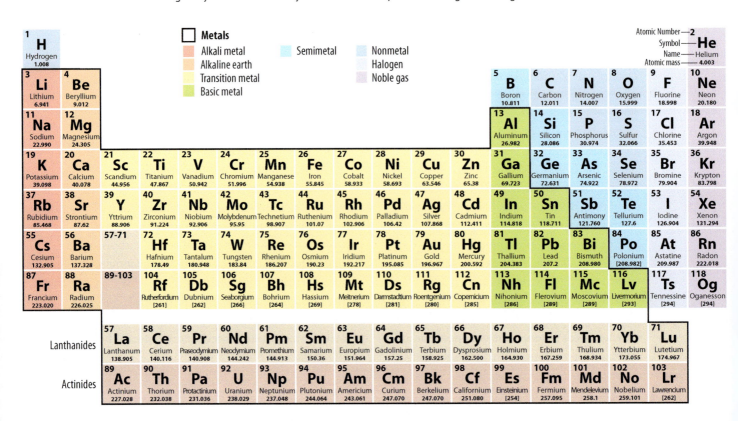

of steel. The process also made steel production much faster and considerably lowered production costs, as much as 80 percent less in some cases.

US industrialist Andrew Carnegie licensed Bessemer's process and in the 1870s started the first large-scale steel production in the US. His main product was steel rails for the rapidly expanding railroad lines across the country. In time the US would become one of the leading steel producers in the world, which it remained until the 1970s.

Today 90 percent of all metal produced in the world is steel. Most of it is produced in Asia, with over half of it produced in China. The US produces less than five percent.

Copper

Element 29 on the periodic table, copper is not quite as conductive as silver, but nevertheless is the main element used for electric wires due to its greater availability and lower cost. It is easier to process than iron, and is ductile in its natural state, meaning that it can easily be drawn out into wires. Most of the world's copper is mined in Chile, but the US also has large copper mines in the Southwest. Copper is by far the most common metal used for electrical wiring and in electronics.

But copper isn't suitable for all electric uses. It's not of much use as a lightbulb filament, for example. Thomas Edison, along with others pursuing the invention of the lighbulb, experimented with a wide variety of materials for a filament that was conductive but with enough resistance to glow brightly, and at the same time not burn out. Element number 74, tungsten, has become the best metal for this purpose, and has been used for lightbulbs from the late 1800s through the 20th century. It is only recently being replaced by electronic lighting such as LCDs.

Other metals

Aluminum, number 13 in the table, is even more abundant in the Earth's crust than iron, making up eight percent of it. But like iron it isn't found in a pure state. It wasn't until the 19th century that processes were developed to extract it from ore and make metals from it.

Aluminum has unusual characteristics: it isn't subject to magnetism but is highly conductive of electricity, and doesn't easily corrode or rust as iron does. It is much lighter in weight than iron but still strong. It is usually alloyed with one or more other metals such as zinc or magnesium. It is used in motors, generators, transformers and related electric equipment.

Titanium, number 22, is another metal useful for its lightweight strength and resistance to corrosion.

Modern mobile devices require a number of precious metals. Along with copper and aluminum, they contain minute amounts of gold, silver, platinum, and palladium. They also require some rare earths: yttrium, lanthanum, terbium, neodymium, gadolinium and praseodymium. These are not particularly rare but are difficult to mine and extract.

Semiconductors

Bordering the metals on their right side in the periodic table are the semimetals, including two elements, silicon and germanium, which are most often used as semiconductors in electronics. These are materials whose electrical conductivity can be controlled, making them useful, for example, as switches. Silicon, being very common, is most often used, but to function as a semiconductor requires a minute addition of another element such as phosphorus or boron.

Semiconductors will be discussed in more detail in the chapter on electronics.

Plastics and synthetics

Although major advances were happening in energy and steel toward the end of the 19th century, household items and consumer appliances, including cases for cameras and early communication equipment, were still being built out of natural materials: everything from wood and leather to animal bones and tortoise shells.

Electric wire insulation was also an issue. At first wires were being wrapped in woven fabric or paper to insulate them. The first use of natural rubber for this purpose was done with gutta-percha, a type of rubber obtained from trees in Southeast Asia that can be molded in hot water and hardens after it cools. In 1848 Michael Faraday suggested it as a material for wire insulation, after which it was used for the first underwater telegraph cables, and ultimately for the first trans-Atlantic cables laid in 1858 and 1866.

But natural rubber is not cheap or plentiful, nor were other natural materials. The search was on for synthetic substitutes.

The first plastic

In the 1860s a New York firm offered a $10,000 reward for a substitute for ivory, for the manufacture of billiard balls. The prize was claimed in 1869 by **John Wesley Hyatt**, who devised a method of treating cotton fiber cellulose with camphor, resulting in the first plastic. It could be modeled into any shape.

This was the beginning of the plastics revolution. Now any number of consumer items could be made inexpensively out of this new material called celluloid.

Celluloid was used for the first film rolls by Kodak in the 1880s, replacing glass plates. It was, however, still made of natural materials.

The first truly synthetic plastic, **Bakelite**, was invented in 1907 by **Leo Baekeland**. It was completely synthetic, made by mixing two chemicals—phenol and formaldehyde—and could be mechanically manufactured into any shape. Soon all manner of consumer items from jewelry boxes to appliances were being made with it, as well as cases for cameras and electronics.

Modern plastics

World War II spurred research into synthetics in order to provide better military equipment and to preserve dwindling natural resources. Out of this research came nylon, originally used for parachutes, rope and body armor among other military gear, and plexiglass for airplane windows.

Plastics were now being made out of petroleum, which was inexpensive and abundant. After the war markets became saturated with plastic consumer goods, demand for which increased as world economies recovered from the Great Depression and the war.

Petroleum could also be made into synthetic rubber, solving the need for inexpensive electric insulation.

Plastics and polymer materials made consumer electronics affordable, beginning with transistor radios and televisions in the 1960s and extending to modern digital devices. It also made them lightweight and portable.

However, the convenience of plastics has not come without problems. Plastic pollution is now a major environmental concern, as is oil extraction and refining.

Science in the modern world

From the 17th-century start of the Enlightenment, through the industrial revolutions and into the beginning of the Modern Era, innovations were largely driven through the use of science—observation, hypothesis and experimentation—to solve technological problems. Each inventor would build upon the discoveries of predecessors, gradually improving upon each other's methods to make machines that in the end were not only utilitarian but marketable.

Some of the early scientists might be described as dilettantes, men of status, education and means, who had the resources and time to do experiments (and most were men; women were socially discouraged from such pursuits). Volta, born into Italian nobility, is an example and Franklin, although technically not an aristocrat, was a celebrity, easily socialized with elite society, and was financially well off. Others came from humble backgrounds, such as Faraday, who was apprenticed at the age of 14 to become a bookbinder, but had the discipline and ambition to educate himself.

There was both competition and cooperation among the innovators. One way that they learned from each other was thanks to improvements in printing throughout the 19th century, which allowed scientific journals to be published and widely distributed, and in which inventors would often describe their discoveries and breakthroughs. These would be distributed internationally, making it possible to keep up to date with contemporaries in other countries.

As we've seen, it took the work of many people to arrive at practical uses for

Edison's Menlo Park lab.   Andrew Balet / Creative Commons

electricity. In the early years of the 19th century they mostly worked independently from each other, or in small teams.

This began to change as technology became more complicated and as financial interests began to become involved in new industries. In this trend, Edison can be given credit for another innovation. He started probably the first large-scale research facility with his Menlo Park lab, which had several dozen employees. His lab foreshadowed how research would largely be conducted in the 20th century: Although there would still be celebrities and outsized personalities, technological and product development would increasingly be conducted by large teams. Companies would increasingly have research and development departments, entirely dedicated to inventing new and marketable products. In the Modern Era and the Digital Age, scientific and technological advances mostly come from the types of facilities that Edison pioneered.

Industrialization and society

All of these technological advances, from mechanization of labor to new energy sources and new means of communication, contributed to profound social changes over the course of the 19th and 20th centuries. The practical application of steam power and then electricity to every type of industry, combined with better materials and machining capabilities, moved most of humanity from largely agricultural lives where most things were made by hand to an industrial existence, where now most things were made by machines, and increasingly livelihoods shifted to manufacturing. At some point in the 20th century, depending on the global region, more people were working in manufacturing than in agriculture, and living in urban areas.

And by many measures the quality of life improved for much of the human population. Average life spans grew longer as did average prosperity, as industrial production made more goods affordable and accessible. Education and literacy levels rose steadily: At the beginning of the 19th century less than one in five adults worldwide could read and had been enrolled in formal education; by the end of the 20th century it was more than four out of five.

Of course it wasn't all bread and roses. Societal upheavals tend to cause disruptions and provide opportunities for abuse and oppression. Factory work made for long and dreary days in exchange for low wages, and in some cases was hazardous. Worker protections such as 40-hour work weeks, paid overtime, child labor laws and government oversight through safety regulations only came after hard-fought labor strikes and political battles in the 20th century.

Modern communication technology

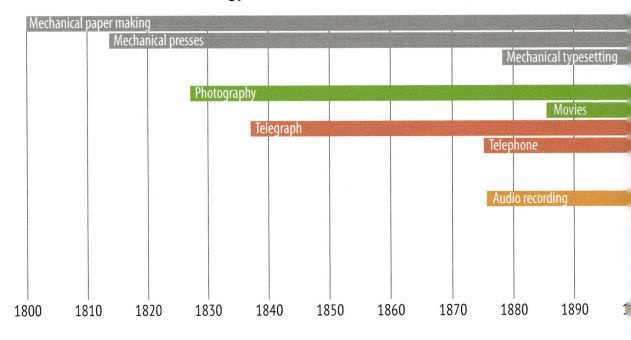

Industrialization made warfare far more brutal, but it also contributed to improved medical care. As shocking as war fatalities were—the two world wars each took tens of millions of lives—disease always took far more, as it had through all of human history.

With greater prosperity and food security, better education and improved health care leading to longer life expectancies, human population has increased dramatically over these two centuries, from one billion in 1800 to six billion in 2000.

And communication and access to news and information saw dramatic transformations. Combined with greater populations and higher literacy rates, consumption of media of all kinds increased dramatically, giving rise to influential industries involved in the commercial production of movies, TV and radio shows, music, newspapers, magazines and books, and finally all the content on the Internet. At the beginning of the 19th century the media audience would have been about 100 million literate people, who would have only had access to books and newspapers of a few pages, and for whom news from any distance would have taken days or weeks to arrive. Two hundred years later the media audience was almost all of the six billion people in the world, with access to all of the modern forms of media delivered on print and digital platforms and nearly instant access to news from across the world. This was made possible by all of the technological discoveries, breakthroughs and inventions during this remarkable time period, which will be covered in the following chapters.

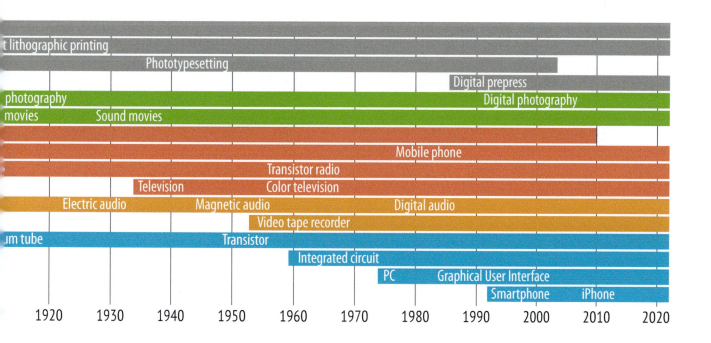

Industrial printing

By the start of the 19th century, there had been little change in printmaking technology since Gutenberg's press. Paper was still being made by hand much as it had been since its invention in China 1,700 years earlier, and presses, although more elaborate, still operated in the same way as Gutenberg's, with type slugs set and inked, the paper positioned and the press bar pulled, all by hand.

The print industry was well established in most of the world. Printing houses employed a large workforce using what were called common presses, Gutenberg-style flat-bed and platen presses with hand-set type.

But rapid change was coming, as the first Industrial Revolution reached its apex and inventors sought their fortunes by designing machines to replace all that manual labor. Print technology would change rapidly over the next two centuries, first with the introduction of mechanical steam-powered presses, then rotary and continuous roll-fed presses that could print on both sides of the paper at once, and intricate machines for manufacturing complete lines of type in a single operation.

And then print technology would go in an entirely different direction, shifting to lithography, which allowed for flat printing plates without the need for type slugs at all. Lithography also made color printing more practical.

Paper making would also become mechanized, and wood pulp would largely replace rags and cotton, as large paper mills were built to satisfy the growing demand of the print industry.

And the demand was great. Even in the 20th century when competing electronic media appeared, the market for newspapers, magazines and books grew from year to year up to and through the start of the Digital Age. The 19th and 20th centuries were the golden age of printing.

Paper machines

At the start of the 19th century there were several inventors in pursuit of a machine to manufacture paper. The first one to succeed in building a working machine was **Nicolas-Louis Robert**, who received a patent for it in France in 1799. His device was operated by a hand crank, which lifted pulp out of a water tank with a series of small buckets and deposited it on a moving wire mesh belt, which would pass through a set of rollers to press and dry it, forming a roll of paper in the end.

The patent was held by Robert's employer, Saint-Léger Didot, a French publisher, who with his brother-in-law John Gamble, entered into an agreement in England with brothers **Henry** and **Sealey Fourdrinier**, who expanded on the concept and built a more elaborate machine. It is described on pages 120-121.

Robert paper machine

1. Crank is turned by hand, beginning operation.

2. In the head box, pulp is lifted out of water tank and deposited on wire-mesh conveyor belt.

3. The belt carries the pulp layer along. A shaker bar shakes it side-to-side to evenly distribute the pulp.

4. The pulp layer is carried under a set of felt rollers which dry and press it, thus producing a continuous sheet of paper.

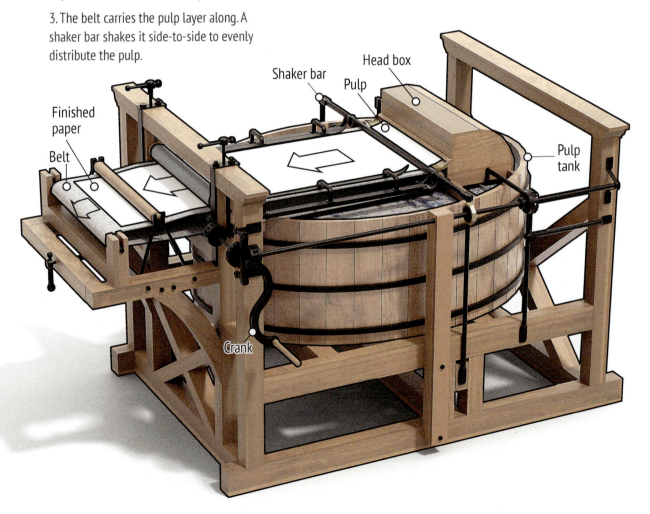

A competing concept was developed in 1809 by an Englishman, **John Dickinson**, which used water power. His concept was to have a rotating cylinder made of wire mesh, into which water would be drawn by suction. Pulp in the water would as a result stick to the cylinder's surface, from which it was transferred to a conveyor belt to make a continuous sheet of paper.

In 1817, **Thomas Gilpin** built a machine based on Dickinson's concept in Brandywine Creek, Delaware, in the US, using the river to power it. His paper was used by a Philadelphia newspaper, *Poulson's American Daily Advertiser*, starting in 1818, marking a first for US papers.

We don't know what Gilpin's machine looked like. The illustration below is based on patent application drawings.

Dickinson paper machine

Pulp from a tank is released into a basin, in which a cylinder with a mesh surface is turned by water power. Water flows into the cylinder through its porous surface, causing pulp to stick to its surface.

The pulp is then transferred to a wire mesh conveyor belt, which carries it through felt rollers to create a finished, continuous sheet of paper.

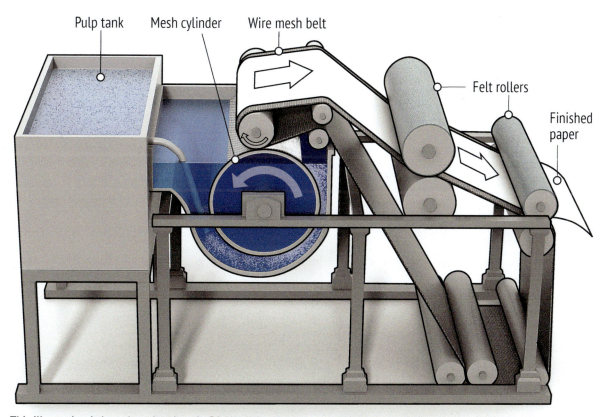

Pulp tank   Mesh cylinder   Wire mesh belt   Felt rollers   Finished paper

This illustration is based on drawings in Dickinson's patent application. There is no record of what the machine actually looked like or precisely how it operated.

The Fourdrinier process

The Fourdrinier brothers, who had invested in Nicolas-Louis Robert's machine, made significant improvements to it and in 1806 unveiled a continuous paper-making machine that formed the future basis for most modern paper mills. Rather than using Dickinson's concept, Robert's method of distributing a layer of pulp along a mesh conveyor belt and through a series of rollers and drying felts became the standard for the industry.

There have been incremental improvements to the process over the decades. The biggest change came in the mid-19th century with a shift away from rags and plant materials such as cotton and flax to wood as a source of pulp. A shortage of rags was becoming an urgent problem, one for which several solutions had been proposed, even including a suggestion that Egyptian mummy wrappings be used, presumably because so many were being discovered in ancient tombs.

Fourdrinier paper machine

Pulp tank
Pulp material is shredded in the tank to make pulp.

Headbox
Pulp slurry is dispensed to the wire mesh belt from here.

Belt
Slurry is spread out on moving wire mesh conveyor belt. The mesh allows water to drip out.

Wire mesh belt

The problem was solved by improved and steam-powered machines that could grind logs into chips, and devices that could render those chips into pulp. One of the latter was the Jordan refiner, patented by **Joseph Jordan** in 1858, that uses a rotating grinder to separate wood into fibers of consistent length. It is now a standard piece of equipment in typical paper mills.

The use of wood for pulp dramatically dropped the cost of paper making, and the new mills greatly increased production, which in turn underpinned a new era of plentiful and inexpensive print products from newspapers to magazines to books. The term 'pulp fiction,' applied to inexpensive paperback novels, originates from this time, a reference to paper made from wood pulp. And inexpensive woodpulp paper combined with mechanical presses made it practical for many newspapers to begin daily multi-page editions.

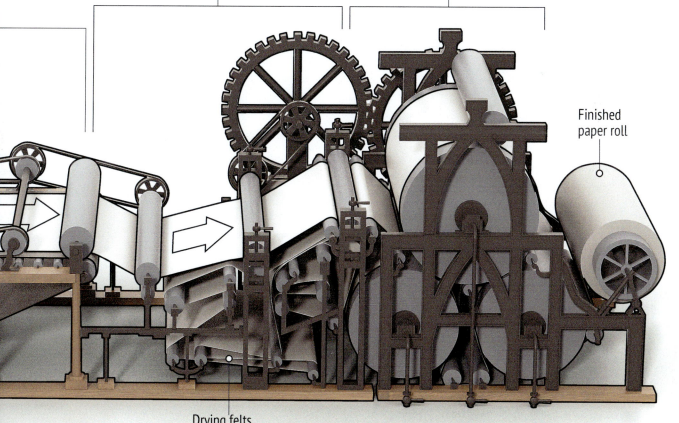

Press rolls
Paper goes through first set of rollers. Canvas felt belts begin drying the paper.

Drying rolls
More felt belts finish drying the paper.

Finished paper roll

Drying felts

Modern paper plant

Advances in pulp making technology by the mid-19th century allowed for wood as a source for paper manufacture, largely replacing rags and other plant fibers. The process depicted here is essentially the way most paper plants have operated from the mid-19th century to present times.

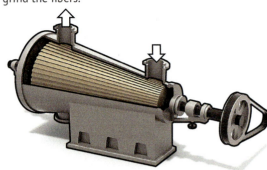

Jordan refiner
Patented by Joseph Jordan in 1858, this device renders wood fibers into a consistent pulp. The inner conical cylinder seen in this cutaway view rotates to grind the fibers.

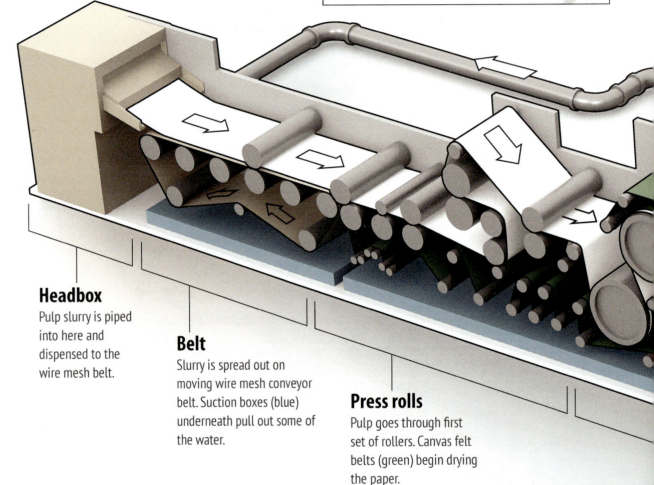

Headbox
Pulp slurry is piped into here and dispensed to the wire mesh belt.

Belt
Slurry is spread out on moving wire mesh conveyor belt. Suction boxes (blue) underneath pull out some of the water.

Press rolls
Pulp goes through first set of rollers. Canvas felt belts (green) begin drying the paper.

This is a simplified diagram of a modern industrial paper mill, showing only the key components in the manufacturing system. A typical plant today has more devices for creating and filtering pulp, as well as recycling and anti-pollution systems.

A modern mill would also have machinery for cutting, folding and packaging different kinds of paper at different sizes and for different purposes, creating a range of paper products.

Pulp preparation

Wood logs are stripped of bark and shredded in a grinder, then bleached and refined into a pulp slurry.

Recycled paper can also be added to the slurry, going through a separate pulping process afer being de-inked.

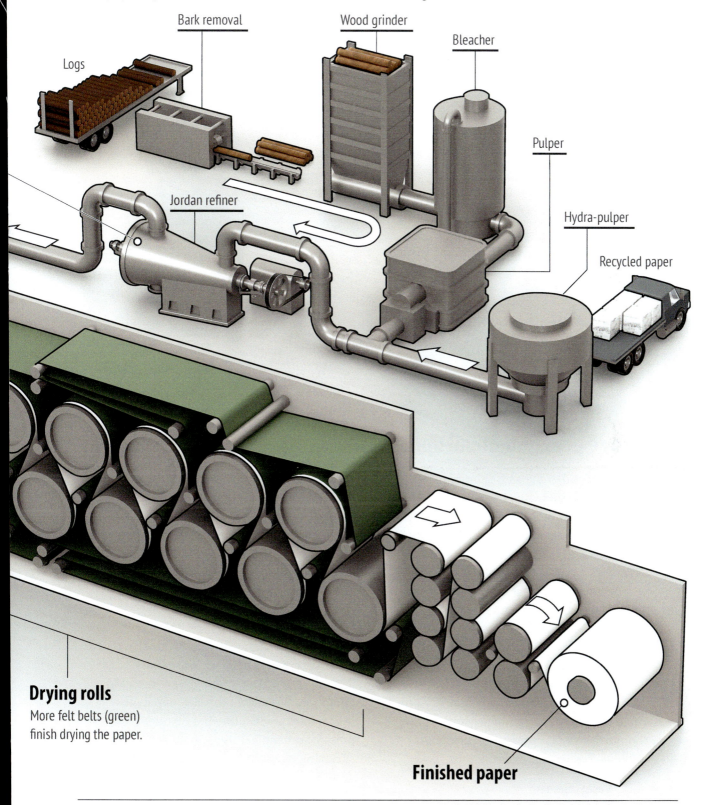

Logs

Bark removal

Wood grinder

Bleacher

Jordan refiner

Pulper

Hydra-pulper

Recycled paper

Drying rolls
More felt belts (green) finish drying the paper.

Finished paper

Printing presses

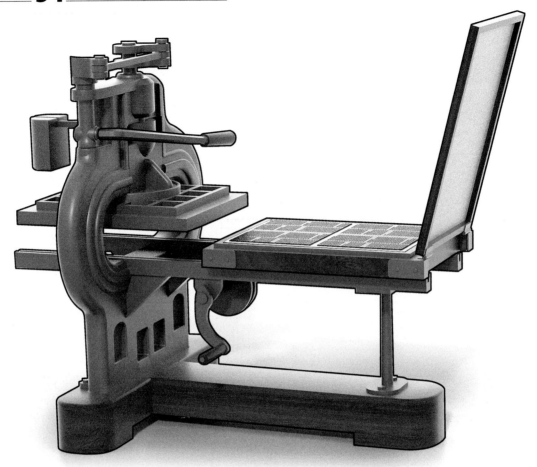

Stanhope press – manual operation

By the end of the 18th century printing presses still worked on the same principles as Gutenberg's press, with type being set in a form and inked, all by hand, and each sheet printed one side at a time with a pull of the press bar.

The most significant improvement was in making the frames out of cast iron, as wooden ones tended to warp and crack with time and use. The iron presses were more precise and durable.

There were also a wide selection of press designs and types, from industrial to table-top sizes. The Stanhope shown above, along with similar presses—Colombians, Albions, Fosters and Washingtons—was among the most common in large shops. The Stanhope had a unique screw that increased the pressure at the end of the bar's pull by decreasing its rate of descent, resulting in higher quality prints.

Charles Stanhope designed his namesake press in the late 18th century and declined to patent it, which contributed to its popularity. There are numerous variations on its design, many of which are on display in museums across the world, and perhaps some still in operation. Because of the lack of patent, it's unknown when the first Stanhope press was manufactured. The oldest surviving one is dated to 1804.

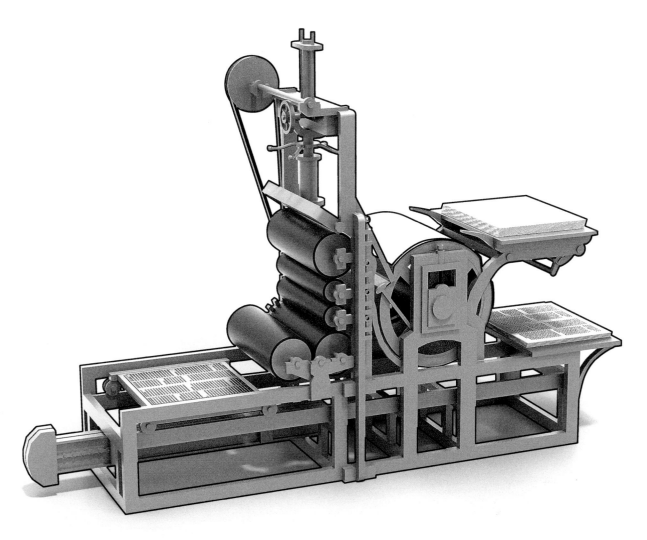

Koenig press – beginning of mechanization

Mechanization came to press design with the invention of the first steam-powered machine to enter production. It was built by **Friedrich Koenig** and **Andreas Bauer**, two German engineers, although its first use was in England by a London newspaper.

Koenig patented a steam-powered cylinder press in 1814. *The Times of London* became the first client, and began using it to print newspapers on November 29, 1814. Capable of printing 1,100 single-side sheets per hour, it was substantially faster than hand presses. It could also handle newspaper-size sheets: Stanhope presses could only print half a newspaper page with each pull.

Koenig's press still required manual type setting and placement of the paper on its large central cylinder, but inking and impressions were done mechanically with steam power.

Koenig and Bauer subsequently designed a press that would print on both sides of the paper at once, which they called the Perfecting Machine. They then began work on a web rotary design which would print from a roll of paper. However, Koenig died in 1833 before that press could be completed. Bauer continued to lead the company until his death in 1860. The Koenig & Bauer company is still in operation today, selling printing equipment.

Koenig single cylinder operation

1 After the character slugs are composed, the form is placed in the rolling form bed. A blank sheet of paper is manually attached to the impression cylinder.

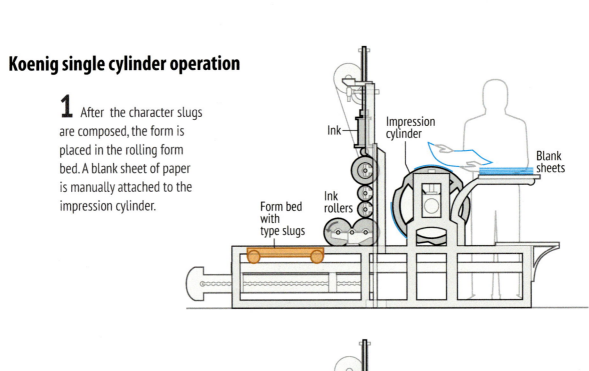

Ink

Impression cylinder

Blank sheets

Form bed with type slugs

Ink rollers

2 The press begins to operate. As the impression cylinder rotates, the form bed rolls under the ink rollers, inking the slugs, and continues on to meet the impression cylinder and the paper sheet attached to it, printing it.

3 The impression cylinder stops every third of a rotation, allowing the printed sheet to be removed and a new sheet attached. The form bed returns to its starting position to be re-inked for the next sheet.

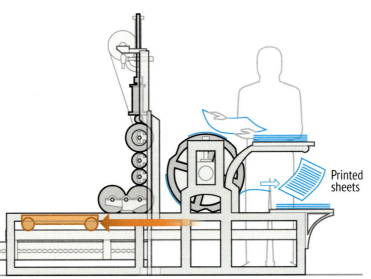

Printed sheets

Press evolution

Koenig and Bauer's 1814 press began a succession of increasingly more intricate and efficient steam-powered mechanical presses that automated the printing process and dramatically increased output. They next designed a double cylinder press capable of printing two pages simultaneously from the same form, which rolled back and forth between the two cylinders to do the impressions.

The rotary press

In 1847 **Richard March Hoe** patented a press in which the type slugs were attached to a rotating cylinder rather than a flat bed. This allowed it to print multiple sheets with each rotation. His patent showed a version with four impression cylinders; various subsequent versions had as many as ten. But it still required hand feeding of paper sheets. The press was so large that operators had to stand on platforms to feed the sheets.

The web-fed press

William Bullock's 1863 press eliminated the need to hand-feed sheets, instead using a paper roll from which sheets were mechanically cut. The press also printed on both sides of the sheet through the use of two slug cylinders.

His press soon went into operation at papers in Cincinnati and Philadelphia, eventually reaching a capacity of up to 30,000 sheets an hour, compared to Keonig's first press which did 1,100 sheets an hour.

Koenig double cylinder press

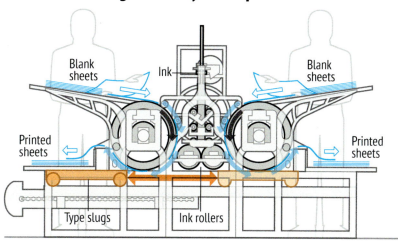

Hoe rotary press

Bullock web-fed rotary press

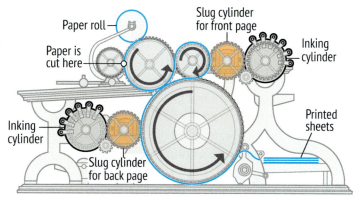

Typesetting

Linotype and Monotype machines

After press innovations had succeeded in automating almost every aspect of the printing process, the one remaining job that was still done manually was the setting of type slugs. This was time consuming and expensive, both in manpower and in the need for thousands of character slugs which needed to be periodically replaced as they wore out.

In the late 19th century a variety of machines were proposed to automate typesetting, and several of them at least partially succeeded in mechanically setting traditional type slugs. But a more complete solution, one that both cast and set type, came from **Ottmar Mergenthaler**, who in 1885 completed the **Linotype** machine. A marvel of the Industrial Age, it was a device of incredible intricacy, consisting of over 36,000 parts. Thomas Edison is anecdotally said to have declared it "the eighth wonder of the world."

The Linotype produced entire lines of type (thus the name) as single bars through the use of character molds called matrices, each of which had a character shape engraved in its side. These were lined up by the operator through the use of a keyboard, after which molten metal was injected into them, all within the machine. The resulting bars were much easier to compose in the press, and subsequently could be melted down for reuse.

Mergenthaler's machine was a commercial success. Its first use was at the New York Tribune, in July 3, 1886. Entering into business with a consortium of newspaper publishers, The Mergenthaler Printing Company went into production and the Linotype became an industry fixture, effectively making the setting of type by hand an obsolete practice.

Mergenthaler himself had a contentious relationship with his investors, eventually leading to his resignation in 1888 and to starting a new company, Ottmar Mergenthaler & Co., in Baltimore.

In 1891 the two companies agreed to merge as The Mergenthaler Linotype Co. But Ottmar didn't live long to enjoy its success. He died of tuberculosis in 1899 at the age of 45.

In 1911 the product name was changed to Intertype, but it was essentially the same machine. By the mid-20th century more than 100,000 of the devices were in use worldwide. There are still a few in operation to this day.

The only successful competitor to the Linotype was the **Monotype** machine, built by **Tolbert Lanston** and brought to market in 1900. Originally the keyboard unit was separate from the casting unit, and produced a perforated ribbon which was fed into the caster, instructing it on the positioning of matrices. Rather than producing a line of type as a bar, it produced individual character slugs, but already typeset and ready for the press. In some ways this was better, for it provided greater control over letter spacing, and made it easier to correct operator errors.

Monotype machines were manufactured until 1967.

The Linotype machine

There have been numerous variations on the Linotype design as improvements have been implemented, but they all are essentially operated the same way, by typing on a keyboard to line up matrices, and then injecting molten metal into them to form a line of type.

They can be powered by any source, from steam to gas engines to electricity. There were even kerosene-powered models for remote locations. The illustration above depicts a mid-20th century model that was powered by electricity, with a gas burner for the molten metal pot.

How the linotype machine works

Matrices

Matrices

Each matrix is a thin brass form that has one or two character shapes engraved in one edge. If there are two, the second one is usually the italic version of the character. They are of different thicknesses depending on the character width. They are contained in a magazine at the top of the linotype machine, which typically has from 72 to 90 channels, each holding up to 20 matrices of a particular character.

Character shape

Back edge

Front edge

When the operator presses a key on the keyboard, a matrix is released from the magazine and slides down to the assembler, where the matrices are arranged into a line. The front edge of each matrix has the character painted on it so that the operator can check for accuracy.

Assembler

This is a line of type set in linotype

Words are separated by spacebands, which are thicker at the bottom than the top. A clamping device moves them up or down to adjust the space between words in order to make justified lines all the same width. This illustration shows the back side of the matrix line.

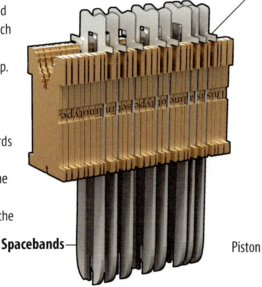

This is a line for type set in linotype.

Spacebands

Casting

After a line is composed, the matrix line is mechanically moved from the assembler to a slot on the mold disk, behind which is a pot containing a molten mixture of lead, antimony and tin kept at around 500 degrees F (260 degrees C). A piston forces the molten metal into the slot behind the matrices and into their character forms, casting a slug. This automatic process happens in about seven seconds.

Metal pot and mold disk

Molten metal

Matrices

Piston

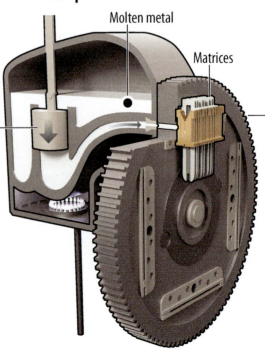

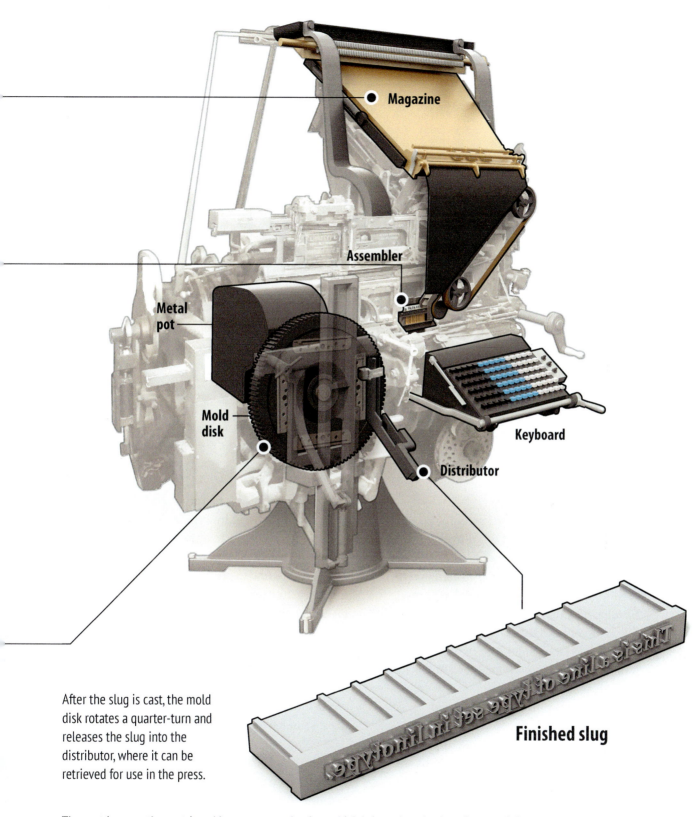

Magazine

Assembler

Metal pot

Mold disk

Distributor

Keyboard

After the slug is cast, the mold disk rotates a quarter-turn and releases the slug into the distributor, where it can be retrieved for use in the press.

Finished slug

The matrices are then retrieved by an arm mechanism which brings them back to the top of the magazine, where they are returned to their respective channels. Unique ridge patterns in the tops of the matrices are keys that guide them to the proper channel.

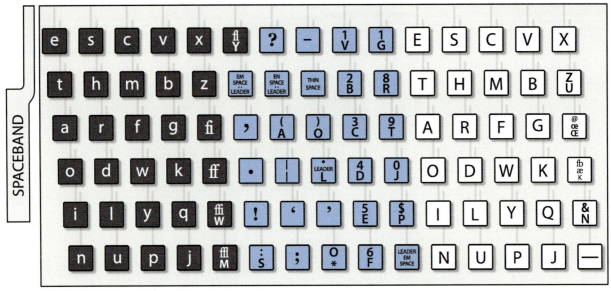

A typical Linotype keyboard.

Keyboards and Linotype

The earliest devices that used a keyboard date to the early 18th century, starting with a 1714 patent taken out by Englishman Henry Mill for a 'machine for transcribing letters'. Little is known about his device aside from the patent, but it appears to have been similar to a typewriter.

At least six different 19th-century men have been credited with inventing the typewriter, and all may have created similar devices. The one most often given credit, American **Christopher Latham Sholes**, patented his typing device with fellow inventor **Samuel W. Soule** in 1868. It had keys laid out in two rows in a manner resembling piano keys in black and white.

Upon further product testing and research, Sholes came up with the QWERTY keyboard layout, the one in common use today with most Latin-based languages. One of the problems he was trying to solve was key jamming, so he tried to not have any commonly used letters next to each other.

The Linotype keyboard

As shown above, this keyboard layout is very different from typewriters. There are separate keys for upper and lower case letters, and others for functions specific to the Linotype machine.

It took two years of apprenticeship to become a qualified Linotype operator, which allowed entry to a profession in great demand. The population of Linotypists grew exponentially through the early 20th century. 33,000 of the machines were in use by 1916.

It was a job that required speed, concentration, some math skills (one had to calculate line widths), and accuracy, since making a typographical error ruined the entire line. If a wrong matrix was dropped to the assembler, there was no way to return it.

A common practice on making a mistake was to run one's fingers down the left two columns of keys, signaling the compositor not to use that slug. But once in a while "etaoin shrdlu" was missed and made it into publication.

Modern printing

By the end of the 19th century printing practices were becoming well established with mechanical rotary presses using linotype. These machines were capable of keeping up with the ever growing market for all the printed products that were becoming common in everyday life, from daily newspapers to magazines and inexpensive paperback books.

There were several limitations to this type of technology, however. Even with linotype, typesetting was expensive and time consuming. Preparing a press run took many hours of work by a team of linotypists and press setters. And that was after the initial and considerable expense of the linotype machines and the presses, and the ongoing maintenance, repair and energy costs of these enormously complicated machines.

Also, there was a growing demand for photographs, illustrations and graphic elements. These required extra steps on the existing presses, with images screened and etched to separate plates.

And there was increasing demand for color. This required several press runs, one for each ink color, which greatly increased costs.

A new printing method, lithography, had appeared in the early 19th century, and had the potential to solve all these problems. It allowed printing from a flat surface, didn't need typesetting, was well suited for visual reproductions, and although still requiring several press runs was ultimately more practical for color printing.

Lithography found niche markets in the 19th century for posters and art reproductions. But in the 20th century improvements to the process gradually allowed it to compete with letterpress. By the second half of the century it became the industry standard for the great majority of commercial printing, which is where it stands now.

Lithography

Lithography changed how most commercial printing was done, and eventually made Linotype obsolete.

Alois Senefelder, a German playwright, is credited with its invention in 1796 CE. In search of an inexpensive method to reproduce his work, he noticed that when he drew on a sheet of limestone with a grease pencil, the surface became permanently marked, and if he moistened the stone's surface (limestone is very porous), the greased areas would stay dry. If he then inked the surface, the ink would only stick to the dry areas. He could then press a piece of paper on top and produce a print.

He had invented a way to print from a flat surface. In a hundred years this would begin to radically change print publication.

At right is a limestone plate and prints made from it. The image is drawn on the stone surface with a grease pencil, in reverse.

To make a print:
• The surface is moistened. The water only sticks to the blank, non-greasy areas.
• Ink is applied, which only sticks to the dry areas.
• A sheet of paper is laid on top and rubbed or pressed, creating the print.

The print depicted here is from A. Hoen & Company, a 19th-century American print shop that achieved a high reputation for the quality of its work.

Lithography didn't have an immediate impact on the commercial print industry. Writing or drawing on slabs of limestone was not practical for periodicals or books, and there was no way to do typesetting. At first it was mostly adopted by artists to make fine art prints. French Romantic painters such as Delacroix, and later, Post-Impressionists including Toulouse-Lautrec and Gauguin made lithographic fine artwork, as did the American artist James McNeill Whistler, as well as many other American artists.

For commercial purposes lithography was mostly used for art posters and reproductions of paintings. Currier & Ives in New York City began making lithographic prints of idyllic scenes in 1825, as did a number of other commercial print shops. At first they were printed with black ink and then hand tinted with watercolor. Later lithographers started using several stones to create color prints, one for each ink color. Sometimes as many as 30 stones would be used for a single print.

A lithographic stone being used on a Stanhope press. There are also a number of presses designed specifically for lithography.

Rotary lithography

In the 1870s in England a method was devised for the purpose of printing on tin cans, which couldn't be done practically with a flat printing plate. This required transferring the printing surface from the flat stone to a flexible sheet that could then be wrapped around the cylinder of a rotary press. At first cardboard was used, but this was improved upon by using aluminum or zinc sheets, the surface of which could be chemically treated to act in the same manner as limestone, with the areas meant to print repelling water and allowing ink to adhere.

Soon this method was applied to printing on paper. Rotary lithographic presses allowed much higher volumes of reproductions than printing from flat stones, and such presses started appearing toward the end of the 19th century for commercial use.

Offset lithography

In 1901 an American lithographic printer, **Ira Washington Rubel**, discovered by accident that printing to a rubber blanket and then to the paper produced a better quality print than printing directly to paper from the metal printing plate. His press had a rubber-coated impression cylinder, the cylinder that provides pressure to the paper from underneath. He neglected to load paper into his press, resulting in the ink printing to the rubber cylinder instead of to paper. When he then ran paper through the press, it got printed on both sides. He noticed that the backside, the side printed from rubber, was of better quality than the one from the metal plate.

From this discovery offset lithography was created. It adds a cylinder with a rubber blanket between the printing plate and the paper, transferring the ink from the plate to the blanket to the paper.

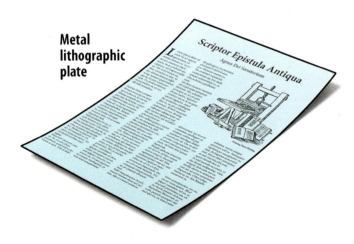

Metal lithographic plate

Scriptor Epistula Antiqua
Agnus Dei Sanatorium

Offset lithographic printing

The lithographic plate is wrapped around a cylinder in the press. Between it and the paper is a cylinder wrapped with a rubber blanket.

As printing begins, the plate is first coated with water, and then with ink, which only sticks to the areas that repelled the water. The plate then transfers the ink to the rubber blanket, which in turn applies it to the paper as it travels underneath.

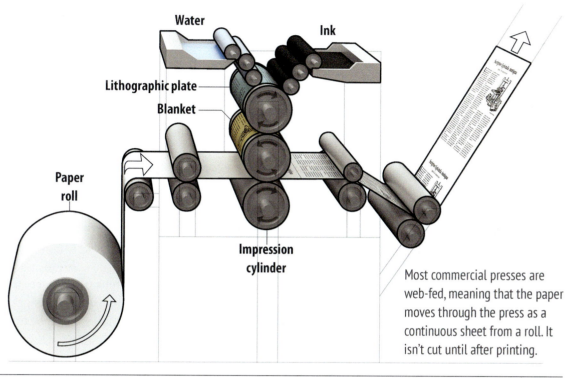

Water

Ink

Lithographic plate

Blanket

Paper roll

Impression cylinder

Most commercial presses are web-fed, meaning that the paper moves through the press as a continuous sheet from a roll. It isn't cut until after printing.

Double-sided printing

Lithography makes it simple to print both sides of the paper at the same time, by adding another set of rollers underneath.

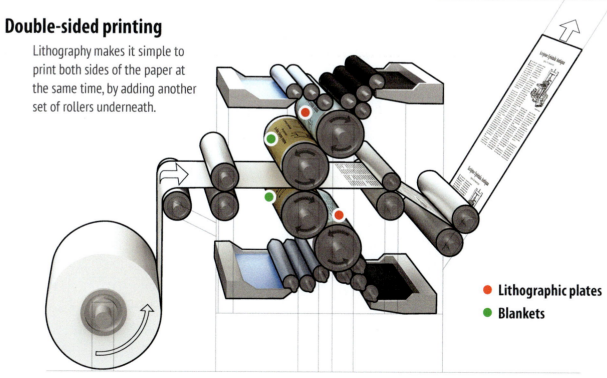

● **Lithographic plates**
● **Blankets**

Phototypesetting

The last major hurdle to lithographic printing for publications was the lack of a method for setting type. One practice was to first set the type with a Linotype machine, print a single page on a letterpress printer, and then use that for paste-up to make a lithographic plate. Clearly this was not efficient.

René Alphonse Higonnet, a French engineer, and **Louis Moyroud** demonstrated the Lumitype in 1946, a device that produced single columns of text on photo-sensitive paper by projecting a strobe light through a disk with letter shapes cut out of it. In the US it was marketed as the Photon.

In 1947 the Intertype corporation, the descendant of the Linotype company, introduced a version of the Linotype that substituted a camera sytem for the hot metal casting part of the machine, that similarly printed text to photo paper. It was called the Fotosetter. Monotype followed with a similar machine, called the Monophoto, which also produced a column of type on photo paper.

The earliest models were called blind, in that the operator couldn't see the typed results until the paper exited the machine. These systems typically consisted of two parts, a perforating machine with a keyboard that output a paper tape with punch hole patterns, and the actual phototypesetter that produced the text on paper when the tape was fed to it.

Later versions used magnetic tape or punch cards instead of paper tape. And then came machines with cathode ray picture tubes, which not only allowed the operator to see the text as they were typing but used the light from the display to expose the photo paper.

The resulting columns of text were then pasted up on boards to design the pages from which printing plates would be made.

Perforator

Early phototypesetting systems used a keyboard device to perforate a paper tape with a pattern of holes designating characters. The tape was then fed into a teletypesetter to produce a column of text.

Tape

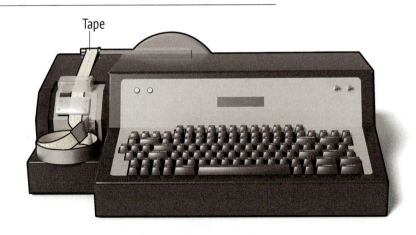

Tape

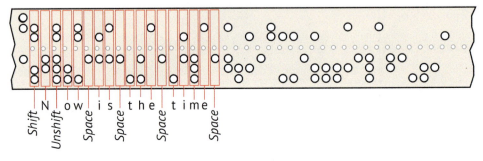

Shift N Unshift ow Space is Space the Space time Space

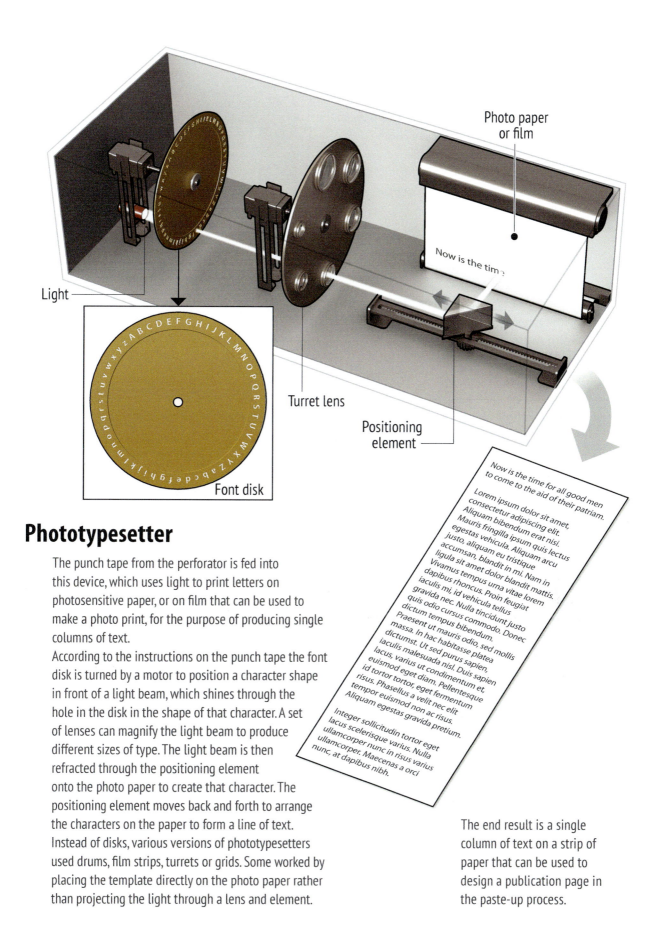

Photo paper
or film

Light

Turret lens

Positioning
element

Font disk

Now is the time

Now is the time for all good men
to come to the aid of their patriam.

Lorem ipsum dolor sit amet,
consectetur adipiscing elit.
Aliquam bibendum erat nisi.
Mauris fringilla ipsum quis lectus
egestas vehicula. Aliquam eu tristique
justo, aliquam eu tristique
accumsan, blandit in mi. Nam in
ligula sit amet dolor blandit mattis.
Vivamus tempus urna vitae lorem
dapibus rhoncus. Proin feugiat
iaculis mi, id vehicula tellus
gravida nec. Nulla tincidunt justo
quis odio cursus commodo. Donec
dictum tempus bibendum.
Praesent ut mauris odio, sed mollis
massa. In hac habitasse platea
dictumst. Ut sed purus sapien,
iaculis malesuada nisl. Duis sapien
lacus, varius ut condimentum et,
euismod eget diam. Pellentesque
id tortor tortor, eget fermentum
risus. Phasellus a velit nec elit
tempor euismod non ac risus.
Aliquam egestas gravida pretium.

Integer sollicitudin tortor eget
lacus scelerisque varius. Nulla
ullamcorper nunc in risus varius
ullamcorper. Maecenas a orci
nunc, at dapibus nibh.

Phototypesetter

The punch tape from the perforator is fed into
this device, which uses light to print letters on
photosensitive paper, or on film that can be used to
make a photo print, for the purpose of producing single
columns of text.

According to the instructions on the punch tape the font
disk is turned by a motor to position a character shape
in front of a light beam, which shines through the
hole in the disk in the shape of that character. A set
of lenses can magnify the light beam to produce
different sizes of type. The light beam is then
refracted through the positioning element
onto the photo paper to create that character. The
positioning element moves back and forth to arrange
the characters on the paper to form a line of text.
Instead of disks, various versions of phototypesetters
used drums, film strips, turrets or grids. Some worked by
placing the template directly on the photo paper rather
than projecting the light through a lens and element.

The end result is a single
column of text on a strip of
paper that can be used to
design a publication page in
the paste-up process.

Paste-up process

In the lithographic system, pages are designed on a board by pasting the different paper components—columns of text, photos and graphic elements—onto a board the size of the page to be printed.

As offset lithography became common, composing rooms were more likely to be equipped with X-acto knives, razor blades, rulers, tape and glue instead of type slugs and forms.

Often a hot wax machine was used for paste-up, which would coat the back of the paper with a layer of melted wax, facilitating positioning the paper on the board.

Picas and points

Another necessary instrument was the pica pole, a ruler that measures in traditional typesetting units of **picas** and **points**. This measurement system dates back to the 16th century, although there was not universal agreement on the actual size of the units. Today the units are somewhat more standardized and the system is in common use by both designers and printers.

In digital systems today there are six picas to an inch, and 12 points to a pica. A measure might be designated as 12p3, which means 12 picas and three points.

Column widths are typically measured in picas and points, but character heights are measured only in points, as in 16-point Garamond or 36-point Helvetica. Column heights are more often measured in number of lines of type.

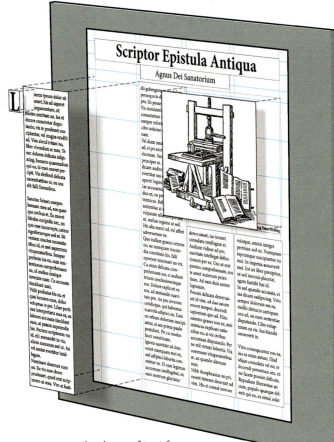

A column of text from a phototypesetter being glued in position on a paste-up board, along with an illustration, in preparation for making a printing plate. The large letter L would have to be printed and glued separately, as would each block of text, including the headlines.

Pica pole

Plate making

Plates for lithographic printing are made by photographing the paste-up board and using the resulting film to prepare the plate surface.

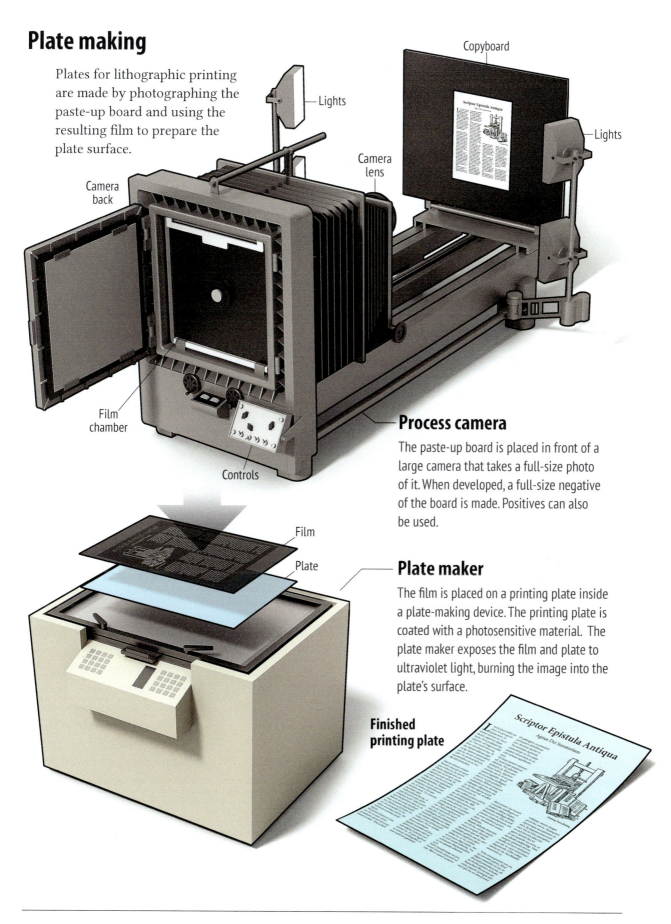

Lights

Copyboard

Camera lens

Lights

Camera back

Film chamber

Controls

Process camera

The paste-up board is placed in front of a large camera that takes a full-size photo of it. When developed, a full-size negative of the board is made. Positives can also be used.

Film

Plate

Plate maker

The film is placed on a printing plate inside a plate-making device. The printing plate is coated with a photosensitive material. The plate maker exposes the film and plate to ultraviolet light, burning the image into the plate's surface.

Finished printing plate

Scriptor Epistula Antiqua
Agnus Dei Sanatorium

Color printing

The earliest known practice of color printing was not on paper but on textiles, in both Asia and Europe as early as the 4th or 5th centuries BCE, at first using stamps and then woodblocks. In Asia before paper was invented, silk was used not only as fabric but as the earliest material for writing and illustration, so it seems likely that this was the origin of woodblock printing on paper.

Printing in color can be done by using several woodblocks, one for each color, to produce a composite image. It's unknown when the practice began but color block prints became common in China and Japan by the 11th or 12th centuries CE.

Color theory

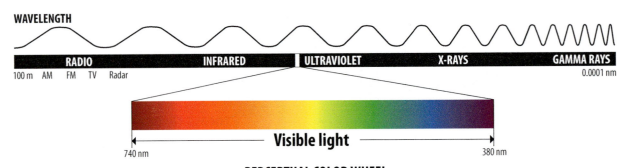

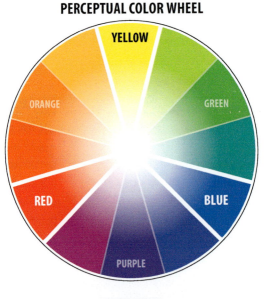

PERCEPTUAL COLOR WHEEL

Visible light is a narrow band of all the wavelengths of electromagnetic energy emitted by a source such as the sun or a lightbulb. We see those waves as the colors from red to purple, with all the rainbow colors in between.

People have attempted to chart color relationships since the 1700s, beginning with **Isaac Newton**, who, with the use of a prism, was the first to demonstrate that white light could be separated into the spectrum colors. He also demonstrated that mixing two colors produced a third, such as mixing blue and red light to produce purple.

The color wheel most people are familiar with is created by taking the band of visible light and bending it around in a circle, as shown here. In this model, blue, red and yellow are the primary colors, which are colors that can't be made by mixing other colors but by mixing them can produce the rest of the colors.

The perceived color of objects in the real world is caused by the particular wavelengths that are reflected off of their surfaces. For example, a lemon appears yellow because it only reflects yellow light, absorbing all other wavelengths.

COMPLEMENTS

Primary	Secondary
Blue	Orange
Red	Green
Yellow	Purple

In Europe block books were sometimes printed with several ink colors, but most often color was added by hand after printing with black ink. Gutenberg's bibles were printed leaving blank spaces for color elements to be hand painted, which was the common practice, as exemplified by the varied copies of the Nurenberg Chronicle, whose block prints were hand colored. Some liturgical books were printed in both black and red ink, requiring two press runs. Typically press runs were a few hundred or at the most in the low thousands, likely making it more economical to hand color each book than to do multiple runs.

Lithography in the 19th century made color reproductions of artwork popular.

The quality of these prints could be remarkable. This new industry is credited with democratizing art by making affordable prints of well-known works available to the public.

Commercial color printing became more common in the 20th century, particularly with magazines. With improvements in lithographic offset printing, color pages became more common in many publications, with the exception of newspapers, which rarely offered it until the 1980s. Even today most newspapers only print color on the front page and on section covers, and on inside pages only for ads if the buyer pays for it. And most books, unless there are color photos or artwork, aren't printed in color.

Key dates in color printing

1346 CE: The earliest found color woodblock print, from China. The practice is undoubtedly older than that.

1816: Godefroy Engelmann and **Charles-Philibert de Lasteyrie**, two Frenchmen, obtain a patent for 2-color chromolithography, using two lithographic stones to produce a single image. In 1837 Engelmann patented the same process for 3- and 4-color printing.

1843: English Botanist **Anna Atkins** self-publishes the first book entirely of photographs, on the topic of algae, using a direct contact method called cyanotype.

Dec. 22, 1855: The *Illustrated London News,* in producing an 8-page Christmas Supplement insert, prints the first color illustrations in a newspaper.

1893: Illustrator **William Kurtz** patents a color separation process using cyan, magenta and yellow ink colors, establishing standard process colors.

1894: *The New York World* prints the first full color comics page.

1906: The Eagle Printing Ink Company adds black ink to Kurtz's color separation process, establishing the standard process ink colors as CMYK.

1930s: Many magazines are by now printing in full color.

1954: *The St. Petersburg Times* in Florida introduces full color into its news pages.

1958: *The Orlando Sentinel*, also in Florida, begins to print in color.

1982: *USA Today* begins publication as a full-color, national newspaper.
By this time, most publications were being printed through offset lithography using phototypesetting.
In 1983, about half of all US daily newspapers were using some color. By 1990, nearly all of them were using some color at least once a week.

CMYK: Process colors

William Kurtz, a German-American illustrator, obtained a US patent in 1893 for printing using three ink colors: **cyan**, **magenta** and **yellow**.

There was already an existing understanding of how colors in the visible spectrum worked, and that blue, red and yellow worked well as primary pigments, that is, colors that couldn't be created from other colors but by mixing them in various amounts could produce all other colors. **Isaac Newton** discussed this color theory in his 1704 work *Opticks*, and a number of 17th-century European intaglio artists had been experimenting with printing in those colors. Kurtz found, however, that cyan and magenta worked better for printing inks than blue and red.

By standardizing these ink colors, a wide range of colors could be obtained with only three printing plates. This significantly lowered the cost of color printing.

The K stands for black, which was also added to what came to be called the **process printing ink colors** of cyan, magenta, yellow and black. K is short for key, as the black plate is used to line up the other three plates during printing.

The CMYK color model has become the industry standard for commercial lithographic printing.

Subtractive colors

A model called **Subtractive Color** is most often used to explain how the process color inks work together. In this model, cyan, magenta and yellow are the primary colors, and mixing varying percentages of them can produce a range of other colors. Mixing all three together makes black.

The subtractive term refers to how inks behave according to the color theory described on the previous page. They absorb all wavelengths of light except for the one you see, which they reflect. So an image of a lemon is printed with yellow ink, which reflects only the yellow wavelength. Similarly, an image of an apple is printed with a mix of yellow and magenta inks to make red, and thus only reflecting red light.

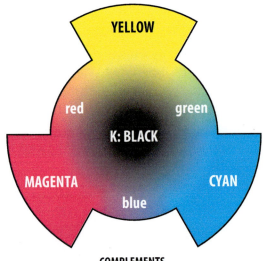

SUBTRACTIVE COLOR WHEEL

YELLOW • red • green • K: BLACK • MAGENTA • blue • CYAN

COMPLEMENTS

Primary	Secondary
Cyan	Red
Magenta	Green
Yellow	Blue

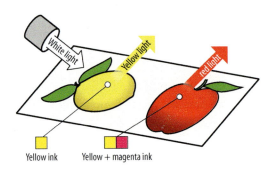

Yellow ink   Yellow + magenta ink

Color ranges

Colored ink on paper cannot, of course, replicate every color in the natural world. In fact, the **gamut**, or range, of colors that we can see is much wider than those that can be created by mixing various amounts of CMYK inks together, as the images at right demonstrate.

But cyan, magenta and yellow are not the only colors of ink that are made. Ink manufacturers such as Pantone and Toyo, two of the largest printing ink distributors in the world, offer thousands of different ink colors.

Spot colors

If an ink of a different color than cyan, magenta or yellow is used, it is called a **spot color**. It will require its own printing plate and set of rollers if added to a print run in an offset lithographic press.

Spot colors widen the gamut of colors that can be reproduced on a press, as one would expect, although it still covers only a portion of all visible colors. Some spot colors are also expressly made to use with certain types of paper, such as paper coated with sizing or wax as opposed to uncoated paper such as newsprint, or with surfaces of different tints or brightness. They can also have added textures making them appear metallic, for example.

It is also possible to use one or two spot colors along with black without using any process colors at all. These are called duotone or tritone prints.

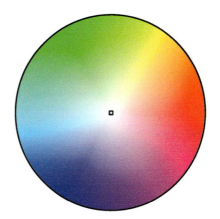

Visible light gamut

Process colors gamut

Spot colors gamut

Four-color printing

In order to print an image with process ink colors, four different lithographic plates have to be produced, one for each ink color. A typical commercial press will have a different set of rollers for each ink color. The roll of paper travels through each set in succession, with each ink color being printed on top of the previous one. In this way, different colors are created by mixing the inks.

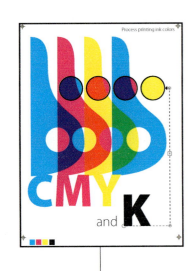

Process printing ink colors

CMY and K

Cyan plate

Magenta plate

Four-color offset lithographic printing press

This cut-away diagram shows the principal parts of an offset web-fed press.
Each of the printing plates is wrapped around a plate cylinder for its respective color.

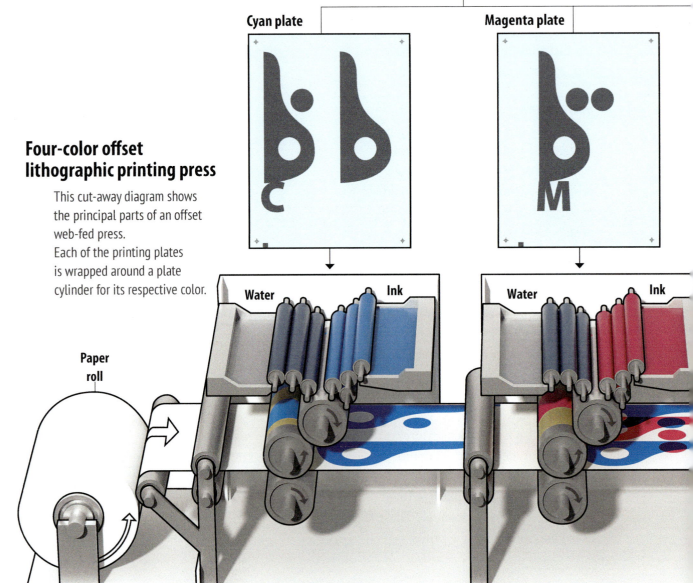

Water | Ink | Water | Ink

Paper roll

Large offset presses typically have more than four sets of rollers, often as many as eight. This allows them to print additional spot colors if desired, or to add a clear coat or some other finish.

The largest presses, particularly for newspapers, can be two stories tall and larger than a train locomotive. Fed from paper rolls as wide as four feet, they can print hundreds of thousands of complete newspapers or magazines, each consisting of dozens of pages, in a few hours. Additional machinery folds and stacks them, ready for delivery.

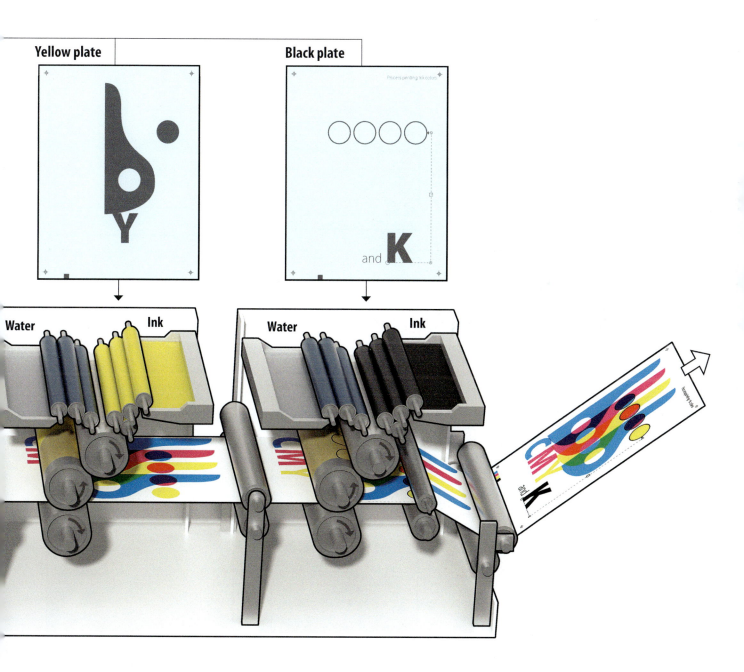

Color line screening

Each process color printing plate for a color photograph has to be created with a dot pattern in order to simulate lighter and darker shades. Before the digital age this was done by photographing a print of the original photo through a filter that blocked all colors other than the one intended for that plate, and also a fine-mesh screen to create the dot patterns.

This would be necessary for any color element on the page that requires a shade other than 100 percent of any of the ink colors. Creating different shades of a spot ink color would also require screening.

Societal change

Along with every other impact that the industrial revolutions had on the way people lived and worked, the mechanization of paper production and printing had transformative societal effects.

Labor shift

The change in printing methods contributed to the larger labor shift from manual to factory work throughout the 19th century. Mechanization in the paper-making and press industries erased many traditional jobs. Paper machines eliminated all the manual tasks of pounding pulp and pulling individual sheets with a mold and deckle. Steam powered presses now only needed workers to feed paper into mechanical rotary presses and collect them at the other end. In a few decades even that was replaced by web-fed presses that cut, folded and stacked the finished product. And typesetting was eliminated by the linotype and monotype machines.

As with jobs in other industries that were being replaced by mechanization, there was resistance. When *The Times of London* bought Koenig's single-cylinder press in 1814, they were careful to install it in a separate building and to keep it hidden from their printers, fearing their reaction.

But there is not much evidence in the paper and print industries of the strikes, sabotage and disruption that other types of industries experienced at the start of the first industrial revolution. In fact, due to the rapid increase in the sheer volume of material being printed, press mechanization likely increased the size of the print workforce, although many of the jobs would no longer be classified as skilled labor.

The changes did create one skilled labor class. By the late 1800s the linotype machine required a new workforce of professional operators. Due to the skills needed, they were well-paid and much in demand, creating a profession that lasted for nearly a century. Maintaining and repairing the machines also required considerable expertise, as complicated as they were. And operating increasingly complex printing presses required a trained workforce as well, creating more middle-class jobs. As older, traditional jobs were eliminated, they were replaced with jobs in mechanical technology.

Literacy

The increasing availability of newspapers, magazines and books in the 19th and 20th centuries brought dramatic increases in public literacy rates. The global average increased from 12 percent to nearly 80 percent between 1800 and 2000. In most of the industrialized world the rate was over 90 percent by 1940, and has been at virtually 100 percent since 1990. In contrast, most of Africa and the Middle East didn't rise above 50 percent literacy until about 1990. North Africa and the Middle East still have the lowest rates in the world, on average around 65 percent.

Education

As literacy increased, the concept of education for the general public also began to take root in the industrialized nations. It's estimated that prior to 1820, less than one out of five people globally were ever enrolled in formal education. From this point on formal education grew, as one would expect, at about the same rate as literacy, reaching a global average of 82

Literacy rates by country, 1750-2015

Estimated rates of basic literacy in Western Europe and the US among inhabitants 15 years and older.

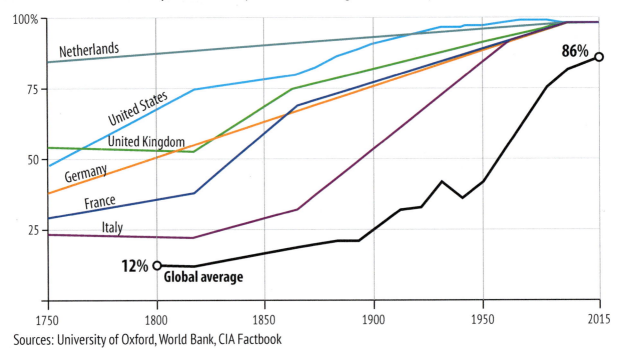

Sources: University of Oxford, World Bank, CIA Factbook

percent in 2010. In industrialized countries, particularly in Western Europe and the US, some level of formal education was being offered to the majority of the population by the start of the 20th century.

The disparity between the industrialized West and the rest of the world has been stark. Prior to World War II, Eastern Europe, Asia, Latin America and Africa provided limited access to formal education. In Africa and the Middle East the rate was below 20 percent until the 1950s, keeping the global rate below 50 percent until about 1950.

Societal influence

In the West, large political and societal shifts started to be manifested throughout the 19th century and into the 20th, leading up to World War I. Late in the 18th century there had been two revolutions, one in the US and one in France, the first successful but the second disastrous, resulting in chaos and a return to authoritarian rule, first under Napoleon and then a return to royalty. Nevertheless a trend away from authoritarian rule was beginning in the West, as it had in the 15th century when literacy took hold in Europe and royal and church authority began to come under question if not yet openly rejected.

The 19th century's vastly more efficient printing presses stoked this growing anti-establishmentarianism. The presses provided access to new ideas as well as current political and civic information. The arrival of large-circulation newspapers made it possible for people to read daily accounts

Percentage of population enrolled in formal education, 1820-2010

Percentage of inhabitants 15 years and older who had received some formal education.

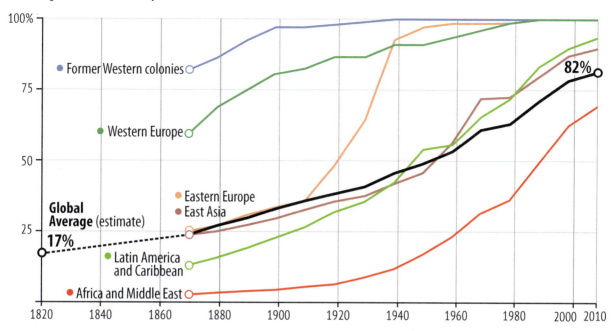

Sources: OurWorldinData.org; Van Zanden et al: 'How Was Life?: Global Well-being since 1820'

of governmental activities, and this began to spur demand for more accountability. Gradually the conditions were building for rejection of the royal houses which still ruled Europe and much of the rest of the world through colonization.

This would culminate in 1914 with the start of World War I. Thanks to the telegraph and telephone, newspapers could now provide first-hand, daily accounts of escalating casualty numbers and descriptions of the brutality and senselessness of modern warfare, itself made more cruel by the vastly improved machinery of war. Improvements in photography and movies made the news even more graphic.

There is general agreement among historians that the war was a societal turning point. Throughout the 20th century more and more countries turned into republics with some form of democracy, and eventually most colonies gained independence. The political landscape at the end of the 20th century was starkly different from its beginning.

The reasons for this are undoubtedly complicated, but increased access to news and information, coupled with greater levels of literacy, was likely a significant factor. And this was only possible because of the technology that greatly increased the number and distribution of publications worldwide.

And newly emerging media would also exert social influence: Movies, radio, TV, video, and the Internet, as we shall see in the following chapters.

Photography and Film

Photography is the process of creating an image by capturing light. It relies on a method of focusing reflected light on to either a light-sensitive chemical surface or, in the digital age, to electronic sensors.

The oldest surviving photograph was taken in 1826 or 1827 by the French inventor Nicéphore Niépce. It is called '*View from the Window at Le Gras*', depicting, as the title suggests, some buildings viewed through a window. The exposure took over eight hours.

Niépce had taken an earlier photo in 1822, but it was destroyed in an attempt to make prints from it. In 1829 he partnered with one of the best-known photo pioneers, Louis Daguerre, but the partnership did not last long as Niépce died in 1833. Daguerre moved the technology along, reducing exposure time from hours to minutes.

By the mid-1800s, photography was becoming practical enough to become commercialized. But it was not a medium of mass communication: Daguerre's photos could only be reproduced by taking a second photo of them.

Two developments made photos more widely available. First was the invention of film, introduced by George Eastman in 1884. From film negatives multiple copies of prints could be easily made. Eastman founded the Eastman Kodak company, and introduced their first roll-film camera in 1888.

The second development was the invention of halftoning, also in the 1880s, which allowed photos to be printed on presses. Now newspapers and magazines could include photos on their pages.

Photography then led to movies. Thomas Edison unveiled his kinetoscope in 1891 by showing a short animated scene, introducing the new medium to the world.

The 20th century saw numerous advances such as color, and polaroids, and the perfection of movie-making. In time the possession of a camera became affordable and common, and most people had large collections of personal photos. It opened up the world for people, who could now see places and events far removed from their lives.

Photo history

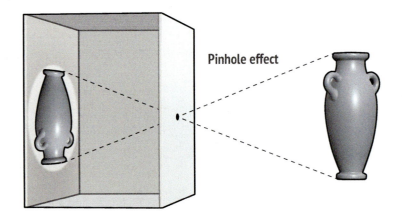

Pinhole effect

The pinhole effect has been known since antiquity. When light comes through a small hole in the wall of a dark room or box it projects an upside-down image of the outside scenery. This is a common way to look at solar eclipses. Aristotle wrote in 350 BCE of doing this to observe an eclipse.

Leonardo DaVinci described a pinhole device in 1485 CE as a way to study perspective. The German astronomer Johannes Kepler described a device called a **camera obscura** in 1604, essentially a box with a pinhole in one end. Dutch painters such as Johannes Vermeer used this device as a way to trace objects and scenes in preparation for a painting.

Camera obscuras gained popularity in the 19th century for artwork and education, and became more sophisticated, with lenses to focus the light. And they were used for the first experiments in photography in the early 1800s.

Camera obscura

Cutaway view of a typical 19th century camera obscura. Light coming through the lens is reflected off the mirror up to the glass pane. An artist could place a piece of paper on the glass in order to trace the reflected image.

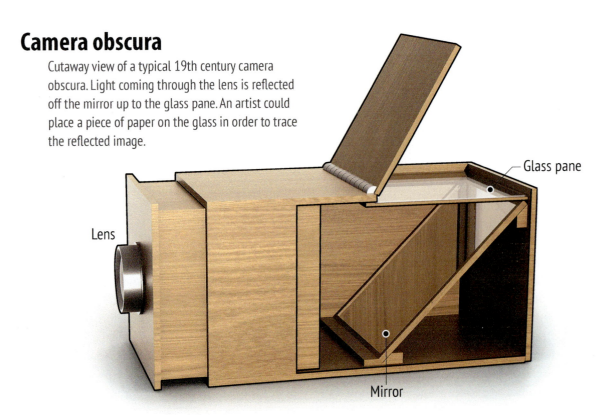

Glass pane

Lens

Mirror

The oldest existing photograph, 'View from the Window at Le Gras' by Nicéphore Niépce, taken in 1826 or 1827. The exposure took over eight hours.

Earliest photographs

The properties of light-sensitive chemicals have been known since the 1700s, when several researchers made observations about them. In 1802 Englishmen Thomas Wedgwood and Sir Humphrey Davy described their experiments of placing leaves and artwork on top of paper and leather coated with silver nitrate and exposing them to sunlight. They found they could produce images but had no way of preserving them.

Nicéphore Niépce of France is credited with being the first person to make and preserve a photo, although his method was rudimentary. At first he was looking for a way to make etched printing plates without the need for an artist. He experimented with coating litho stones and metal and glass plates with asphaltum, a petroleum-based chemical, dissolved in oil of lavender, placing them in a camera obscura and leaving them exposed to sunlight for several hours. The areas of the plate that received the most light became hardened. He then dissolved the still soft unexposed areas with a solvent, creating a fixed negative image. His plan was to then etch with acid the areas of the plate thus exposed, in order to make a printing plate. But through experimenting with direct contact exposure of the plate on a sheet of paper, he discovered he could make a positive image, thus producing the first photographic prints.

He reportedly made his first such photograph in 1824 using a litho stone in a camera obscura pointed out his window, but it was later destroyed when he tried to make copies of it. He repeated the experiment in 1826 or 1827, this time with a pewter plate, producing the image shown above, the oldest known existing photograph. The exposure took over eight hours.

Daguerrotypes

In 1829 Niépce entered into partnership with **Louis Jacques Mandé Daguerre,** who was performing similar experiments. But the agreement was short lived: Niépce passed away four years later of a stroke. He never profited from his work, dying destitute.

Daguerre refined the process over the next few years, using more sensitive chemicals such as silver nitrate, and found a way to reduce exposure times to 20 minutes. He called his product **daguerreotypes**, and in 1839 sold the rights to the French government in exchange for a lifetime pension for himself and for Niépce's estate.

Now in the public domain, and as further advances in the chemistry along with faster lenses reduced exposure times to under a minute, and then to a few seconds, studios began offering daguerreotype portraiture to the public. By 1850 one could get one's portrait taken in any major city in the industrialized world. Each photo was unique: the process produced a single image that could only be reproduced by photographing it again.

1850s camera

A typical mid-19th century camera. It didn't have a shutter, viewfinder or film. Operators had to look through the lens from the back and focus it by sliding the back of the camera back and forth. They then coated a glass plate with nitrocellulose and soaked it in a silver nitrate solution for a few minutes to make it light sensitive. The plate was then mounted in the back and the lens cap removed to begin the exposure.

The exposure would take a few minutes, so the camera would have to be mounted on a tripod. When done the plate was placed in a developing solution to make the image appear, and then a stop solution to fix it, all of this done on the spot.

A photograph of Abraham Lincoln taken in 1864 by photographer **Anthony Berger**.

It was thought that Andrew Jackson was the first president to be photographed, in 1845, but a daguerrotype of John Quincy Adams was recently discovered, dated to 1843.

Lincoln was well documented photographically. There are at least 130 photos of him, the earliest from 1846 or '47.

From glass to film

At mid-19th century there was nothing automated about the practice of photography. Every step from beginning to end required on-the-spot preparation and development of the photo plate with chemical coatings and baths.

This would change with the invention in 1884 of flexible film by **George Eastman**, along with machine-coated printing paper. Eastman founded the **Eastman Kodak** company, which in 1888 offered for sale a pre-loaded roll film camera, making photography available to anybody who could press a button and who could afford the initial cost of the camera, which was fairly expensive.

Flexible roll film not only made photography far more convenient, it made it easy to make multiple prints from the negatives. The darkroom method was now fairly standardized: Negatives were dipped in a series of chemical baths, and then used to make prints on photo-sensitive paper using a light-projecting enlarger. Roll film and darkroom developing would become standard in photography for the next hundred years until the digital age.

By the start of the 20th century photography became much more affordable as well, as inexpensive cameras, film and developing came on the market.

1888: Kodak film camera

After George Eastman created flexible roll film, his company, Kodak, introduced a camera that anybody could use. It came preloaded with a 100-shot film roll. All the user had to do was press the shutter button and wind the film to the next shot.

When the roll was done, the user mailed the entire camera back to Kodak, where the film would be developed, prints made and the camera reloaded.

It wasn't cheap. The camera cost $25, which is about $680 in 2020 dollars. Prints and a reload cost $10, about $270 today. Optionally owners could develop the film themselves. A new roll cost $2, about $55 in 2020 dollars.

This camera is the predecessor to the much more affordable Brownie line of Kodak cameras which started in 1900 and lasted through much of the 20th century. They had the same box design.

The modern age

There would be steady improvements to both cameras and the photo development process throughout the 20th century. Some key moments:

1900: The **Kodak Brownie** goes on sale, a cardboard camera that sold for $1 (about $30 in 2020 money). The film could be mailed to Kodak to be developed inexpensively as well. This camera made photography available to anyone.

1912: Kodak releases the **Vest Pocket Kodak**, an affordable camera for the general public small enough to fit in a jacket pocket.

1913: The **Tourist Multiple** becomes the first successful 35mm camera. It could hold a 50-foot film roll and shoot as many as 750 exposures. It was too expensive for most consumers, however.

1925: The **Leica 35mm** camera is released. Its popularity would cement the 35mm format as standard for most cameras for the rest of the 20th century.

1934: Kodak releases pre-loaded 35mm film cassettes. Up till then photographers had to load their own cassettes.

1935: Kodachrome color film is released.

1957: The Japanese **Asahiflex Pentax** single lens reflex camera (SLR) with instant mirror return is released. There had been SLRs before but they were not popular. This camera popularized the type, and soon companies such as Nikon, Canon, Minolta and Fuji were making SLRs for the consumer market.

1912: Vest Pocket Kodak

A foldable camera small enough to fit in a jacket pocket when closed, this camera gained popularity with the general public both in the US and in Great Britain, especially among World War I soldiers. Over two million were sold by the time it was discontinued in 1926.

And it was affordable. Its price was the equivalent of less than $200 in today's money.

The negatives were postage-stamp size, just 1 5/8 by 2 1/2 inches. The most common model had two shutter speeds, 1/25 and 1/50 of a second.

The viewfinder had to be looked through from above, so the camera was held at waist level to frame a shot.

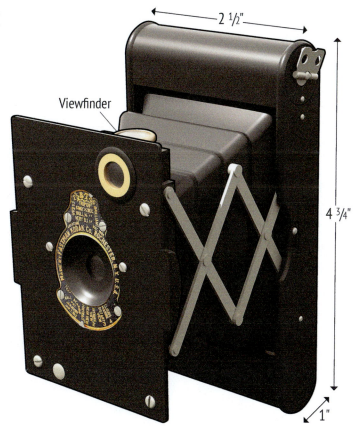

Viewfinder

2 1/2"

4 3/4"

1"

1925: Leica 35mm camera

The Leica's ease of use and compact size combined with a high-quality lens made it a market success. Although not the first camera to use 35mm film, the Leica 1, shown here, and subsequent Leica models popularized this film size.

It was designed by Oskar Barnack, a Leitz engineer, in 1913, but World War I delayed production until 1924. It went on the market the next year.

At $114 it was too expensive for the average consumer—that's about $1,700 in 2020 money—which limited its appeal to professionals and the well-to-do.

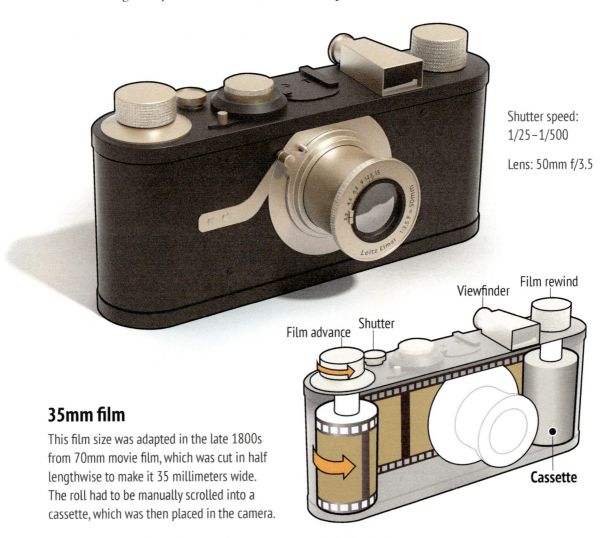

Shutter speed: 1/25–1/500

Lens: 50mm f/3.5

Film advance

Shutter

Viewfinder

Film rewind

Cassette

35mm film

This film size was adapted in the late 1800s from 70mm movie film, which was cut in half lengthwise to make it 35 millimeters wide. The roll had to be manually scrolled into a cassette, which was then placed in the camera.

36mm

35mm

24mm

Single lens reflex

The purpose of a single lens reflex system is to allow the photographer to look directly through the camera lens instead of through a separate viewfinder. This is accomplished by having a mirror redirect the light coming through the lens to a viewfinder until the shutter is released, at which point the mirror swings out of the way to expose the film.

With the earliest cameras, the only way to aim was to look directly through the lens prior to installing a glass plate and exposing it. Several later 19th-century designs did use a mirror that allowed the photographer to look down from above the camera to look through the lens, and then manually pull the mirror out of the way to take the photo.

In 1934 a Russian camera, the **Cnopm**, is cited by some as the first true SLR, with a mirror that automatically retracted on shutter release. A German 35mm SLR, the **Kine Exakta**, was also marketed at about the same time, with the same features.

The camera that popularized SLRs was made by Asahi, a Japanese company. In 1957 they released the **Pentax**, a 35mm SLR that featured instant return of the mirror after each shot. Earlier cameras required the film to be advanced in order to return the mirror to its viewing position.

Another innovation was the prism, which allowed the viewfinder to be at eye level, while also flipping the image, which otherwise is upside down when seen directly through the lens.

The Pentax was commercially successful and set the standard for the industry. Soon other major camera companies such as Canon, Nikon, Minolta and Fuji released similar SLR models. Most high-end and professional cameras have since been SLRs.

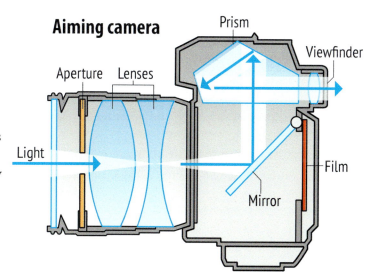

Aiming camera

Prism

Viewfinder

Aperture Lenses

Light

Film

Mirror

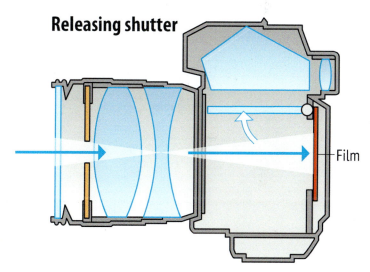

Releasing shutter

Film

Printing photos

The Civil War was one of the first wars to be documented by photographers. But those photos didn't appear in newspapers of the time, due to a technological problem: printing presses couldn't reproduce the different tones in a photograph.

At the time almost all images in print were etchings and engravings. In fact, photos, including those taken during the war, were often copied by artists to make versions for the press. The reason for this is that etchings can be printed with solid black ink. As the enlargement below shows, the technique relies on series of fine lines which are printed with solid ink. This creates the effect of lighter and darker tones.

U.S. Army

An etching depicting the burial of the dead on the Antietam battlefield during the Civil War, published in *Frank Leslie's Illustrated Newspaper* in 1862.

Halftoning

The first photo to be printed on a press was in 1880 in *The Daily Graphic*, of a shantytown in New York. It was achieved through a process called **halftoning**, which converts a photograph's different tones into dot patterns, with larger and smaller dots in order to make darker and lighter areas.

Halftoning was first patented for use on fabrics by Englishman **William** **Henry Fox Talbot** in 1852. No one individual gets sole credit for adapting it to printing on paper, but by 1880 the process had been sufficiently developed to be used commercially.

Sometimes called **linescreening**, the process involved placing a fine-mesh screen in front of the print of a photo and photographing it again.

The fineness of the screen is largely determined by the quality of the paper to be printed. It is measured in the number of rows of dots per inch, or lines per inch, abbreviated as lpi. For lower quality, uncoated paper such as newsprint, the standard is 85 lpi. At the other end of the scale, for a high-quality magazine on coated paper the line screen can be as high as 150.

Levels of gray before halftoning

93%   54%   17%   77%

After halftoning

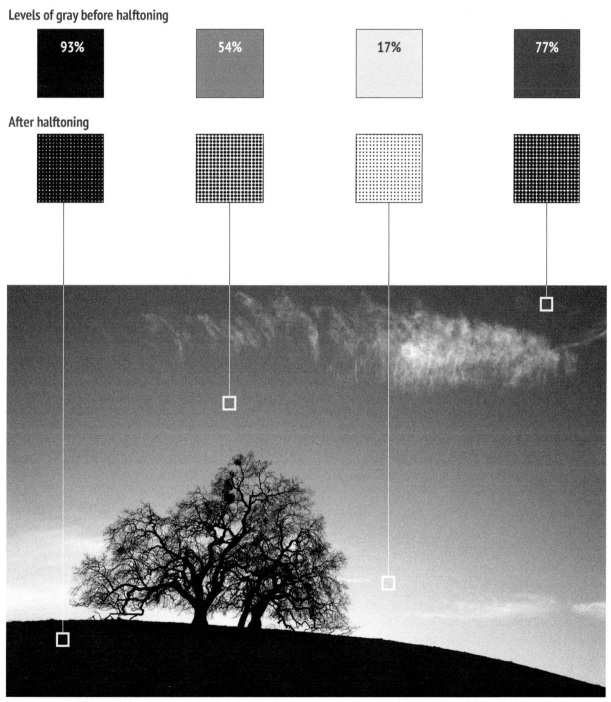

Mark Yamamoto Photography, used with permission

Moving pictures

The invention of movies introduced a new medium of communication to the public—light. Before there were movies the only mass-produced images were of ink on paper, including still photographs. But now light generated from electricity was the medium, projected through a series of translucent photo frames in rapid succession to create the illusion of motion. Now not only static reality could be captured but movement, reality as it changes over time, could be recorded and replayed at will.

Predecessors

The idea of manipulating light to create movement wasn't new when movies were invented. Shadow puppetry had been practiced since antiquity. And the concept of projecting images with light was described by several Renaissance inventors, including Leonardo da Vinci. But their implementation wouldn't happen until optical lenses were created, which arrived with the invention of both the telescope and the microscope in the early 17th century.

Taking advantage of the new lenses, the earliest known image projector, the **magic lantern**, was created in the mid-17th century by **Christiaan Huygens**, a Dutch scientist and inventor. It was the opposite of a camera obscura; instead of taking light in, it projected a sequence of images painted on glass slides through a lens and onto a wall. Since electricity and lightbulbs didn't exist yet, it relied on candle light.

The magic lantern is more accurately the predecessor of the slide projector, but can be considered an important step toward the making of animated images. (This was not Huygens' greatest accomplishment. He is better known for numerous contributions to the study of physics, mathematics and astronomy, and is considered one of the founders of modern science).

Magic lanterns became popular throughout the 18th and 19th centuries for both entertainment and education, only falling into disuse with the arrival of true movies in the 1890s.

The technical problem

With the invention and ongoing improvements in still photography, the idea of animating pictures was taken up by numerous inventors. But it wasn't as easy as one might imagine. First, two devices are required—a camera capable of shooting a rapid sequence of photos at a fraction of a second each, and a projector to show them with equal speed.

And second, both camera and projector shared the same technical problem: Simply dragging a film strip in front of a lens doesn't create a sequence of individual frames, and dragging a sequence of frames

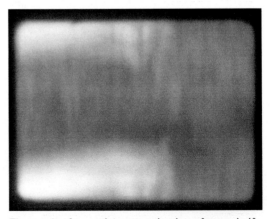

The result of a continuous projection of a movie if the film strip is simply dragged in front of the light source without pausing each frame and without a shutter mechanism.

in front of a light source and projecting it through a lens doesn't make a movie. The result in either case is a blurry, indecipherable streak.

In order to make it work, each frame in the camera has to pause for a split second to be exposed, and pause at the same rate in the projector as light is shone through it. And light has to be blocked by a shutter until the next frame is in position, otherwise both the film and the projection are blurry. That requires two intricate, finely balanced machines that work in coordination.

First attempts

Here are the early inventions that made movies a reality:

1832: The Fantascope. Belgian **Joseph Plateau** invented a projector that addressed the exposure problem. In front of a rapid succession of drawings reflected in a mirror, he placed a spinning cardboard disk with slits cut into it. The slits isolated each drawing for a split second, allowing the succession of drawings to create an animation. Plateau had invented the shutter, something that even still cameras wouldn't get until several decades later.

1878: Chronophotography. British photographer **Eadweard Muybridge** made his famous galloping horse movie by placing a series of cameras in a row and releasing their shutters in sequence as a horse galloped by. This is one of the very first actual photo animations.

In 1879 Muybridge made a device he called the **Zoopraxiscope**, which projected images from painted glass disks, similar to a Magic Lantern, but rapid enough to create animation. This is sometimes cited as the first movie projector. He made a second set of disks between 1892 and 1894 that consisted of drawings printed on the disks photographically and then hand colored.

1887-1889: First motion picture camera. In 1886 Frenchman **Louis Le Prince** made a multi-lens camera capable of shooting a movie. With 16 lenses, it was capable of shooting at 16 frames per second. But because each of the lenses was at a slightly different angle, the result was an image that wobbled around.

In 1887 he was successful in creating a single-lens movie camera, and in 1888 he shot what is considered the oldest existing motion picture on film, the **Roundhay Garden Scene**, a short clip (two seconds long) of some of Le Prince's family walking in a garden. He then made at least two more movies, one of Leeds Bridge and another of his brother playing the accordion.

Le Prince then invented a projector using an arc lamp to project his film clip onto a screen, and showed it in 1889.

Unfortunately his work was never well documented, as he mysteriously disappeared after boarding a train from Dijon to Paris in September 1890.

A still image from Louis Le Prince's 1888 film, *Roundhay Garden Scene.*

The Kinetograph

In 1888 **Thomas Edison** filed a patent for an "Optical Phonograph", a hand-cranked device which would project a moving image from photos on a cylinder, each 1/32 of an inch wide. His lab made three movies for this device. They were called *Monkeyshines*, each consisting of a couple of his workers making gyrating and arm-waving movements.

This was not the direction he ended up taking, however.

With the use of Eastman's celluloid film, Edison's lab created both a movie camera, the **Kinetograph**, and a viewer, the **Kinetoscope**, in the early 1890s. The work was largely done by Edison's employee **William Dickson**.

Only one Kinetograph was made. It was used to shoot the first movies shown in the Kinetoscope, notably one of Dickson doffing his hat while bowing, and the first movie to receive a US patent, *Fred Ott's Sneeze*, which lasted all of five seconds.

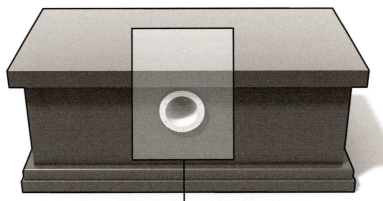

Interior mechanism

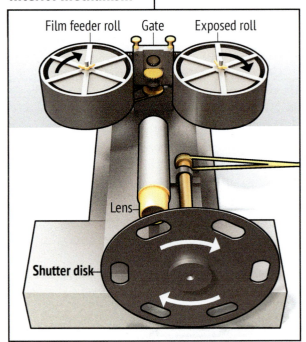

Film feeder roll — Gate — Exposed roll — Lens — Shutter disk

Kinetograph

This movie camera was operated by an electric motor. It was large, about two and a half feet wide, which combined with its need for electricity, limited its use to the studio. The motor turned a series of gears and shafts connected by pulleys, which pulled the film through a gate where each frame was shot, while a shutter disk with holes cut into it rotated into position to expose each frame and then block the light as the film advanced to the next frame. A stop-start mechanism caused the film to pause at the moment of exposure. The film size was 35 mm.

Still from a 3-second movie showing William Dickson bowing while removing his hat..

The Kinetoscope

With its commercial release in the mid-1890s, Edison's single-person movie viewer became for many people their first film experience. It played a filmstrip up to 50 feet long that was looped around a series of rollers, which lasted about 40 seconds.

The first prototype was demonstrated in 1891, and its first public showing took place in 1893 at the Brooklyn Institute of Arts and Sciences.

In April 1894 the first Kinetoscope parlor opened in New York City on Broadway, becoming the first public movie venue in the world. It had ten coin-operated machines, each with a different movie. They could be seen individually, or for half a dollar one could see them all.

It was a commercial success, and soon parlors opened up in Chicago and San Francisco, followed by numerous other cities in the US and ultimately around the world. Its popularity lasted until projected movie houses made it obsolete in the early 20th century.

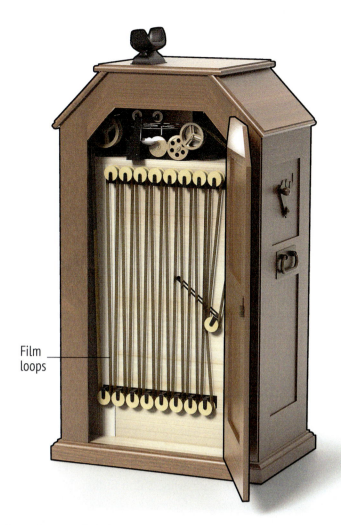

Film loops

Interior mechanism

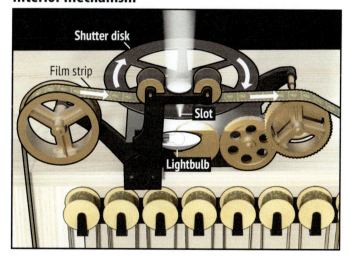

Shutter disk
Film strip
Slot
Lightbulb

The Kinetoscope had a stop-start mechanism to pause each frame, and a shutter disk with a single slot in it to act as a shutter. As each frame stopped, the rotating shutter disk's slot would sweep between the film and the light source, allowing the frame to be quickly projected upwards. The disk would then cover the light to allow the film strip to move forward to the next frame.

The Cinématographe

French inventor **Léon Bouly** made the first version of this camera in 1892, but lacking funds to further develop it he sold the rights to the **Lumière Brothers**. They made some improvements and in 1895 released their version of the camera.

The device was unique in that it worked as both camera and projector. By opening up the back and projecting light through the lens it could be used to show the movies it had earlier recorded.

It was operated with a hand crank instead of electricity, which made it far more versatile than Edison's studio-bound electric-powered camera. It could be used anywhere.

The brothers made their first movie in 1895, *Workers Leaving the Lumière Factory*. By December they had made ten films of about 50 seconds' duration each, and showed them in what might be the first commercial screening of projected film, at the Salon Indien du Grand Café in Paris.

In spite of their success, the brothers quit the film business in 1905 in favor of still photography equipment. They later developed a functional color photo process.

Film roll

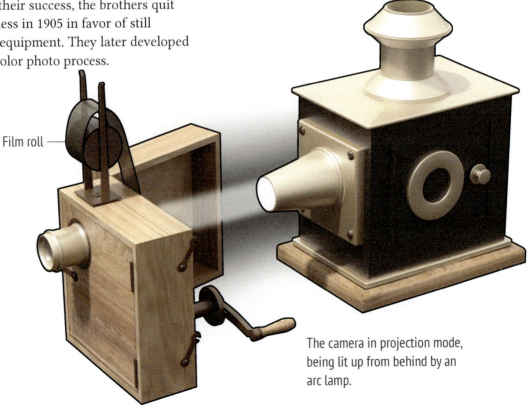

The camera in projection mode, being lit up from behind by an arc lamp.

1912 Bell & Howell camera

The Bell & Howell Model 2709 was the studio camera most often used in the silent film era. It was used to make many of the classic films from that time, from Charlie Chaplin to Buster Keaton to the Keystone Kops.

Donald Joseph Bell had been working in Illinois as a projectionist in the early 1900s as movie houses were first appearing. He met **Albert Howell** at a machine shop that made projector parts. In 1907 they started a business making and repairing cameras and projectors, and within a year gained an industry reputation for developing a system to reduce the distracting amount of flickering that was common in early movies.

Their first camera, released in 1910, was made entirely of wood and leather. By 1912 they began selling the metal-body Model 2709, a hand-cranked movie camera that soon dominated the industry and set the standard for the basic design and operation of movie cameras for most of the twentieth century. Some early Disney animations were done with this camera in the 1930s, and it was still being used up and into the 1950s.

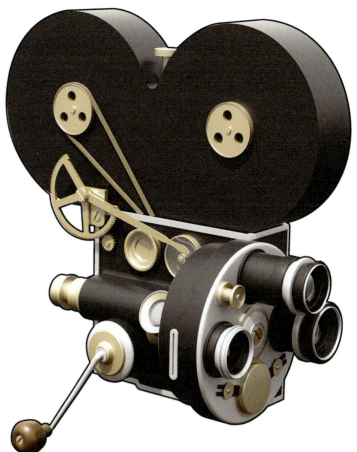

The two men's partnership was short-lived. In 1916 following a dispute Howell bought out Bell, who was never again associated with the company.

The Bell & Howell company was successful through much of the 20th century and still exists in name but no longer makes cameras.

Frame rate

Virtually all cameras and many projectors in the early 1900s were hand cranked, which made for variations in film speed, which is measured in the number of frames shown per second. It's commonly believed that silent films typically had a 16 frame-per-second rate, but the actual rate depended entirely on the camera and projector operators. Camera operators often varied the rate depending on a particular scene, speeding it up, for example, for an action scene or slowing it for dramatic moments.

In fact, the Bell & Howell camera had an optional motor drive, but most operators preferred the hand crank.

With the arrival of sound movies in the late 1920s, however, it became necessary to standardize frame rates, which eventually became 24 frames per second.

Projector technology

The film advance and shutter systems that are essential for projecting a movie were first innovated by the early film pioneers such as Edison, but there was room for improvement. One of the problems was a noticeable flicker as the shutter opened and closed with each frame advance (this is where the slang term 'flicks' for movies came from).

Bell and Howell addressed this problem with a three-bladed shutter that showed and hid each frame three times instead of just once, smoothing out the rapid transitions from light to dark. They also developed a shuttle device to precisely advance the film strip incrementally, frame by frame.

By mid-twentieth century projector technology was standardized through these innovations, and most projectors used the same or similar devices.

Film as a medium is one of the last analog technologies to be replaced by digital equivalents. Up until the 2010s some movies were still being distributed on celluloid film, and some film-makers resist the move to digital. There are still film projectors in use in the world as of this writing.

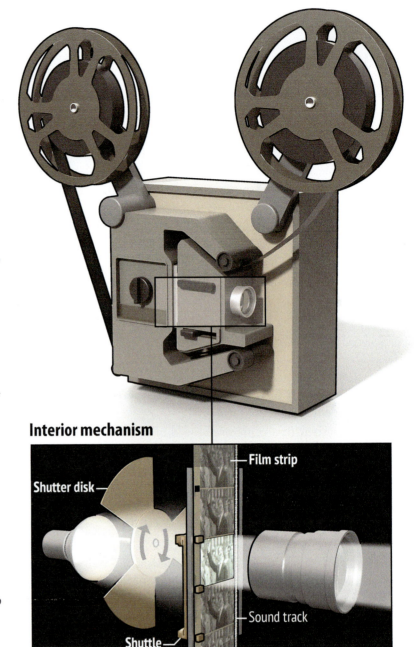

Interior mechanism

Film strip
Shutter disk
Sound track
Shuttle

The shutter and shuttle mechanisms in both movie cameras and projectors are nearly identical. The shutter blocks light momentarily while the shuttle, whose teeth insert themselves in the film strip's holes, moves back, up and forward to grip the film and pull it down by a frame, after which the shutter moves out of the way to light the new frame.

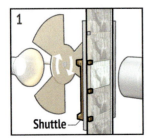
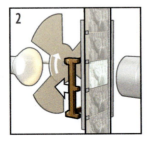
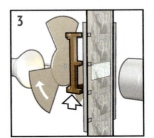
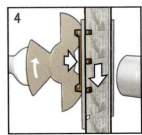

Shuttle

Color film

One significant drawback with photography from the beginning was the lack of color. Although certain materials proved to be light sensitive, none were yet known to be sensitive to specific wavelengths, so there didn't seem to be any way to have a plate or film strip naturally record color. Until a method to do so could be devised, the only option was to hand tint photos after the fact.

The first semi-successful experiment in this was done in 1861 by Scottish physicist **James Clerk Maxwell** and photographer **Thomas Sutton**. They photographed the same image—a multi-colored ribbon—three times, with each shot through a different colored filter, red, green and blue, and then projected the three images through magic lanterns, each through a filter with its corresponding color. When lined up, the three photos combined to make a color image.

While interesting, it was not a practical solution. But it did demonstrate a novel concept of how color works, based on theory going back to Isaac Newton's 1666 use of a prism to separate light into the distinct colors of the rainbow. Maxwell theorized that red, green and blue were primary colors of light from which all the other colors could be made.

Maxwell would eventually be proven right, but not in his lifetime. He died in 1879 at the age of 48, well before color technology became practical for either still or motion photography. He is, however, remembered for several more important

Maxwell and Sutton's 1861 color photo of a ribbon.

discoveries, including demonstrating that electric and magnetic fields travel through space at the speed of light in the form of waves. Einstein credited him for having laid the foundation for the special theory of relativity, and many consider him the most important 19th-century scientist in establishing the field of physics.

Color printing on paper also had not yet been fully solved by the time of Maxwell's death, although it was further along with innovations in lithography. But color photos and movies wouldn't become fully developed and practical until several decades into the 20th century, and not affordable for the public until well into the second half of the century. In order to understand the technical problem to be solved, one must first understand how color works in both print and projected images, and how Maxwell's work was relevant.

Color theory

Photography includes two platforms: images printed on paper and images projected by light. And they each rely on two different but complementary models of how color works.

In the chapter on printing we already looked at how the cyan, magenta, yellow and black ink system came about, which is the basis of the **Subtractive** model. This applies to the effect of white light being reflected off of a physical surface: The apparent color of that surface is due to the particular wavelength that is reflected, since the material absorbs, or subtracts, all the other wavelengths. And it happens that cyan, magenta and yellow, called the process colors, serve well as the primary colors in this model. Mixing different percentages of them can produce a wide range of other colors when printing with ink, and also when making prints of photos. Equal amounts of the three colors results in black.

As Maxwell demonstrated, however, the best primary colors to use when projecting light are red, green and blue. This is called the **Additive** model, in that adding together different amounts of light in these three colors produces a wide range of other colors. White light results from equal amounts of all three colors.

The additive model is useful when making transparencies for both slide and movie projections. It is also the color model in electronic devices such as televisions, and in digital devices including computer monitors and mobile phones; in effect anything that emits light instead of reflecting it.

You might notice on looking at the two diagrams to the right that the two models are inverses of each other, with the primary colors in one being the secondary colors in the other. This became relevant in the pursuit of practical color for photos and movies.

Subtractive color model
Reflected light

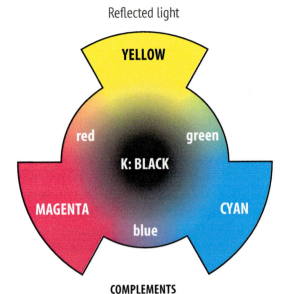

COMPLEMENTS	
Primary	**Secondary**
Cyan	Red
Magenta	Green
Yellow	Blue

Additive color model
Emitted light

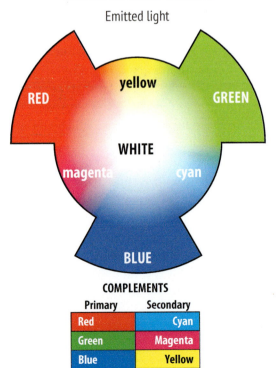

COMPLEMENTS	
Primary	**Secondary**
Red	Cyan
Green	Magenta
Blue	Yellow

Gamuts

The gamut, or range, of colors that can be reproduced varies by platform and the quality of the reproduction, but RGB light displays have a wider range than ink on paper.

Visible light gamut

All the colors that are visible to the human eye.

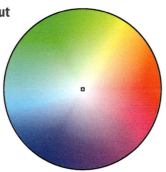

Process colors gamut

The range of all visible colors that can be reproduced with CMYK inks on paper.

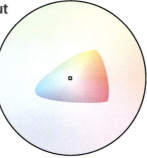

Spot colors gamut

The range of all visible colors that can be reproduced by adding additional spot ink colors to the process colors.

RGB gamut

The range of all visible colors that can be reproduced with red, green and blue projected light.

Color film for photos

First practical color film

In the 1880s photo plates that were sensitive to blue and green light became available, and by the early 1900s the process was possible but still not commercially practical.

It was the Lumière brothers, already known for the Cinématographe, who came up with a practical product, the **autochrome**. They demonstrated the process in 1904 at the French Academy of Science, and in 1907 began marketing autochrome plates used for photographing and projecting still images. The method relied on embedding thousands of minute grains in the transparency, each creating red, green or blue colors when lit up.

The plates could be used in existing cameras, but required considerably longer exposure times, at least a second in bright sunshine and ten seconds if it were cloudy. In a studio, exposures might require as much as 30 seconds. The color didn't become visible until light was shone through it.

Color prints

Making color prints required a return to the subtractive color model, since negatives would have to be composed of the opposites of red, green and blue, respectively, cyan, magenta and yellow. The film negative would have to be composed of materials that would produce these colors when developed.

There were two systems created for this purpose. One required a specialized camera with which to take sets of color separation negatives. The other system used what was called a **tripack**, which had three layers of emulsions on one film strip, each layer sensitive to one of the primary colors.

The first system was impractical in that it required investing in new equipment and taking multiple exposures to produce a single photo. The tripack system, however, resulted in lower quality photos since light had to pass through three layers of emulsion, which softened the exposure. Nevertheless the tripack achieved commercial viability.

American inventor **Frederic Ives** developed the first practical tripack system. Its three stacked sheets of film, each between two glass plates, were sensitive to, from top to bottom, blue, green and red light. Each layer then had to be developed separately before being combined into a single image.

Modern color films

Two professional musicians and amateur photographers, **Leopold Mannes** and **Leopold Godowsky**, invented **Kodachrome**. In 1931, based on their own efforts in pursuit of color film, Eastman Kodak hired them, where they completed their work. The film went on sale in 1935.

The exposed film is black and white, but dyes are added during development to make reverse-color negatives from which color prints can be made. The developing process was too complicated for photographers to do on their own, the film had to be developed by the company, which made it expensive to use. Nevertheless it made color photography accessible to anyone who could afford it.

In 1936 the German company Agfa, which had been making additive color plates since 1916, also released a multi-layer color film, which they called **Agfa-Neu**. It was easier to develop than Kodachrome, but also expensive.

In the late 1940s Kodak released a color slide film, **Ektachrome**, which when developed produced a positive transparency. It was also easier to develop, and became popular with both amateurs and professionals, including many *National Geographic* photographers due to its higher speed. Agfa made a similar film, as did other companies such as Fuji.

By the 1970s the cost of the films had come down enough for most people to use. Film processing labs began appearing, offering inexpensive and fast developing, bringing color photography into common use by the general public.

Film photography continued well into the digital age, until inexpensive digital cameras came on the market in the late 1990s and early 2000s. Kodachrome was discontinued in 2010.

Tripack color film

The film has three emulsion layers, each one specifically sensitive to a different part of the visible light spectrum.

Red
Green
Blue
LIGHT

Light passes through all three layers, each of which captures only the wavelength of light to which it is sensitive.

The three emulsions aren't in color, they simply have different light and dark areas specific to their sensitivity.
In the lab they're developed separately and color is added through a dye process. They're then combined to make the final color image.

Color film for movies

Kodachrome could also be used to make movie film, but it wasn't of sufficient quality for the commercial studios. It was available to amateur and home movie makers. Color film for studio movies actually started much earlier, with the first experiments in the 1890s.

Hand tinting

From the very beginning in the 1890s movies were often hand tinted to set mood. A scene might be tinted blue to simulate a night setting, for example.

Next came hand painting, where certain parts of each frame had color added, usually with the use of a stencil to maintain consistency from frame to frame. Edison made a short movie called *Annabelle Serpentine Dance* in 1895, in which the dancer's white veil appears to change colors, using this method. The French director Georges Méliès made fantasy movies with hand colored scenes, and the Pathé film company, founded in 1896 by two brothers, employed as many as 100 colorists for the task. Pathé, incidentally, would become the world's largest film production company in the early 1900s, and is still a major production and distribution enterprise.

Hand painting continued into the 1920s, as did film tinting; in fact Kodak began marketing pre-tinted film in 1921.

But at the same time progress was being made in actually filming in color.

Film for movies works according to the two color models: They are either additive or subtractive. The first successful attempts were additive, which was done in a manner similar to Maxwell's color photo projection, by placing color filters in front of the camera lens during both filming and projection. But ultimately subtractive methods proved to be the best answer to the color problem.

Kinemacolor

Recently discovered in Britain's National Media Museum were two films made by Englishman **Edward Raymond Turner** in 1901 and 1902, which are now thought to be the earliest color films ever shot. Turner had invented a camera and projector system using an additive method, in which black and white film was both shot and projected through alternating red and green filters to simulate a limited range of colors, one frame green and the next red. Both the camera and projector had two lenses and ran two film strips at the same time. They had to operate at twice the typical frame rate in order to achieve this effect, so that in viewers' eyes the two alternating colors blended together.

Turner died suddenly in 1903, and in 1906 his system fell into the hands of **George Albert Smith**, who improved it and made it into the first commercially successful process, **Kinemacolor**. (Smith was an unlikely inventor, his first career was as a stage hypnotist and psychic

A still from Smith's 1908 movie *A Visit to the Seaside*, shot in Kinemacolor.

Additive color movies

Kinemacolor and the first version of Technicolor made color movies through the use of colored filters both in filming and projecting. The film itself didn't have any colors.

It relied on two of the three additive primary colors, red and green, but technical limitations prevented adding blue, so it could only produce a limited color range.

1 **The camera** had two lenses and recorded the scene with two filmstrips at the same time, one through a red filter and the other through a green one.

2 **Negatives:** The two film strips each captured a negative image of a different part of the visible light spectrum.

3 **Positives:** The films were developed and reversed into positive images. These were the images that were projected.

4 **The projector** was similar to the camera, having two lenses behind two color filters. The two film strips were projected together. When the two images were properly lined up, they blended together to create a range of colors.

The end result, of course, omitted blue light. It was hard enough to get two projections to line up; three probably would have been close to impossible. Blues and purples were considered the most expendable. They showed as dark grays and blacks.

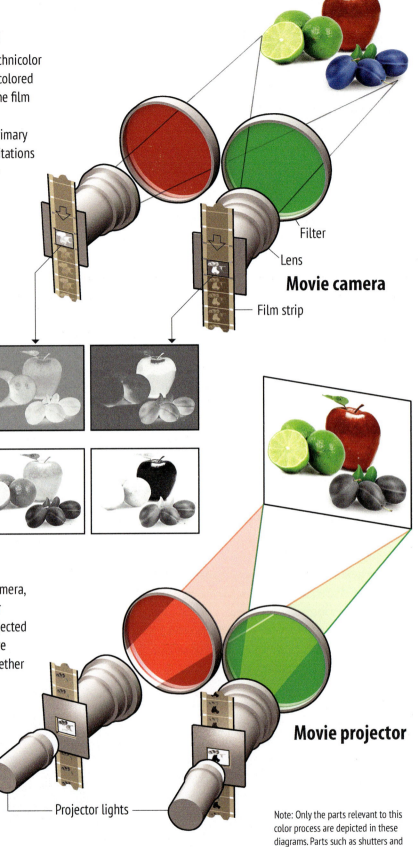

Movie camera

Filter

Lens

Film strip

Movie projector

Projector lights

Note: Only the parts relevant to this color process are depicted in these diagrams. Parts such as shutters and film reels are omitted for clarity.

PHOTOGRAPHY

who began adding simple animated photo shows at the end of his stage performances, leading to his interest in movies.)

The first film Smith made was a 1908 eight-minute short titled *A Visit to the Seaside*. The first public showing of Kinemacolor movies was in early 1909, consisting of 21 short films shown at the Palace Theatre in London. Smith also did a demonstration in late 1909 at Madison Square Garden in New York City.

Financial success was limited, however, mainly due to the expense of the specialized equipment, and perhaps also due to middling quality: It was almost impossible to get the two colors to line up perfectly, resulting in a halo effect. Smith's studio was ultimately put out of business in 1914 after losing a patent infringement suit.

Technicolor

This was the next successful system and dominated the industry for several decades. Many early iconic movies are in technicolor, such as *The Wizard of Oz*, *Gone with the Wind*, *Singing in the Rain*, and Disney's *Snow White and the Seven Dwarfs* and *Fantasia*. In fact, nearly all major studio releases from the 1930s to the 1950s were shot in technicolor.

Herbert Kalmus, **Daniel Comstock** and W. Burton Wescott founded the Technicolor Motion Picture Corporation in 1914 (Wescott left in 1921). They did not find immediate success. It took close to two decades before they arrived at the rich, full-color process that made Technicolor famous.

Over time there were four versions, the first starting in 1916 and known as **Process 1**. It was a two-color additive process similar to Kinemacolor and using red and green filters, and also required a special camera and projector running at twice the normal frame rate, but different in that instead of frames alternating between red and green the two frames were shown at the same time.

Process 1 was less than successful, however. The image from the projector's two lenses had to be merged together with prisms, which required a great deal of technical expertise to operate. That, along with the expense of the equipment, didn't attract many customers. In fact only one film was produced with it, *The Gulf Between,* in 1917.

Process 2 produced film through a subtractive method. It was still filmed the same way as process 1 with a split film, but the negatives were then combined to produce a single film strip in which the colors were actually present in the film. This meant that a special projector was no longer needed. The first film to use this method was released in 1922, *The Toll of the Sea*.

The first film made with **Process 3** was *The Viking* in 1928. This process wasn't much different from its predecessor, except for the way that dyes were used to create colors during development of the film strip.

With this version, Technicolor became popular in 1929 and 1930, to the point that it seemed like all Hollywood movies would be in color. But the economic crash that resulted in the Great Depression forced most studios to cut back on expenses. And Technicolor was substantially more expensive than black and white film.

Full color range

In 1932 work was completed on a new Technicolor three-strip camera, adding blue to the previous red-green spectrum. This was **Process 4**, which was capable of producing the first films with a full range of colors.

Walt Disney was the first film-maker to try it out on a Silly Symphony cartoon,

Flowers and Trees, in 1932. It was a hit with the public, convincing Disney to enter into an exclusive contract for the system.

It is sometimes stated that *The Wizard of Oz*, released in 1939, was the first feature-length Technicolor movie, but that is incorrect. The first live-action movie to use it was *The Cat and the Fiddle*, a Metro-Goldwyn-Mayer musical, in 1934. Other movies that preceded *Wizard* included *The Trail of the Lonesome Pine* in 1936 and *Robin Hood* in 1938.

There were limitations to its use. The camera was massive and weighed more than 400 pounds. It was so noisy that it had to be enclosed in a sound-deadening case. And due to the need to expose three film strips instead of one, the set had to be flooded with light, often baking the scenery and the actors. Temperatures reportedly reached 100 degrees Farenheit at times on the set of *The Wizard of Oz*.

In additon, its operation required a special film crew that was overseen by a Technicolor director (*see biography below on Natalie Kalmus*) who might dictate set changes, sometimes to the annoyance of the film director. And the film had to be processed in Technicolor's labs, which took time and at no small expense.

Nevertheless the superior quality of Technicolor gave it an edge over other systems, and it dominated the market up to the 1950s. Due to the dye process, colors could be made more vibrant and even artificially enhanced during development, resulting in striking visuals. To this day movies filmed with it are considered to have the highest quality color. Fortunately the dye process also made them resistant to fading over time, so they are well preserved.

The end of Technicolor

In 1950 Kodak released a 35mm color negative film, and then in 1952 a studio-quality tri-pack color film that didn't require a three-strip shooting process and that could be developed with standard

Natalie Kalmus 1882-1965

The wife of Technicolor co-founder Herbert Kalmus, Natalie was actively involved in the development of Technicolor from its inception and is often credited as one of the developers of the process.
She served as the executive head of the Technicolor art department and as the company's on-set representative.

She has numerous film credits from the 1930s and 1940s as the color director of nearly all Technicolor feature films. She has 404 film credits listed on the IMDb website.
She is the author of a book, *Color Consciousness*, published in 1935. Natalie and Herbert were divorced in 1922 but continued living together until 1944.

methods more quickly and at less expense than Technicolor's dye process. Although not capable of the same vibrancy, it was of sufficient quality to progressively capture the market. The last feature film that used Technicolor was *The Godfather Part II* in 1974.

Other types of film

Most film is 35mm, but in the 1950s 70mm film started trending. It offered a wide-screen experience intended to compete with the increasing popularity of television. *Oklahoma!* was the first feature film released in this format, in 1955. One system, Super Panavision 70, was specifically designed to be projected in theaters with a curved screen. *Lawrence of Arabia*, in 1962, was one of the most well-known films using that method.

Other notable 70mm movies include 1959's *Ben Hur* and *Sleeping Beauty, The Sound of Music* in 1965, and *2001: A Space Odyssey* in 1968.

But the novelty didn't last. After a number of flops, combined with the extra expense in both filming and projecting, wide screen movies have largely been relegated to IMAX productions.

3D movies is another specialty format. Its roots extend back into the 19th century, with various experiments to produce stereoscopic images that appear to show objects in three dimensions. In the 1890s British inventor **William Friese-Greene** obtained a patent for a 3D film, but the necessity of having to look through a stereoscope made it commercially impractical. This was later solved with disposable cardboard glasses with one lens tinted cyan and the other red.

The first film to use the glasses was 1922's *The Power of Love*. Since then 3D has fallen in and out of fashion numerous times. The first 3D color film was *Bwana Devil* in 1952, which led to a brief period of popularity with the format, but it faded before the decade was out, mostly due to the technical difficulties and expense of the process: Like the first color movies, it requires two film strips running simultaneously.

In the mid-1980s **IMAX** brought a resurgence of 3D, and the 2000s brought another resurgence, starting with 2004's *The Polar Express* and perhaps culminating with *Avatar* in 2009.

Transition to digital

Reel-to-reel film has lasted well into the digital age, longer than most other analog platforms. But increasingly it has given way to digital. In 2014 Paramount Pictures became the first major studio to announce that it would no longer release 35mm films to the US market. Its last reel film was *Anchorman 2: the Legend Continues*. Just a year earlier *The Wolf of Wall Street* was the first major feature film released solely in digital form.

Most commercial studios have been incrementally switching to digital production. The transition is problematic and expensive, especially for theaters—a digital projector costs anywhere from $60,000 to $150,000. But it is an inevitable trend, which in the long run is projected to save studios billions of dollars.

Technicolor camera

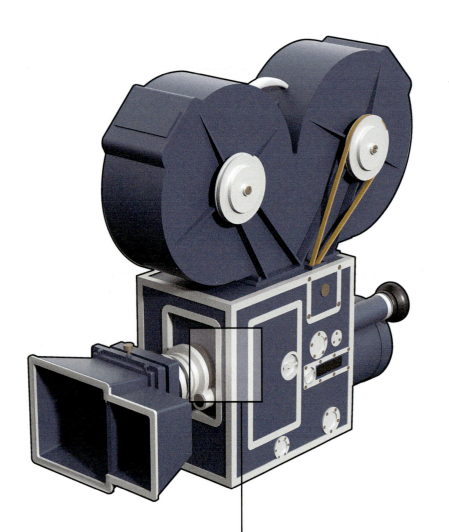

This is a 1930s three-film strip, full-color movie camera used to shoot Technicolor film.

It weighed between 400 and 500 pounds, and was so loud that it had to be enclosed in a sound-muffling enclosure.

It recorded color by running three film strips simultaneously, each capturing a different spectrum of light: red, green and blue.

The strips were then developed and dyed their respective colors in the lab, before being combined to make the final color film.

Subtractive color system

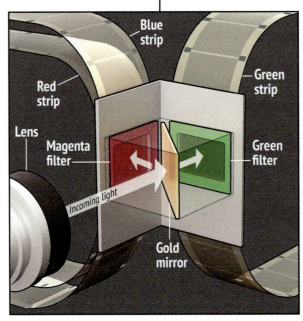

How the camera operates:

1 Light entering through the lens strikes a mirror with gold flecks embedded in it, making it semi-opaque.

2 Some of the light passes through the mirror to reach a green filter and a film strip behind that.

3 The rest of the light is deflected sideways to a magenta filter, behind which are two film strips, one sensitive to blue light and the other to red light.

Subtractive film processing

Technicolor was able to achieve full color in film in the 1930s by using a subtractive color method somewhat similar to color printing on paper. The process uses cyan, magenta and yellow dyes. Here are the steps:

1 A camera running three film strips at the same time shoots a scene. The light coming in through the camera's lens is split with a prism, directing a different range of the light spectrum to each film strip.

2 The result is three negative film strips, each specific to one of the three additive primary colors.

3 The strips are developed and reversed into positive images.

4 Each strip is dyed with the original color's complement: cyan for red, magenta for green, and yellow for blue.

5 The three strips are combined into one to make the final film strip, in a process called dye transfer.

6 In the final step, a black and white copy of the scene is added to increase contrast. This is called the key, the same as it's called in offset printing: the K in CMYK.

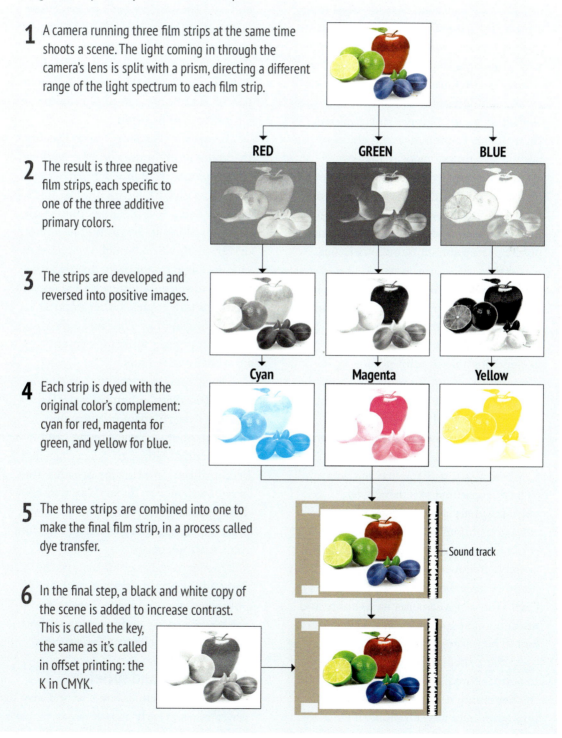

RED GREEN BLUE

Cyan Magenta Yellow

Sound track

The impact of photos and film

Photos do something no painter or sculptor can do: They freeze reality at a moment in time, allowing anyone to experience that moment long after it has passed. And by doing that photos can have great influence over us, with the power to relate events and to change perceptions. Of course photos can be manipulated, and in that way they can tell lies. But that doesn't diminish their power to influence and change people's impressions of reality.

And that's what photography and its progeny, movies, did: They provided a new medium through which people got news and information, and influenced public perception on numerous issues.

Photojournalism

But this didn't really start happening until photos and movies were more broadly distributed. Even though it became possible to print photos in newspapers and other print media by the 1880s, the practice didn't become common until the 1910s, when the concept of photojournalism began to appear in the public consciousness.

World War I was the first big war to be documented extensively by photographers. Cameras were by now compact and with fast shutter speeds, and could take photos in less light, making it possible to cover live action, which wasn't possible in earlier conflicts such as the Civil War when cameras were bulky and needed long exposure times, and subjects had to be posed.

Soldiers themselves were the first to start taking photos of the war. At the beginning of the war independent photographers weren't allowed close to the front lines. But soldiers with their Pocket Vest Kodaks recorded both the brutality and banality of trench warfare and sent the images back home. Soon newspapers were publishing these photos.

In an attempt to control the medium, the army started designating certain individuals as official war photographers, for the first time making photojournalism a professional position.

Magazines especially started seeing the value in photographs. The *National Geographic* started as a scholarly journal in 1888, with little or no photos. In 1905 it published a few full-page photos of Tibet, marking its beginning as a photo-driven publication, which increased its circulation exponentially. In 2015 its worldwide circulation exceeded six and a half million copies. Other popular magazines such as *Time* and *Life* also relied on photographs for content interesting to readers.

Newspapers were slow to the table, but by the 1960s, when they started moving toward offset lithographic printing, photos started being used more prominently. Although magazines had been printing in color for decades, the first newspaper to do so daily was *USA Today*, starting in 1982. Soon, however, most newspapers began using color on their section covers.

Thanks to these publications, the demand for photos created jobs for photogaphers, and magazines and newspapers were soon relying on both staff photographers and freelancers.

Photography and society

The introduction of low-cost and easy-to-use cameras as early as 1900 began to make

A World War I photo taken by British photographer **Ernest Brooks** in 1916 during the Battle of the Somme, showing wounded British soldiers together with captured German soldiers returning from the front. Brooks was one of the best known photojournalists covering the war.

photos a part of people's lives. It became normal for most people to record not only important events but also everyday life. By the mid-20th century it was common for people in the industrialized world to own a camera and to have photo albums documenting their families and social circles. Photos have been fully integrated into almost all people's stories of themselves.

This of course includes movies, first with home movie cameras and projectors— Kodak released Super 8 film in 1965 for amateur use—and then with video beginning in the mid-1970s.

The greatest impact of photos has been in its use in print media, in magazines, newspapers and periodicals, in fact in virtually all print publications, fundamentally changing the way that news is reported, stories told and products marketed.

Movies and society

The impact of movies is hard to overstate. They quickly became a primary source of entertainment for the public, edging out live performances such as vaudeville. As movie houses gradually opened in even the most rural of communities, all demographic sectors of society were having the same cinematic experience. This even extended across cultures: Charlie Chaplin movies were viewed around the world, and as the film industry matured it became normal practice to release movies to international markets.

This wasn't a problem with silent movies, and although at first it was an impediment with soundtracks, the issue was solved with either subtitles or by dubbing the speech. Language hasn't been a barrier: The majority of popular movies have enjoyed large audiences in multiple countries. In fact, movies are among the most popular international forms of entertainment, crossing cultures and languages, at least equal to if not more so than music, with the exception of a few bands such as the Beatles or the Rolling Stones.

And film was essential to popularizing television. Prior to the invention of video tape, everything on TV was either live or filmed, and movies on film became a key time-slot filler for most stations.

With such exposure, movies gained the power to influence culture, as people picked up everything from fashion trends to speech idioms from the stars they admired, and learned of historical events through movie reenactments, albeit often with less than rigorous academic accuracy.

Photography timeline

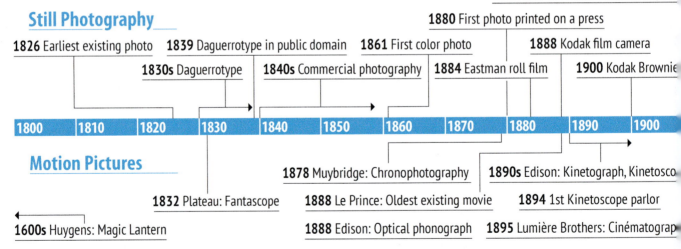

Still Photography

1904 Lumiére Autochrome color phot

1880 First photo printed on a press

1826 Earliest existing photo   1839 Daguerrotype in public domain   1861 First color photo   1888 Kodak film camera

1830s Daguerrotype   1840s Commercial photography   1884 Eastman roll film   1900 Kodak Brownie

1800 1810 1820 1830 1840 1850 1860 1870 1880 1890 1900

Motion Pictures

1878 Muybridge: Chronophotography   1890s Edison: Kinetograph, Kinetosco

1832 Plateau: Fantascope   1888 Le Prince: Oldest existing movie   1894 1st Kinetoscope parlor

1600s Huygens: Magic Lantern   1888 Edison: Optical phonograph   1895 Lumière Brothers: Cinématograp

Movies in many ways have served as social unifiers by providing a common narrative experience through all levels of society and across diverse cultures.

The visual world

Pictorial artwork, of course, extends far back into prehistory, but until technology made it possible to reproduce illustrations, they could only be seen in person. With the invention of printing, copies of etchings and engravings could be seen by a larger audience, but for the average person this would be an infrequent event. Pre-industrial book printing was usually limited to a few hundred copies and usually only enjoyed by members of the literate elite. Even into the Industrial Age methods of picture reproduction were technologically limited until close to the beginning of the 20th century.

Both color lithographic printing and moving pictures, as they became broadly available in the early 20th century, were a novel experience for the public. This is attested to by the fascination with the earliest movies, in spite of their being only seconds long and showing mundane activities. Within decades photo magazines such as *Life* and *National Geographic* had wide circulation, and for a majority of the population going to the movies was for a time an almost weekly activity.

Through these publications and films, society at large was introduced to depictions of the world they hadn't seen before. By many measures this exposure had profound impacts on societies in most parts of the world, as visual story telling became a part of people's everyday lives.

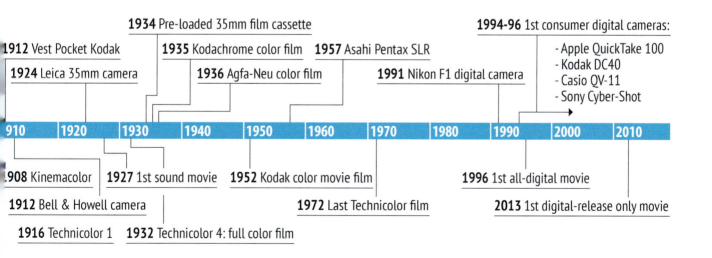

Electronic Communication

The field of electronics is about controlling an electric current, to not only start and stop it but to alter its characteristics: To vary its power and frequency, in order to make machines do specific tasks.

As we discussed previously, the practical use of electricity began in the 19th century with the first electric motors and generators, the lightbulb, and power grids. The first use of electricity for communication was the telegraph, an early 19th-century invention. But all of these uses only needed a steady electric current that was simply switched on and off.

The discovery that an electric current creates a field around it consisting of radio waves inspired many inventors with the possibility of wireless communication, and its pursuit led to a greater understanding of how electricity works, and the necessity of modulating it in order to achieve this goal. This led to the discovery of the first semi-conductors, which allowed a weak current to control a strong one—necessary for broadcasting a radio signal—and ways to modify the signal to allow it to carry sound. These discoveries led to the invention of the radio, followed by television.

The pursuit of ways of recording sound also began in the 19th century, and was at first purely mechanical, but in time was converted to an electric pattern, allowing it to be synced with movies, and then combined with TV broadcast signals.

By mid-20th century magnetic tape made it easier to record both audio and video, making content production easy and affordable.

And then came the silicon microchip and integrated circuits, which made available to the public a vast range of portable and affordable electronic devices in the second half of the century.

Electronics radically changed the way the public accessed information and communicated with each other, even before the Digital Age. Radio, TV, movies and audio media had profound societal influences unlike any prior era.

Electronic components

The term electronics didn't come into use until the 1940s. Prior to that it was called radio engineering, in reference to the first devices to rely on electronics.

There are several different components needed by most electronic devices. They range from simply turning a circuit on and off to altering the characteristics of the current. Early inventors found several methods to execute these tasks.

Coherers

For a radio to work, the first requirement is, of course, to be able to receive a radio signal. The first device for this purpose was called a coherer, invented by French physicist **Édouard Branly** in 1890. It was a glass tube inside of which were two electrodes and some loose metal filings. When a strong enough radio signal passed through it, the metal filings would clump together, closing the circuit between the electrodes.

These were used for the earliest radio receivers. Their drawback was a lack of sensitivity to weak signals.

Crystals

Jagadish Chandra Bose, an Indian scientist, discovered that certain minerals in crystal form could be used to focus reception to just the desired frequency in a radio. In 1901 he submitted a patent for the use of a galena crystal for this purpose, which was granted in 1904.

Crystal radios gained in popularity in the 1920s when the first radio stations

Crystal radio set

① Coil
Radio waves captured by the antenna create a magnetic field around the coil, which consists of copper wire wrapped around a cylinder.

② Tuner
Sliding this back and forth allows the operator to choose a frequency, which is carried through the wire to the crystal.

It doesn't need an electric power source to operate. Crystal sets popularized radio in its early days, when some communities were still not electrified.

③ Crystal
A piece of crystalline mineral such as quartz or galena, this acts as a filter and one-way valve, allowing only the desired frequency through. A thin wire called a cat's whisker completes the connection to the crystal. It has to be positioned at just the right spot to work. These were eventually replaced with less-fickle diodes.

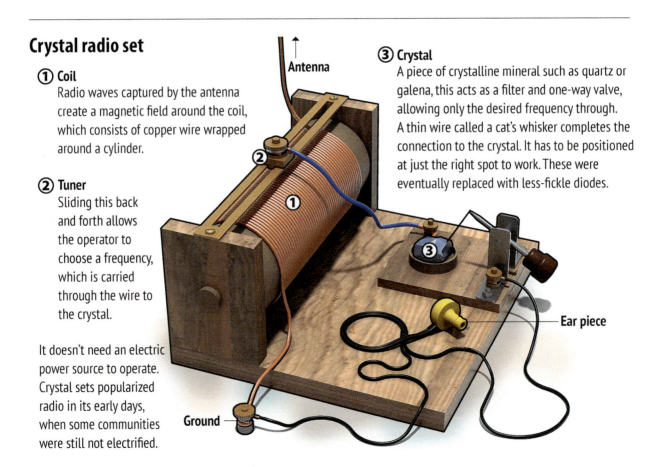

Antenna

Ground

Ear piece

began to broadcast. Anyone could build a simple one, which could operate even without electricity. The US Bureau of Standards published plans on how to build one in 1922, and inexpensive kits went on the market.

Vacuum tubes

The thermionic vacuum tube for use in electronics was developed by English physicist **John Ambrose Fleming** in 1904 while working as a consultant for Edison. The term **thermionic** refers to the release of electrons when an element is heated.

The concept of vacuum tubes wasn't new. They had been experimented with and used as novelty items in the 19th century, filled with gases that glowed different colors when a current ran through them. Besides Edison, Tesla had also experimented with them. What Fleming found was a way to use them as an electronic component in radios.

Diodes: In Fleming's tube, a plate was heated, causing it to release electrons which then flowed to a positively charged plate, completing a circuit. The tube's purpose was to restrict the current flow to one direction. This is necessary to keep a radio signal clear of interference, which is what crystals do. This type of tube is called a diode. It also came to be called a **valve**, which was the common term at the time.

Triodes: Austrian **Robert von Lieben** and American **Lee de Forest** both developed the triode independently but at the same time, in 1906-1907. This type of tube has the added function of controlling the strength of the signal through the addition of a charged grid between the negative and positive plates. As a result, it could be used to amplify the signal.

There are also tetrode and pentode tubes, with additional grids. They do the same thing as triodes; the extra grids add stability and improve performance.

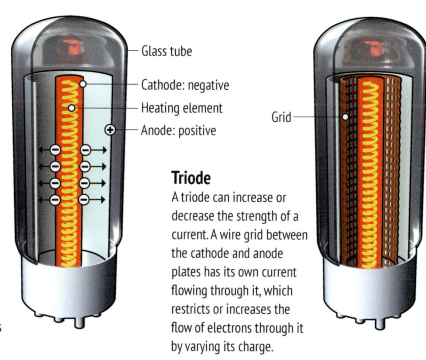

Vacuum tubes

There are many different types of vacuum tubes for different purposes. Here are the two most basic kinds.

Glass tube
Cathode: negative
Heating element
Anode: positive
Grid

Diode

Acting like a crystal, it restricts an electric current to one direction of flow. Heating the central cathode causes it to release electrons, which flow to the positively charged anode plate, completing a circuit. The vacuum in the tube allows the electrons to flow unimpeded. The heating element is controlled by a separate current.

Triode

A triode can increase or decrease the strength of a current. A wire grid between the cathode and anode plates has its own current flowing through it, which restricts or increases the flow of electrons through it by varying its charge.

Transistors and integrated circuits

Vacuum tubes, or valves as they were called, proved useful as both switches and amplifiers, and came into common use in the 1920s in radios and then in other electronic devices, including televisions, and the earliest electronic computers. Their advantages included greater reliability and control than crystals. But their significant drawback was that they tended to burn out after a while, just as incandescent lightbulbs do. As machines grew more complicated, using hundreds or even thousands of tubes in some cases, this became a major maintenance problem. The British Colossus computers used during World War II for decoding enemy messages, for example, had as many as 2,400 tubes, and the largest MIT-IBM computers of the 1950s had 55,000 tubes.

In addition, vacuum tube devices would never be small enough or light enough to be truly portable. Computers occupied entire rooms, and required significant power to operate in order to heat up all those vacuum tubes. So the research for a smaller, more reliable way to control electricity got underway in the 1940s.

Transistors

William Shockley, **Walter Brattain** and **John Bardeen** created the first transistor in 1947 at Bell Laboratories in New Jersey (Bell Labs is a subsidiary of AT&T), for which they were awarded the Nobel Prize in Physics in 1956. The compact transistor that is most commonly used today was invented by **Mohamed Atalla** and **Dawon Kahng** at Bell Labs in 1959, and is referred to as the MOS, an acronym for Metal Oxide Semiconductor.

Transistors can perform all the functions that vacuum tubes can, but are much smaller, consume much less power and are much more durable. So they quickly replaced tubes in virtually all electronics. (Vacuum tubes are still used in rare applications. Audiophiles claim that they work better for playing music, for example.)

Transistors are made of a semiconductor material, most commonly silicon but occasionally germanium. Semiconductors are elements that conduct electricity only under certain conditions.

The first transistor was half an inch in height, gargantuan compared to modern

Junction transistor

This type of transistor performs the same function as a triode vacuum tube, controlling the strength of a current. It is made of a semiconductor material, usually silicon, which changes from an insulator to a conducting material by applying a small current to it. In this way a weak current can be used to control a strong current.

As with vacuum tubes, there are many different types of transistors besides this one.

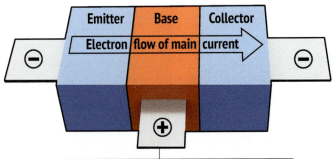

A secondary circuit is connected to the base. When it is off, the main current is blocked. When turned on, the base becomes a conductor, allowing electrons to flow through it at increasing rates as the secondary circuit's strength is increased.

ones, millions of which are on a single chip. It was a **point-contact transistor**, the purpose of which is to control the strength of an electric current. It worked by diverting the current through a piece of germanium, which sat on top of a piece of metal to which was attached an electrode connected to a stronger power source. When the weak current started flowing through the germanium, this allowed the strong current to flow as well. It was doing what triode vacuum tubes do, acting as not only a switch but a current amplifier.

The first design was not practical for manufacture, so in 1951 an improved design called a **junction**, or **bipolar** transistor was unveiled, which worked both as a switch and a variable strength amplifier.

Manufacturers rapidly adopted the transistor, and electronics were transformed. The first computers using transistors appeared in 1957 and 1958, including Philco corporation's UNIVAC.

Integrated circuits

It was common practice by the time transistors became available to combine separate components onto a single circuit board, which would include transistors, capacitors (a passive component to store a small electric charge), resistors and the like.

G. W. A. Dummer, an English engineer whose job was to test electronics under harsh conditions, came up with the idea of a component that combined all those separate ones into a single block. Doing so would likely improve overall reliability. He published his concept in 1952, but didn't know how to actually create an integrated circuit.

The first functioning integrated circuit was designed in 1958 by **Jack Kilby** of Texas Instruments. With it the company built a tiny computer for the Air Force that was contained in a 6.3-cubic-inch case, that was as powerful as a comparable computer in a 1,000-cubic-inch case, and that weighed only 10 ounces, compared to the 30 pounds of the conventional computer.

Silicon Valley

But the Texas Instruments computer was not very reliable. This is where the story turns to **Robert Noyce**, and the start of **Silicon Valley**, the legendary center of modern electronic development in California. By now silicon was the element

Integrated circuits

Integrated circuits, also called microchips, combine transistors into one unit on a piece of semiconductor material. By doing so it greatly reduces the size of circuitry for electronics, with billions of microscopic transistors on flat chips just a few inches across. PCs and mobile devices wouldn't be possible without these.

Current manufacturing methods etch the circuits using a photo-lithographic process, literally printing circuit boards with transistors just a few nanometers long (a nanometer is one billionth of a meter. A human hair is about 100,000 nanometers wide).

An Apple iPhone's CPU in 2020 had 11.8 billion transistors. The largest integrated circuits have up to 2 trillion transistors.

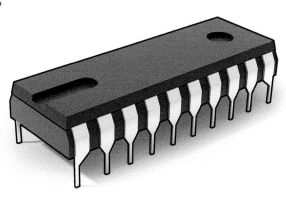

of choice for semiconductors, proving to be less expensive and more useful in some ways than germanium.

Noyce had been working at a lab started by William Shockley, one of the original transistor inventors. Shockley was by several accounts a poor manager who alienated Noyce and a group of other scientists, who left and started their own lab, **Fairchild Semiconductor**. The lab was in Palo Alto, soon to become the heart of Silicon Valley. There, Noyce and his team created their first functional and reliable integrated circuits.

In 1961 both Texas Instruments and Fairchild released the first electronic chips built out of integrated circuits. At first they were expensive and Fairchild's only customer was the US government, along with some defense contractors.

NASA's Gemini space program was one of Fairchild's first customers, using the chips in their on-board computers.

By the late 1960s the price of chips had come down enough to attract commercial manufacturers, including the growing computer industry. Texas Instruments released their first electronic handheld calculator in 1972, followed by similar consumer products using electronic chips.

Integrated circuit chips set the foundation for the future development of personal computers, followed by mobile devices. Palo Alto and Silicon Valley became the site of hugely successful startups such as Apple and Hewlett-Packard. By then Noyce had left Fairchild and started the **Intel** corporation in 1968 along with **Gordon Moore**. Intel is the world's largest producer of semiconductors.

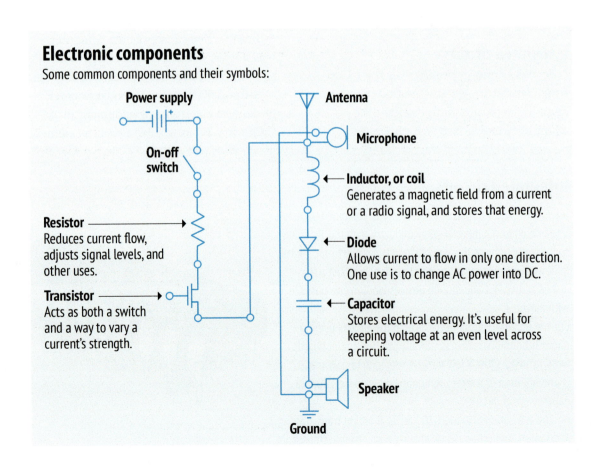

Electronic components

Some common components and their symbols:

Power supply

Antenna

On-off switch

Microphone

Resistor
Reduces current flow, adjusts signal levels, and other uses.

Inductor, or coil
Generates a magnetic field from a current or a radio signal, and stores that energy.

Diode
Allows current to flow in only one direction. One use is to change AC power into DC.

Transistor
Acts as both a switch and a way to vary a current's strength.

Capacitor
Stores electrical energy. It's useful for keeping voltage at an even level across a circuit.

Speaker

Ground

Electronic devices

From coherers to integrated circuits, electronics enabled modern communication platforms to emerge. At the beginning of the 20th century print was the dominant means of mass communication. By the end of the century it was largely electronic media.

Here are the principal pre-digital electronic media and technologies:

The telegraph: This was the first communication device that operated on electricity. Invented in the early 19th century, it remained in wide use well into the 20th century.

The telephone: This was the first device that required something more than a simple on-off circuit. Invented near the end of the 19th century, by the mid-20th century a majority of residences and businesses in the industrialized world had one.

Radio: This was the first true mass communication platform that ran on electricity. Its development required new ways to convert sound into electric patterns, to broadcast radio waves over long distances, and then to convert the signals back into sound. It was for radio that first vacuum tubes and then transistors were invented.

Television: The first TVs were a combination of mechanical and electric components, but they became entirely electronic by the time widespread broadcasting began in the 1940s. Within three decades virtually every household in the US and much of the industrialized world had a television, and it became the most used media device in the world, overshadowing radio as a primary source of news and information.

Audio: The first devices to record and play back sound were completely mechanical, and only started using electricity in the 1920s. Even then, vinyl records, which rely on a mechanical component, remained popular until the Digital Age.

Magnetic tape: Recording sound and images as magnetic patterns on plastic film made producing audio and video content easy and inexpensive, and led to numerous portable consumer products from tape recorders and music players to video cameras and video cassette recorders.

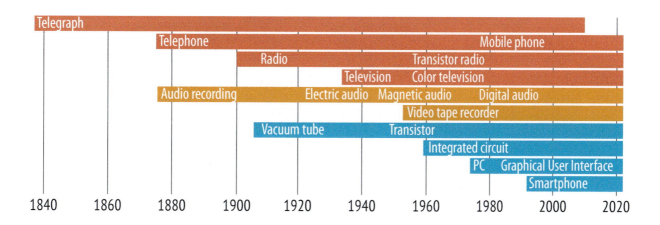

The telegraph

Contrary to popular belief, Samuel Morse was not the first inventor of the electric telegraph. That honor may belong to **Francis Ronalds**, an Englishman, who in 1816 created a system with two dials marked with letters around their edges, one at either end of an eight-mile-long wire. Static electric impulses rotated the disks to a particular letter. He presented it to the British Admiralty, who rejected it as "wholly unnecessary." He did publish his work, and parts of it were used in subsequent devices.

Optical telegraphs

Even before that there were what are sometimes called optical telegraphs, which are simply lines of towers with some type of visual signaling system, such as semaphores. An operator in each tower would watch the next tower with a telescope and pass any messages down the line. The origins of this concept go back into antiquity, as do the use of flag semaphores at sea, but the first known large-scale deployment of such a system happened in France beginning in 1792, when engineer **Claude Chappe** and his brothers built 556 stations stretching for a total of 3,000 miles, fanning out from Paris in five lines extending to the country's borders. It was subsequently used by the French military in their incessant wars with virtually all their neighbors, Great Britain and Austria in particular.

The French system was used well into the 19th century, even after other countries had adopted electric telegraphs. Sweden also built a similar system that was nearly as extensive. Both systems, however, had

Telegraph transmitter

The operation is simple: When the key is pushed down onto the contact, an electric circuit is completed, causing the coils in a receiver at the other end of the line to generate a magnetic field, pulling its bar down. In the years before electricity became available, the transmitter was attached to a battery.

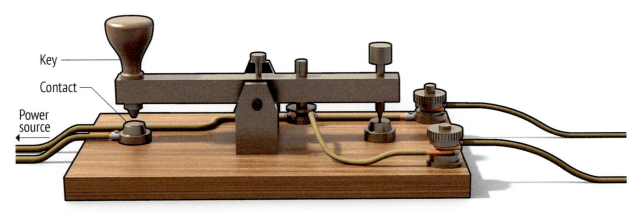

Key
Contact
Power source

International morse code

• Dot	A •—	E •	I ••	M ——	O ——•	U ••—	Y —•——
— Dash	B —•••	F ••—•	J •———	N —•	R •—•	V •••—	Z ——••
	C —•—•	G ——•	K —•—	O ———	S •••	W •——	
	D —••	H ••••	L •—••	P •——•	T —	X —••—	

vulnerabilities: Bad weather and lack of daylight would limit their use, and they were easily spied on.

Electric telegraphs

The invention of a chemical battery in 1800 by Alessandro Volta and the subsequent observation by several researchers, including Michael Faraday and William Sturgeon, of the connection between magnetism and electricity were necessary first steps for the invention of electric telegraphs. These provided the power source and the method by which they work.

A number of inventors created various versions of telegraphs, including Russian Pavel Schilling in 1832 and Germans Carl Friedrich Gauss and Wilhelm Weber in 1833. Both of these systems were at most only several miles long and never developed commercially.

In the 1830s British researchers **William Cooke** and **Charles Wheatstone** created the first commercial electric system for the British Railway. At first it used six wires to convey electric impulses to five magnetic needles, turning each to specific letters and numbers on a disk, but was later refined to a single needle and two wires, which was more reliable. Their system was highly successful in Great Britain and thousands of sets were built. Some of the lines were still in use as late as the 1930s.

In the US during the same decade **Samuel Morse**, **Leonard Gale** and **Alfred Vail** began work on their telegraph. It was simpler than the British one, and worked with a single key to complete a circuit intermittently, enabling the operator to send a message by a code of short and long pulses. At first the message was recorded on a paper tape

Telegraph receiver

The first telegraph designs had a scrolling roll of paper that the bar punched holes into. Operators found that it was simpler to just listen to the clicks from the bar being pulled down by the coils, and decipher the message by ear.

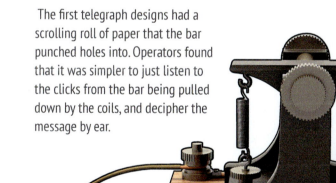

Bar

Coil

1 •– – – –
2 •• – – –
3 ••• – –
4 •••• –
5 •••••
6 – ••••
7 – – •••
8 – – – ••
9 – – – – •
0 – – – – –

Using a dot as a unit of time:

Dot: 1 unit   Space between letters: 3 units
Dash: 3 units   Space between words: 7 units
Space between dots and dashes: 1 unit

with a series of marks, but it became apparent in practice that it was easier for the operators to simply listen to the pattern of clicks, so the tape was replaced with a receiver that made audible clicks.

Morse and Vail created the dot and dash code that came to be named after Morse, and eventually became the global standard. Their first transmission was outside of Morristown, New Jersey, on January 11, 1838, when they sent a message over a wire two miles long. This was the first telegram sent in the US.

In 1843 the US Congress authorized funding for Morse and Vail to construct a line between Washington DC and Baltimore, a distance of about 40 miles. It was completed in 1844. The first message sent was Morse's famous but perhaps a bit melodramatic "What hath God wrought?"

With this success, telegraph lines were soon connecting every major city in the US, operated by private companies. The **Western Union Telegraph** company gained market dominance when it completed the first trans-continental line in 1861.

Other countries began building their own lines throughout the second half of the century, and soon extensive networks extended across continents.

The remaining challenge was to lay a line across an ocean. Messages between the Americas and Europe could still take weeks to be delivered by ship. After several failed attempts, a line was successfully laid between Newfoundland and Ireland in 1858, but only functioned for three weeks, and not very well, before it burned out. A dependable line made of better materials was finally laid in 1866, establishing dependable, rapid communication between the Old and New Worlds.

Telegraphs remained surprisingly resistant to obsolescence despite the invention of telephones. They were widely used around the world through much of the 1900s, perhaps due to the high cost of long distance phone calls until late in the century. Even the Internet took a while to do them in. The last telegram sent in the US was in 2006, over Western Union, and the last one in the world was in India in 2013.

International telegraph lines, 1891

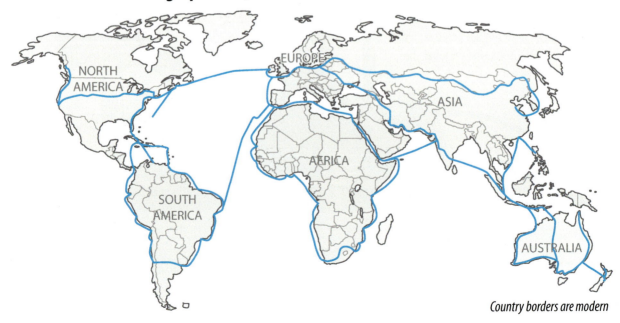

Country borders are modern

The telephone

The telephone is the next logical step after the telegraph. While telegraphs operate simply by turning a circuit on and off, the telephone's circuit is on for the duration of a call. The difference is that now the electric current's strength varies in relation to sound. It's the first device to use variations in the current to transmit data.

As with the telegraph, there were pre-electric precedents. English philosopher Robert Hooke made a string telephone in 1667, consisting of a taught string between two cups. Acoustic phones of this design were sold in the 1800s, although they had limited range, as one would expect. There were also speaking tubes in buildings and ships, which in some cases are still in use.

There isn't a lot of agreement on who invented the electric telephone. While **Alexander Graham Bell** is often given

The first Bell telephone

Alexander Graham Bell's first phone relied on a combination of mechanical and chemical means to change sound into an electrical impulse. The phone's microphone and speaker were later improved with a better design from Thomas Edison.

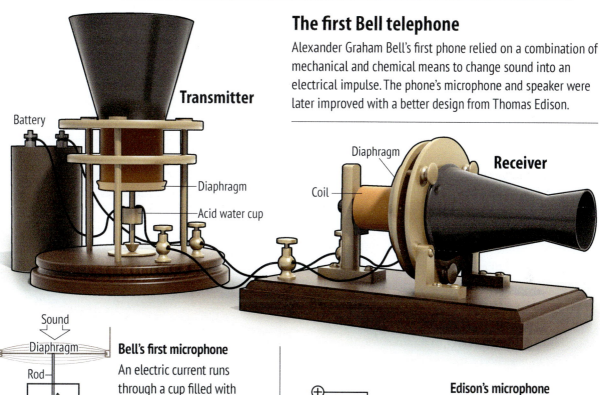

Transmitter

Battery

Diaphragm

Acid water cup

Diaphragm

Coil

Receiver

Bell's first microphone

Sound

Diaphragm

Rod

Acid water

An electric current runs through a cup filled with acid water, which conducts the current.

A steel rod attached to a diaphragm moves up and down as the diaphragm vibrates from sound. The up and down motion of the rod makes the current's strength increase and decrease, translating the sound vibrations into a varying electric pulse.

The electric current then goes to a coil in the receiver, which causes a diaphragm to vibrate and produce sound.

Edison's microphone

To receiver

Front contact

Rear contact

Sound

Diaphragm

Button

Carbon block

This microphone works on the principle that carbon's conductivity varies with pressure. When sound causes the diaphragm to vibrate, it variably compresses a block of carbon, changing the strength of the current flowing through the carbon to the rear contact and on to the receiver.

credit, German inventor **Johann Philipp Reis** had built a functioning one in 1861. When Bell filed his 1876 patent, he beat his closest competitor, **Elisha Gray**, by mere hours for the same device. Some insist the real inventor was **Antonio Meucci**, who shared a laboratory with Bell. The only known fact is that Bell was granted the first patent for a telephone in the US.

Edison also played a role. In 1877 he filed a patent for a better microphone than Bell's, based on the one in Reis' phone. His patent was promptly challenged by Emile Berliner, who had filed a patent on the same idea two weeks earlier. Their dispute wasn't settled until 1886. Theirs was just one of numerous legal disputes, including between Bell and Gray and Bell and Meucci, which were not resolved for years. Meucci's case was never resolved prior to his death in 1889.

Regardless of where the credit lies, telephone technology quickly evolved into a practical system. When Bell filed his patent in January of 1876 he hadn't even built a working prototype yet. It wasn't until March of the same year that Bell succeeded in completing the famous phone call to his assistant **Thomas Watson**, in which he reportedly said "Mr. Watson, come here – I want to see you."

That call was only to another room, but in a series of tests in the same year they succeeded in completing calls over distances of several miles, using telegraph wires. The first ones were only one-way, but in October they succeeded in having a two-way conversation between Boston and Cambridge, over a distance of several miles.

Bell Telephone

Bell at first proposed to sell his device to Western Union, but the offer was declined. In 1877 he founded the Bell Telephone Company, and within a decade had sold more than 150,000 phones, including one to the White House in 1878.

The first phones were essentially intercoms, with only two phones connected to each other. In 1878 the first exchange system was set up in Hartford, Connecticut, allowing calls to be switched to different subscribers. With this the job of phone operator was created.

Phones with numbered rotary dials, allowing the caller to place a call without going through an operator, became available in the early 1900s, and dial phones became the standard for most of the 20th century. They only started being replaced with push-button phones in the 1970s.

Ma Bell

Although the appearance of phones evolved, there was little change to their

THE

AUTOMATIC TELEPHONE

is one of the answers to the modern cry for greater efficiency in everything.

You will never realize the true value of a perfect telephone service until you install the

AUTOMATIC

UNMEASURED, UNLIMITED, AND SECRET SERVICE

ILLINOIS TUNNEL COMPANY
166 Washington Street

Creative Commons

A 1910 advertisement for one of the first rotary-dial telephones.

essential mechanisms until the digital age. One of the impediments to progress was due to monopolization of the market. The Bell Telephone Company became the American Telephone and Telegraph company, better known as **AT&T**, in 1885, and established subsidiaries across North America, each with monopoly control of its region. Anyone wanting phone service had to accept AT&T's terms, including a monthly fee to rent a telephone—the company didn't allow anyone to purchase their phones—and accepting their rates, which were expensive for any call outside the local area. AT&T's dominance earned it the nickname '*Ma Bell.*'

In 1982 US federal regulators forced AT&T to divest its subsidiaries as independent companies, breaking its monopoly power. This gave a foothold to competitors, notably MCI and Sprint, to enter the market, giving consumers more options for phone plans and to own their own phone equipment.

Infrastructure

What did evolve throughout the 20th century was the infrastructure, which continued to expand until most households

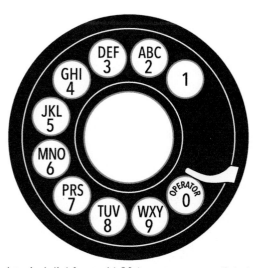

A typical dial for a mid-20th century rotary-dial phone.

and businesses in the industrialized world were connected by at least one phone line. This paralleled electrification, which extended power lines to most urban centers early in the 20th century, but took longer to reach rural areas. In the US rural electrification didn't start happening until the 1930s, when the Roosevelt administration's Rural Electrification plan provided loans to rural communities to build their own electric cooperatives, providing the infrastructure to install phone lines as well.

By the 21st century most of the world had wired access to both electricity and telephone service, with the exception of certain parts of central Africa and south-central Asia, where some regions still have limited access to either.

Mobile phones

The first two-way wireless transmissions of conversation were achieved through radio waves. Such devices were available for military uses during World War II, but they had limited range, the network could only support a few simultaneous links, and the devices were bulky and energy-consuming. Similar devices later became available for vehicles, but had the same limitations. Nevertheless, numerous radio phone networks were established in different locations around the world through the 1950s and '60s.

The first successful use of a handheld mobile phone was in 1973. **Martin Cooper**, a Motorola engineer, placed the call on a **DynaTAC 8000x** phone whose development he had led. In a bit of showmanship, his call was to Dr. Joel Engel, a rival engineer at AT&T.

The phone, which was a prototype, was not very portable, at a weight of 2.4 pounds and a length of 13 inches. And its battery was exhausted after about 30 minutes of conversation.

Cooper continued to lead the development of the DynaTAC, which went on the market ten years later in 1983. Its price of $3,995 (about $10,000 in 2020), along with its size and weight, limited its marketability.

Motorola released a compact phone in 1989, the **MicroTAC**, which was small enough to fit in a pocket, marking the start of consumer mobile phones and their gradual public adoption through the 1990s.

Cellular networks

Of course, a handheld phone is of no value without a network. Since mobile phones are two-way radios, they each need a unique frequency on which to send and receive data. The problem is that there are many more phones than available frequencies. This was solved by dividing a region into sections called cells, each with its own transmission tower. This allows the same frequencies to be used repeatedly, but only once in each cell in the network.

Motorola DynaTAC 8000x, the first mobile phone, first tested in 1973, and put on the market in 1983.
Length: 13 inches
Weight: 1.75 lbs.
Recharge time: 10 hours

Cellular network

Each cell tower covers a distinct area, within which users are each given a unique frequency. The same frequencies can be used in other cells.

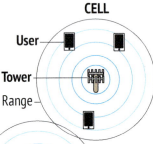

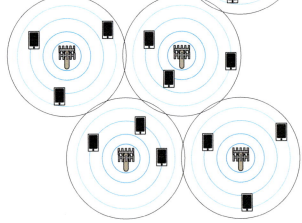

Redrum0486 / Creative Commons
Motorola MicroTAC, first pocket-size flip phone, released in 1989. About 5.5 inches long when closed, it weighed 12.3 ounces, and cost $2,495.

Key dates in phone history

1876: Alexander Graham Bell patents the telephone in the US.

1877: Bell Telephone Company founded.

1879: First phone numbers assigned.

1883: The first exchange was set up between two cities, Boston and New York.

1888: Phones powered by central exchange.

1889: First coin-operated pay phone installed in Hartford, Connecticut. It was created by William Gray and George A. Long.

1892: Rotary dial phone patented. Callers can now place their own calls.

1927: First public trans-Atlantic phone call service, relayed across the ocean by radio.

1955: First trans-Atlantic phone cables.

1962: First communications satellite, Telstar, was launched.
First push-button phone displayed at the World's Fair in Seattle.

1973: First mobile phone call, made with a Motorola DynaTAC, in New York City.

1979: First analog cell phone network, 1G, launched in Japan.

1983: Motorola DynaTAC 8000x phone goes on market.
First commercial cell phone network in the US launched by Ameritech in Chicago.

1989: Motorola MicroTAK becomes available, the first compact flip phone.

1991: 2G launched, adds texting capability. The lithium-ion battery becomes commercially available.

1998: 3G launched, adding the ability to send and receive data over the Internet.

2007: iPhone 1 goes on sale, popularizing multi-function touchscreen smartphones.

2009: 4G launched, providing greater speeds.

2018: 5G begins rollout. Has the potential to provide significantly faster speeds than 4G.

Hedy Lamarr 1914-2000

One of the best known Hollywood actors in the 1940s and '50s, Hedy Lamarr also made a scientific contribution that later proved necessary for cell phone networks.

At the start of World War II, Lamarr and composer George Antheil together patented a method of frequency hopping for a torpedo guidance system, preventing enemy forces from jamming the signal. The invention was later adopted for use with cellular networking, WiFi, Bluetooth and GPS. It changes the frequency over which a device is transmitting when needed to avoid interference.

Lamarr also helped Howard Hughes, whom she was dating, improve aviation design during the war.

Born Hedwig Eva Maria Kiesler in Vienna, Austria to Jewish parents, Lamarr fled to the US in 1937, where she began her Hollywood career, starring opposite some of the biggest male actors of the time, including Clark Gable and James Stewart.

Publicity photo

Dissatisfied with the way she was typecast, Lamarr formed her own production company with several partners in 1945, both producing and starring in several films.

Lamarr and Antheil were given the Electronic Frontier Foundation Award shortly before her death in 2000, and both were inducted posthumously into the National Inventors Hall of Fame in 2014.

Radio

One of the original motivations for developing radio was purely economical. Installing telegraph wires was expensive, limiting the number of places that could have telegraph offices. So sending telegrams wirelessly could be a big money saver for telegraph companies. In fact, radio was first talked about as the wireless telegraph or the radiotelegraph.

And the first radio transmissions were only long and short beeps in morse code. But it didn't take long for inventors to devise ways to transmit voices and sounds, as was already possible by telephone. Radio transmission would quickly go far beyond what telegraphs and telephones could do. It would be the first form of broadcast messaging, in which a large audience could receive the same message as long as they were within range of the signal. This would be the first media platform to rival print for the mass distribution of information.

The challenge

The first successful demonstrations of radio transmission were remarkable considering that the mere suggestion that radio waves even existed was only a few decades old at the time, and evidence of them was even more recent. No one person gets credit, it took contributions from a number of inventors to finally make radio work. But the fact that, upon learning of this new-found phenomenon, they envisioned how to send messages with it shows remarkable vision and ambition.

There were a number of problems to be solved: first, how to generate a powerful enough signal that could be detected from miles away, second, how to limit the signal to a specific wavelength so that a receiver could be tuned to it, and third, how to encode sound waves in the signal that could be converted back into sound by the receiver.

These problems were solved in steps, with radio telegraphy first becoming practical in the 1890s, and the first voice and sound broadcasts in the 1900s and 1910s. By the 1920s the technology was sufficiently advanced for the first commercial radio stations to appear.

The inventors

Guglielmo Marconi is often cited as the inventor of radio, but that is far from accurate. In fact, his 1901 radio demonstration, transmitting three morse code dots across the Atlantic, was not even the first transmission. Here are the significant contributors.

James Clerk Maxwell

Maxwell, a Scottish mathematician, published a theory in 1865 that electricity, magnetism and light were not only related but were different manifestations of a common natural phenomenon. His mathematical calculations demonstrated that electricity and magnetism travel through space as waves, and at the speed of light. Albert Einstein would later give Maxwell credit for providing the basis for Einstein's special theory of relativity, which in part depends on an understanding of electromagnetic fields. Maxwell is often cited as the third most important scientific theorist behind Einstein and Isaac Newton.

Heinrich Hertz

In a series of experiments from 1887 to 1889, Hertz, a German, built a receiver capable of detecting the faint radio waves being emitted from an electric current running through a wire, proving their existence and validating Maxwell's theory.

He was also able to measure the waves' strength and direction, and verified that they traveled at the speed of light.

Later the unit of frequency of radio waves, measured in cycles per second, was named in Hertz' honor.

Sir Oliver Lodge

Lodge, an English physicist, proved the existence of radio waves independently from Hertz. In 1894 he demonstrated a device that rang a bell from a radio signal transmitted a short distance away. Lodge later patented a method for tuning a radio receiver to a specific signal.

Nikola Tesla

Tesla, who invented the AC power generating system that the world now uses, also invented the Tesla coil in 1891. His goal was to transmit electricity wirelessly, a dream never realized. What his coil did was to greatly increase the voltage of an AC current, creating a strong electric field around the coil and causing it to radiate electromagnetic energy, which includes radio waves. The Tesla coil would be an essential component of the first radios, solving the problem of broadcasting a radio signal over long distances.

Tesla would go on to show the effects of radio waves in several demonstrations in the 1890s. In 1898 at an exhibition in New York's Madison Square Garden, he demonstrated radio control of a four-foot-long boat which he sailed around a pool, a prototype for remote controlled toys and drones.

In 1900 Tesla published his goal of a wireless transmission system that could encircle the globe. He thought that signals could be transmitted through the Earth itself, and was able to obtain funding from JP Morgan to build a transmission tower on Long Island, a project he began in 1901. But the funding ran out before

he could complete it and demonstrate its functionality, so we will never know whether his plan could have worked. As far-fetched as the idea might sound, it was not without precedent. The Earth does have some slight conductive properties. Several earlier experimenters, including Samuel Morse, had transmitted signals over short distances through the ground.

Tesla also proposed the possibility of transmitting signals through the upper atmosphere, although he never pursued this avenue.

Ernst Alexanderson

Transmitting a constant signal at a specific frequency was solved by Alexanderson, a Swede. He made a device called an alternator, a massive machine with a rotating disk which, when spinning at high speeds, created low-frequency radio waves which could carry over great distances.

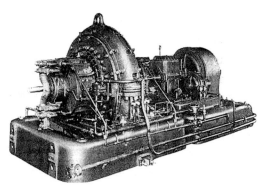

Wikimedia Commons

An Alexanderson alternator. It was very large and heavy, weighing about 50 tons. Its purpose was to generate radio waves at specific frequencies. Radio transmissions wouldn't interfere with each other if each was assigned a unique frequency.

The machine consisted of an electric motor spinning a large disk at very high speeds. The outer edge of the disk was arrayed with magnetic poles. The frequency generated was determined by the speed of rotation and the number of poles on the disk.

The first alternator was built in 1904. They were used until the mid-1920s, when they were replaced by vacuum tube devices.

Alexanderson was awarded 344 patents over his career for devices that would make radio and TV possible.

Reginald Fessenden — first voice broadcast

Fessenden made the first radio transmission of speech in 1900, and the first transmission of sounds across the Atlantic Ocean in 1906. He had been working on a key issue, how to transmit information over a specific frequency. There needed to be a way to tie the information to a carrier signal, and then for a receiver to separate the two in order to read the information.

Fessenden was Canadian by birth but lived and worked in the US. He never earned his high school degree despite completing his studies. He worked for a while in Edison's lab as chief chemist, then briefly for Westinghouse.

In 1900 Fessenden was hired by the US Weather Bureau to develop a radiotelegraph transmitter. He was stationed at Cobb Island in Maryland, where, during an experimental transmission he was able to make his voice heard at another station about a mile away. This is the first reported instance of the sound of a voice being transmitted by radio.

In addressing the problem of combining a carrier signal with sound information, he came up with the solution of modulating the amplitude of the signal, which is the width of the radio waves. This is where we get the acronym of AM radio, which stands for amplitude modulation. By varying the amplitude he could code sound information into the carrier signal, which could be sent at a specific frequency.

Fessenden then employed Alexanderson to build a 50,000-hertz alternator as part of a high-frequency transmitter in Brant Rock, Massachusetts. In January of 1906 they were successful in sending telegraph messages to a station 5,000 miles away in Scotland. That station also reported hearing voice messages between the Brant Rock station and another one in Plymouth.

On December 24 in 1906, the Brant Rock station broadcast speech and music that was picked up as far away as Norfolk, Virginia, and by ships at sea. On the 31st a similar broadcast was heard as far away as the West Indies. The music consisted of Fessenden playing the violin while his wife and daughter sang. Those who tuned in to the frequency of the signal were amazed to hear Christmas carols through their telegraph speakers, which up till then only emitted short and long beeps in Morse code.

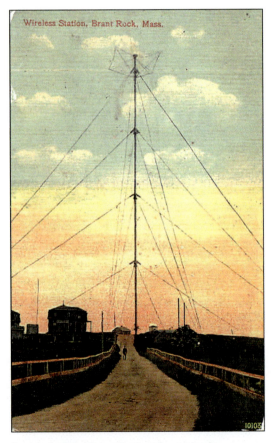

Postcard of the Brant Rock radio station in Massachusetts, site of Fessenden's first cross-Atlantic voice transmission in 1906.

Guglielmo Marconi

An Italian by birth who emigrated to England, Marconi had no formal scientific training. His knowledge of radio transmission was self-taught.

While still a teenager in Italy in the 1890s, he succeeded in sending a wireless telegraph signal more than a mile, but couldn't interest local authorities in his device. Subsequently moving to England with his Irish mother, he continued his efforts, and in 1897 received a patent for the first wireless telegraph system after successfully sending messages as far away as 80 miles. He promptly founded a company in his own name.

In 1900 he announced a plan to send a signal across the Atlantic Ocean. In December of 1901 he claimed to have received a telegraph signal consisting of three dots, representing the letter S in Morse Code, at his station in Cornwall from a station in Newfoundland across the north Atlantic.

There is no definitive evidence to confirm his success. The only other witness was his assistant, and doubts have been cast on the likelihood based on the physics and the crudeness of his equipment. He could just as easily have been picking up random radio noise that sounded like three short dots.

So it may or may not have happened in 1901, but in the next year he was verifiably successful in sending telegraph signals to ships up to 2,000 miles away, although it only worked at night, when solar radiation wouldn't interfere with the radio signals.

His company enjoyed great success through the 1920s. Communication with ships at sea was particularly valuable, something that hadn't been done before in maritime history. Marconi's radio telegraph is credited with saving those that did survive the sinking of the Titanic in 1912 (sadly only 712 out of 2,207 on board, but without radio contact all would have perished), as just one example of the value of this communication.

Marconi enjoyed fame and fortune in England and the US for two decades, but in the 1930s his life took a different turn when he decided to return to Italy, where, to the dismay of some, he joined Mussolini's fascist movement. He died in Rome in 1937 of heart disease.

The patent dispute: Marconi received his second patent in England in 1900. He had been employed by the British Post Office at the time and had developed his system for them, but applied for the patent in his own name. His application also didn't give any details about the contruction of his device, only presenting a closed box along with a general description of its function, but was nevertheless granted the patent.

When the contents of the box were finally made public, it became obvious that Marconi hadn't created anything original but had instead used existing technology already created by Hertz, Lodge and Tesla. Tesla was outraged when Marconi was awarded the Nobel Prize in 1911.

Tesla had patented his coil and other technology by 1900, so when Marconi applied for similar patents in the US, they were rejected. However, for reasons that are still mysterious, in 1904 the decision was reversed and the patents were awarded to Marconi. Speculation generally follows that rich investors in Marconi's company, including Edison and Andrew Carnegie, might have been able to influence the decision.

Tesla sued for infringement but didn't have the financial means to pursue it. It wasn't until shortly after his death in 1943 that the US Supreme Court returned the patents to Tesla.

Radio's golden age

The very first radio stations began broadcasting in the 1910s, but it was in the 1920s that the medium gained popularity. In 1916 Wisconsin station 9XM began broadcasting weather reports in morse code. In 1919 they were able to broadcast speech and music. In 1920 a regular broadcast of entertainment programming began in Argentina, as did broadcasting from station WWJ in Detroit. Also that year in Detroit, unlicensed station 8MK broadcast what is believed to be the first on-air news report.

The **Westinghouse** corporation, Edison's biggest rival, was the first to receive a commercial radio broadcasting license from the FCC in the US, for station KDKA in Pittsburgh, Pennsylvania, and aired the first commercial, for radios. In Great Britain the British Broadcasting Company, BBC, began operations in 1922.

From the 1920s until the rise of television in the 1950s radio became a central communication platform in much of the world. Radio dramas enjoyed considerable popularity. Sporting events were narrated in real time. Franklin Delano Roosevelt was the first US president to have a regular broadcast presence, in a series of talks he called 'fireside chats' between 1933 and 1944. And now the public had a news source other than print, one that could report breaking news much faster, even as events were unfolding.

By the end of the 1930s about 80 percent of Americans owned a radio, some now installed in their cars.

FM radio was patented in 1933 and the first broadcasts began in 1937.

In 1954 the first portable transistor radio went on the market, the **Regency TR-1**. By the 1960s inexpensive, pocket-size radios from Japan started coming on the market.

Although TV eventually overshadowed radio and ended most radio dramas, radio is still an ever-present medium across the world. In 2020 there were about 44,000 radio stations across the globe, with three-quarters of households able to receive at least one signal.

Regency TR-1

This was the first portable transistor radio on the market. Released in 1954, it was made in collaboration between Texas Instruments and the IDEA company of Indiana. It came in a variety of colors, had a 20-hour battery life, and cost $50 ($479 in 2020). About 150,000 units were sold.

By the 1960s similar radios could be bought for around $15 ($125 in 2020).

Broadcasting

Transmitting and receiving

The entire process starts with converting sound to radio waves, broadcasting those, and then for receivers to capture the waves and turn them back into sound.

Transmitter

The oscillator converts an electric current into electromagnetic waves at the station's assigned frequency. The modulator combines the waves with audio input. The signal is amplified and broadcast.

Receiver

A radio's antenna picks up the broadcast. The signal is amplified, and a tuner isolates the desired frequency and sends it to an amplifying circuit where the volume can be adjusted.

Power supply → Oscillator → Modulator → Amplifier

Audio input → Modulator

Signal Amplifier → Tuner → Audio Amplifier → Speaker

Measuring waves

Electromagnetic energy travels in waves of different lengths and strengths. There are two ways to measure length:

• **Wavelength:** the distance from the top of one wave to the next. Usually measured in metric units from meters to nanometers.

• **Frequency:** the number of waves that pass a fixed point in a second. Measured in **hertz** (Hz). Thirty megahertz would mean that 30 million waves went by a fixed point in one second.

Strength is measured in **amplitude**, which is the height of the waves, in metric units.

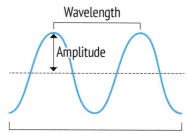

Frequency: If two waves pass by in one second, that would be two hertz.

AM and FM

A broadcast signal needs two parts, the station's frequency which radios can tune to, called the carrier signal, and the audio content: speech, music, etc.

The audio can be coded by altering, or modulating, the carrier signal's amplitude, which is AM, or its frequency, which is FM.

The carrier signal and the **modulating wave**, which is the audio content, are merged to make the broadcast signal, which can be sent by either AM or FM.

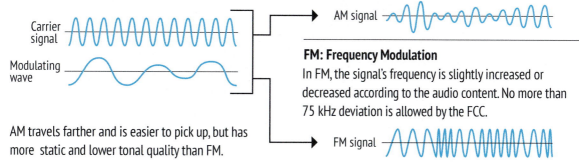

AM travels farther and is easier to pick up, but has more static and lower tonal quality than FM.

AM: Amplitude Modulation

In AM, the amplitude varies, getting alternately stronger and weaker according to the audio content.

FM: Frequency Modulation

In FM, the signal's frequency is slightly increased or decreased according to the audio content. No more than 75 kHz deviation is allowed by the FCC.

Television

Transmitting images as well as sound was envisioned as early as radio was, in the later decades of the 19th century. But of course, it's more complicated, and although there were some partly successful experiments in the early 20th century, television didn't start to gain traction until the 1950s. Radio had a significant advantage in that listeners could make their own crystal sets inexpensively. That couldn't be done with TV, and until there was, first, enough television content being broadcast, and second, affordable TVs for the public to buy, there wouldn't be widespread adoption of the new platform. Still, there was incremental progress through the first half of the century.

Cathode ray tubes

The principal component of all TVs until the invention of LCD screens was the CRT, or Cathode Ray Tube, more commonly called the picture tube. These are essentially large vacuum tubes, with heated cathodes at the back end emitting electrons which cause a phosphor coating on the front of the tube to glow.

Color cathode ray picture tube

CRTs were used for TV picture tubes and computer monitors throughout the 20th century until they started to be replaced by LCD screens in the 1990s and 2000s.

CRTs are vacuum tubes, with electron-emitting cathodes at the back end that light up a phosphor coating on the inside of the tube's front. Phosphor glows when electrons strike it.

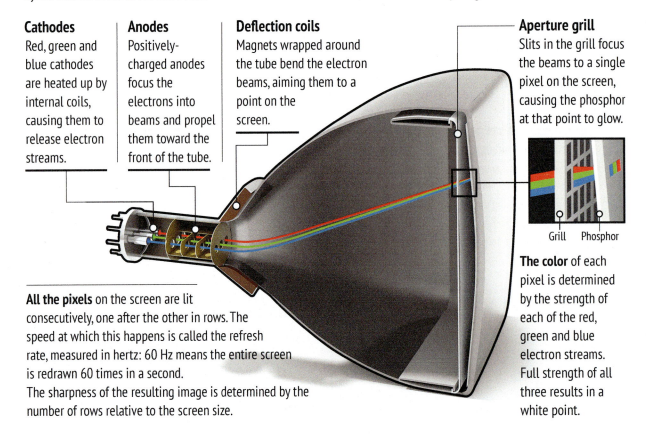

Cathodes
Red, green and blue cathodes are heated up by internal coils, causing them to release electron streams.

Anodes
Positively-charged anodes focus the electrons into beams and propel them toward the front of the tube.

Deflection coils
Magnets wrapped around the tube bend the electron beams, aiming them to a point on the screen.

Aperture grill
Slits in the grill focus the beams to a single pixel on the screen, causing the phosphor at that point to glow.

Grill   Phosphor

The color of each pixel is determined by the strength of each of the red, green and blue electron streams. Full strength of all three results in a white point.

All the pixels on the screen are lit consecutively, one after the other in rows. The speed at which this happens is called the refresh rate, measured in hertz: 60 Hz means the entire screen is redrawn 60 times in a second.
The sharpness of the resulting image is determined by the number of rows relative to the screen size.

The first cathode tube was made in 1878 by **Sir William Crookes**, an Englishman, simply as a demonstration of the existence of cathode rays. It was called the Crookes tube. In 1897 German physicist **Karl Ferdinand Braun** made the first functioning CRT that could display moving images. His device was used as an oscilloscope. Improvements to the tube were subsequently made over the next few decades by a number of researchers until a version that could work in a TV was made.

In 1922 Western Electric put a CRT on the market. In 1926 Japanese engineer **Kenjiro Takayanagi** demonstrated a 40-line CRT TV, and in 1928 he was able to display an image of a human face in half-tones. He went on to create an all-electronic TV in 1935. In Japan he is considered the inventor of Japanese television, but never gained much recognition in the West.

Mechanical TVs

The first TV prototypes relied on mechanical means to produce images, most commonly by means of a rotating perforated disk that converted a subject into dots of light of varying brightness, which were then converted by photoelectric cells into electric impulses. A few early versions could produce static images. In 1925 Scottish inventor **John Logie Baird** demonstrated silhouettes in motion using a disk system, and in 1926 he successfully transmitted an image of a face in motion on a screen. This is often cited as the first television display in history.

Mechanical TVs were offered to the public in 1928 at the same time that the first mechanical TV station began broadcasting, W3XK near Washington DC. But the quality of this system couldn't compete with electronic TVs. W3XK stopped broadcasting in 1934.

Electronic TVs

Philo Farnsworth, the man usually credited with the invention of television, held the first demonstration of his electronic TV for the press in 1928, and in 1929 showed the first electronic displays of a human face, that of his wife. By 1934 he had developed a completely electronic system including a camera.

In short time he founded the Farnsworth Television and Radio Corporation, and took out patents on his invention. The Radio Corporation of America, better known simply as **RCA**, licensed Farnsworth's patents in 1939, and put on the market a TV with a 5-inch by 12-inch picture tube.

First broadcasts

The major US national broadcasters, **NBC**, **CBS** and **ABC**, began as radio networks before they started delivering TV programming. NBC, which was owned by RCA, was founded in 1926 as the first nationwide radio network, providing programming for affiliate stations. It began broadcasting an experimental TV signal in 1931, from the top of the Empire State Building, and began regular TV broadcasting in 1939. One of their first features that year was the Macy's Thanksgiving Day Parade. Sports were also some of the first events to be shown: The first baseball game in May of 1939, between Columbia and Princeton universities, the first football game that fall, between Fordham and Waynesburg universities, and in February of 1940 the first basketball game, between Fordham and the University of Pittsburgh.

CBS was started in 1927 as a radio network (originally as United Independent Broadcasters). It received the second FCC license for TV, on the same day in 1941 as NBC, and promptly began broadcasting.

ABC came about as a result of an FCC ruling against NBC, which actually consisted of two entities, NBC Red and NBC Blue. The FCC issued a rule denying licenses to stations affiliated with networks consisting of multiple entities, in effect, denying licenses to any NBC affiliates. So NBC Blue was sold off in 1941, and eventually became ABC in 1943. It didn't begin TV broadcasting until 1948.

Color TV

The first demonstration of a color TV was a mechanical one made by John Logie Baird in 1928, based on his 1925 mechanical TV, using three disks and red, green and blue light filters. He then made the first color broadcast in 1938, using the same system, to the Dominion Theatre in London. In 1940 he showed a hybrid TV with an electronic black and white display with a rotating color disk. In 1944 he showed a fully electronic color system, the **Telechrome**, using two light guns aimed at cyan and magenta phosphors in a picture tube, creating a limited color range. But Baird's death in 1946 stopped development of a full-color version of the Telechrome.

It was RCA's model that set the standard for the industry, a TV that could display both black and white and color pictures. It achieved this by superimposing a low resolution color display on the higher resolution black and white image. The model was introduced in 1953, and the first color broadcast took place on January 1 of 1954, of the Tournament of Roses parade. But almost no color programming was offered for the next ten years.

In 1964 the FCC approved a standard color system based on the RCA TV, and in the fall of 1965 more than half of all prime-time programming was in color. A year later the entire prime-time lineup was in color.

Also in 1966 General Electric put on the market an affordable, portable color TV, the Porta-Color, spurring the sales of color TVs. By 1972 color TV sales surpassed those of black and white sets for the first time.

Rapid growth

The television audiences were small at first. In 1946 there were only 6,000 television sets in use in the US. But as broadcasting increased, that number skyrocketed. By 1951 there were over 10 million sets, and by 1954 there was a TV set in more than half of all US households. By 1962 ownership had surpassed 90 percent of households, and by 1978 it leveled off at 98 percent, where it has remained, marking it as both one of the most universal and one of the fastest communication platforms to be adopted.

Color TV ownership in the US also increased rapidly, from seven percent in 1965 to 98 percent in 1990, as did the number of households with more than one TV, from four percent in 1955 to 76 percent in 2000.

Along with this the number of commercial TV stations in the US grew from 98 in 1950 to more than 1,700 since 2005.

Other industrialized nations saw similar growth and have about the same levels of ownership. Across the world there are tens of thousands of broadcast TV stations, with over 3,000 each in Russia and China. There are differences in the types of networks though. In the US, until the advent of cable, the market was dominated by the three major networks, NBC, CBS and ABC. In many other countries the dominant networks are state owned or sponsored, such as the BBC in Great Britain and the CBC in Canada. The US has no major state-sponsored network. The Public Broadcasting Service, PBS, established in 1969, is a non-profit program distributor and receives a limited amount of public funding.

Expanding communication

Broadcast networks

When in 1901 Marconi claimed to have sent a radio signal across the Atlantic, there was some doubt, in part because the curvature of the Earth would have blocked a straight path between the two stations. But in fact some radio frequencies can be transmitted long distances because they bounce off the ionosphere, an electrically charged layer of the Earth's upper atmosphere. These are high frequencies between three and thirty megahertz, called shortwave, and a signal in that range can bounce all the way around the planet. So it's a possible explanation for Marconi's claim of success.

But most radio and television signals are not high frequency, and are typically broadcast up to distances of about 35 miles. The range of the signal depends on the power of the transmission equipment, but also geography and atmospheric conditions, and at a certain point, again, the curvature of the Earth. It isn't feasible for a single station to reach an area the size of the US, or even a smaller country such as England

or Japan. So major networks, which produce content, sell licenses to local stations for the rights to broadcast that content. The local stations are usually owned by separate entities, and are called affiliates.

Distribution of content to a network's affiliates posed challenges from the beginning. Most of it is pre-recorded, which in the early years meant shipping media to all the affiliates across the country, at first records for radio and film for TV, and then later magnetic tape. Live events such as sports or political speeches could only be done by sending a broadcast signal through a series of relay stations across the country. For the most part programming was local. This problem was solved in two ways, with satellites and cable.

Satellites

In 1962 **Telstar 1**, the first communications satellite, was launched into orbit and successfully relayed a television signal from the US to Europe. Built by AT&T, it was the first commercial endeavor into space, and

Assigned broadcast frequencies

Each radio and TV station is broadcast on an assigned radio wave frequency, generally somewhere between one hertz and three gigahertz. There are ranges reserved for AM and FM broadcasting.

Each country assigns frequencies through an agency. In the US it's the FCC, or Federal Communications Commission, in Great Britain it's Ofcom, or Office of Communications.

Electromagnetic spectrum

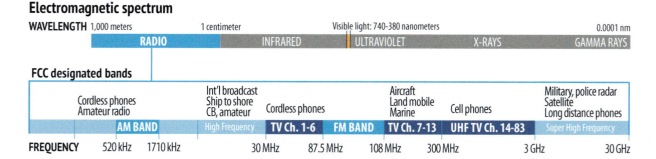

relayed everything from TV to phone calls and other data, but only for the 20 minutes during its three-hour orbit that it was in line with both continents. It also only lasted a few months before its electronics were fried by radiation from US and Russian high-altitude atomic bomb tests.

In 1963 Telstar 2 was placed into orbit, and was soon followed by a string of satellites providing constant relay of communications encircling the globe. In 2020 there were about 2,000 communications satellites orbiting the Earth, relaying all manner of content, including TV and radio to both affiliate broadcasters and, through satellite TV, directly to individual subscribers.

Although inoperable, Telstar 1 was still in Earth orbit in 2020.

Fiber optical cable

The concept is fairly simple and was put into use as early as the 19th century: Light could be directed down a glass tube wrapped in an opaque material for the purpose of illumination, and possibly communication. In fact, Alexander Graham Bell filed a patent for the **Photophone** in 1880, which would have worked on an optical light system. But he decided against pursuing it in favor of an electric phone.

Optical glass tubes were first put into practice in the 1880s in Vienna by doctors for the purpose of illuminating body cavities, and later by dentists for the same purpose.

In the 1920s several patents were taken out in the US, proposing to transmit images through optical fibers. Between then and the 1950s numerous researchers further refined the methods and materials, but were stymied by what is called a high attenuation rate: the rate at which the signal loses intensity over distance, due to impurities in the fibers.

The attenuation problem was solved in 1965 by British scientists **Charles Kao** and **George Hockham**, who demonstrated that silica glass could be made sufficiently pure that it loses very little intensity over long distances.

German physicist **Manfred Börner** achieved a practical fiber optic cable in 1965, which was subsequently used in 1968 by NASA for lunar mission TV cameras.

Further improvements in the technology eventually resulted in materials of such high purity that virtually no data is lost even over long distances. The resulting cables are orders of magnitude more efficient than comparable electric cables.

In 1977 the first use of fiber optical cables for telephone lines began in Chicago by Bell and in London by the British Post Office.

Late in 1988 the first trans-Atlantic fiber optic cable, a type called **TAT-8**, began operation between the US, England and France. It failed in 2001 and was never repaired, but several cables with greater capacity had already become operational.

The growth of cable TV and of the Internet in the 1990s greatly increased demand for fiber optic networks, which rapidly replaced existing copper wire communications networks, and in time cross-ocean cables encircled the Earth.

The Internet bubble of the late 1990s generated massive investments in fiber optic infrastructure, but when the bubble burst in 2000 it caused a string of bankruptcies, most notably **Worldcom** in 2002, the largest such case in US financial history. Left behind were thousands of miles of fiber optic cable with much greater capacity than was needed, based on overly optimistic projections of traffic growth. But the world might be catching up to that capacity as fiber optic cable has become the primary carrier of communication data.

Fiber optic cables

Single fiber cable

Fiber

Multi-fiber cable

Fibers

Steel wires

Underwater cable

Polyethylene sheath
Mylar tape
Steel wires
Aluminum barrier
Polycarbonate
Copper tube
Petroleum jelly
Fibers

Fibers inside the cable are made of a clear material through which light, that is, electromagnetic energy, can travel virtually unimpeded. The outer layer, called the cladding, has a higher refractive index than the core. This causes light beams to reflect off the cladding and stay inside the core.
Individual fibers range in diameter from 0.25 mm to 3 mm.

There are lots of configurations and sizes of cables, with different numbers of fibers.

FIBER CROSS SECTION
Core
Cladding
Light signal

Trans-oceanic underwater cables are composed of multiple layers of insulating materials and steel to protect the fibers.
Signal boosters called **repeaters** are needed to amplify the signal about every 100 kilometers (~60 miles) along the cable line. These are powered by a DC line in the cable.

Underwater fiber optic cable lines

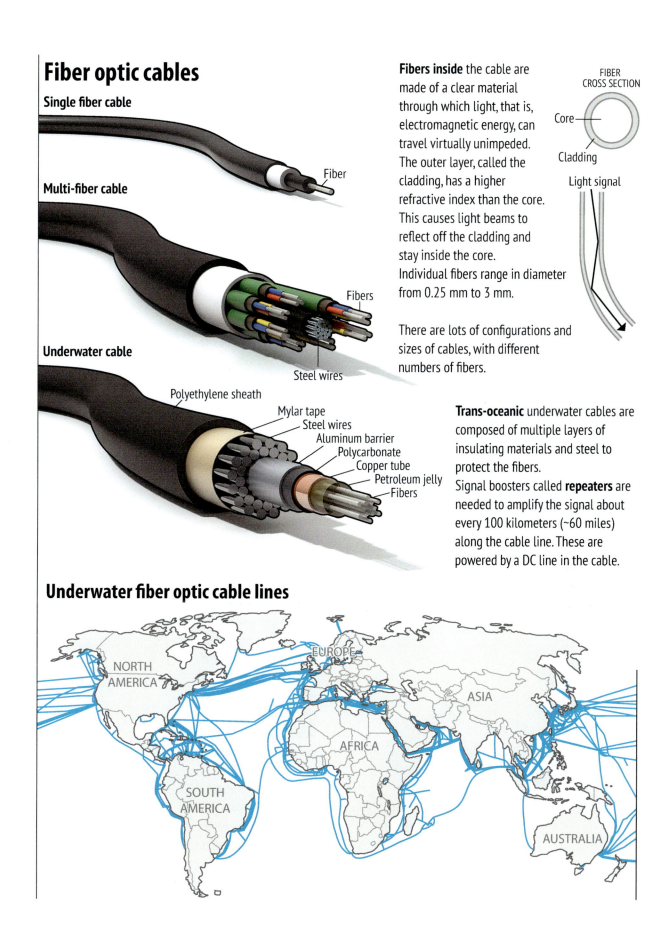

NORTH AMERICA

EUROPE

ASIA

AFRICA

SOUTH AMERICA

AUSTRALIA

Audio

The earliest sound playing devices were music boxes, whose origin is usually attributed to Switzerland in the late 1700s, probably as an offshoot from clock making. Consisting of a rotating cylinder with teeth arranged to pluck metal prongs in the pattern of a song, they were either hand cranked or ran on springs as a mechanical clock would. By the late 1800s music boxes were marketed that had interchangeable cylinders, making them capable of playing a variety of songs.

Mechanical audio players

The first devices that could record and play back sounds were, like music boxes, purely mechanical. The earliest of these date from the second half of the 19th century. They recorded sound through a vibrating diaphragm, usually at the end of a large cone, to which a needle was attached, which would inscribe the vibrations into a rotating cylinder with a soft surface such as wax. The playback would simply do the opposite, with the needle causing the diaphragm to vibrate. As one would expect, they had a limited frequency range and could only record loud sounds.

The earliest such device, the **phonautograph**, was only intended to make a visual recording of sound. It was invented by **Édouard-Léon Scott de Martinville** in 1857. Its needle scratched the sound pattern onto a sheet of soot-coated paper wrapped around a rotating cylinder, and couldn't play the sound back. In 1877 **Thomas Edison** took the device to the next step by changing the recording medium to a sheet of tinfoil, which could then be used to play the sound, but with very limited results. It wasn't until the late 1880s that Edison developed a workable device. Its medium was a wax cylinder into which the sound pattern was engraved.

Phonographs

Norman Bruderhofer, www.cylinder.de
Edison wax cylinder phonograph, ca. 1899.

Mechanical sound recording

Sound collected in the cone causes a diaphragm at its bottom to vibrate, moving a needle up and down and leaving a track of impressions in the rotating cylinder. The louder the sound, the deeper each impression.

Playback does the reverse, the impressions in the cylinder push the needle up and down, causing the diaphragm to vibrate, replaying the sound.

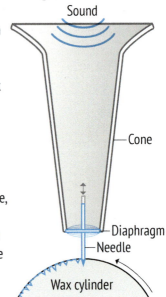

Being completely mechanical, the early devices were either hand cranked or driven by springs that were wound up, much like music boxes.

Edison's target market was for business use. But when a demand for music reproductions started forming, a significant shortcoming of his device was revealed, in that it wasn't possible to make a large quantity of good reproductions from the original cylinder, which was only good for about 25 replays before it wore out.

The Gramophone

In competition with Edison, **Emile Berliner** patented the Gramophone in 1887. His device, which could only play and not record sounds, was the prototype of modern record players, using a disk instead of a cylinder. The disks were at first made out of hard rubber—this was still before modern plastics—until a shellac-based compound proved suitable.

Berliner's system used a negative metal master with which thousands of records could be mass produced by stamping. The player came to be called a phonograph, and the music record industry was launched.

Cylinders continued to be used for a few decades but by the end of the 1920s had been mostly relegated to business dictation uses.

Phonograph record sizes and playing speeds were at first random but in time became standardized, with a speed of 78 rotations per minute, or rpm. 45 and 33.3 rpm didn't become popular until the 1950s. The RCA Victor company introduced a 33.3 rpm 12-inch disk, the first LP or long-playing record, in 1930, but it failed commercially due to a scarcity of players and it being the height of the Depression. This was also the first time that vinyl was used, but the format's lack of success put off further use of the material until World War II, when a shortage of shellac pressured record companies to turn to vinyl.

Norman Bruderhofer, www.cylinder.de

Mechanical gramophone, ca. 1907.

Record grooves

A highly magnified close-up of a single groove in a record's surface would show that the needle is vibrated from side to side instead of up and down as in Edison's phonograph.

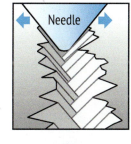

Electronic turntable, a component of a later 20th-century stereo system that would include a separate amplifier and speakers.

Record sizes

Early records played at 78 rpm and had large grooves. Columbia Records introduced microgrooves in 1948. At 33.3 rpm, a 12-inch record's playing time increased from about 5 minutes to 22 minutes per side.

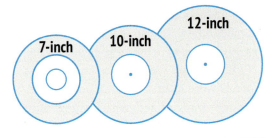

Electric audio

Electricity was first used for recording with microphones in 1925. Electronic microphones were more sensitive and could capture a wider range of frequencies. In addition, the recording could then be improved with the use of the first noise filters for this purpose, and by amplifying or damping specific sound ranges to better balance the overall sound. This was the start of the electronic recording industry, for which sophisticated mixing consoles have over time been developed, giving greater control over every part of a sound recording.

The first electric-powered record players came out the next year in 1926, but were expensive, and good speaker quality had not yet been developed, so they did not sell well. It wasn't until the late 1930s that a combination of price and quality brought them into greater use.

The improvement in microphones in the 1920s and ways to better control sound quality helped the radio industry, as did improvement in the quality of recorded music which could be played over the radio. It also provided necessary technology for the development of television as the first experimental broadcasts began in that era.

Sound in movies

The first attempt at adding sound to movies was made by Edison in 1895, with his Kinetophone. This was a version of his single-viewer kinetoscope with a phonograph added inside the cabinet, which the viewer listened to with earphones while watching the film clip. The sound was music only, and no attempt was made to synchronize it with the movie. Only 45 Kinetophones were made.

Several other attempts were made in the succeeding years to add sound to movies, but successful synchronization was elusive. Also, before the introduction of electric amplification of sound it was difficult to provide enough volume for a large theater.

One solution being pursued was to add the sound track directly to the film strip. In 1919 American **Lee De Forest** obtained a patent for a method to do this through a photographic process. In 1923 he exhibited a series of short films with sound, and soon started **De Forest Phonofilms**, which specialized in producing short films featuring celebrities and music acts. The sound quality, however, was poor, and by 1931 his company closed.

Similar systems were underway in Europe as well. Germans **Josef Engl**, **Hans Vogt** and **Joseph Massolle** patented the **Tri-Ergon** system, also in 1919, which became dominant in Europe by 1930. Like De Forest, it added a sound track directly to the film strip with a photographic process.

A competing method was introduced as **Vitaphone** in 1926. The sound was played on a phonograph that was mechanically linked to the movie projector in order to synchronize them. Vitaphone was started by **Sam Warner** of Warner Brothers studios, then still a small Hollywood studio, under contract with Western Electric. The system was first used for the movie **Don Juan** in 1926, the first feature-length movie to have any synchronized sound, although consisting of only music and sound effects and no dialog.

Sound-on-disk was initially more successful than sound-on-film. It was more economical to produce and had superior sound quality. But it was still prone to syncing problems, increased distribution complications as both film and disk had to be delivered to movie houses, and the disks wore out after only 20 screenings. When electronic sound recording became available it improved the quality of sound-on-film, helping it to eventually out-compete sound-on-disk.

Improvements in speaker quality, now also electronically driven, helped in adding sound to films. AT&T's research division,

Microphones
Microphones convert sound waves into electric currents of varying strength. There are four basic types.

Carbon
First invented by David Edward Hughes in 1878 and improved on by Edison in 1886, this was the first one used in telephones.

It works on a property of carbon: Its conductivity increases when compressed.

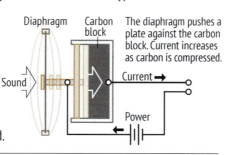

The diaphragm pushes a plate against the carbon block. Current increases as carbon is compressed.

Dynamic
Also called Moving Coil or Magnetophone, it was invented in 1923 by HJ Round.

It works on Faraday's principle that a wire moving through a magnetic field generates electricity.

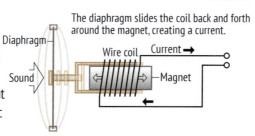

The diaphragm slides the coil back and forth around the magnet, creating a current.

Ribbon
Also in 1923 Harry F. Olson invented the ribbon microphone. Similar to the dynamic, it uses a conductive strip of metal between two magnets to generate an electric current.

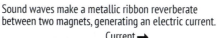

Sound waves make a metallic ribbon reverberate between two magnets, generating an electric current.

Condenser
Invented in 1917 by Edward C. Wente. An improved version, the **Electret**, was invented in 1964 by Gehard Sessler and James West. The Electret is what is used in most phones and mobile devices.

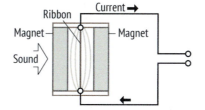

The two plates are conductive. Sound waves push the front plate towards the back plate. The closer the plates are to each other, the more current passes through them.

An Electret microphone. Width: 5 mm.

Holger.Ellgaard / Creative Commons

Shure 55 series
Perhaps the most iconic microphone in history, the Shure 55 has shown up in photos of Franklin D. Roosevelt, who used one for his fireside chats, and in use by celebrities such as Elvis Presley, Ella Fitzgerald and Frank Sinatra.

Sidney Shure started his company in 1925 selling radio parts, and began making microphones in 1932. The 55 Unidyne, a dynamic microphone, was first produced in 1939, and the series has been in constant production since then.

newly renamed as **Bell Labs**, was largely responsible for the improvements in speaker sound quality.

In 1927 Warner Brothers released *The Jazz Singer*, using the Vitaphone system. Although still not including full dialog, the two scenes of star Al Jolson singing were synced with a recording of his actual singing on set, as well as some ad-libbed dialog.

Although often incorrectly cited as the first feature-length sound film, *The Jazz Singer* was a huge financial success, and Warner Brothers subsequently released a string of popular and profitable sound movies, spurring the other Hollywood studios to follow suit. By 1929 all of the major studios had released a "talkie" as they were popularly called. That same year Warner Brothers released *On with the Show!*, the first all-color and all sound feature-length movie, using Technicolor's two-color system.

Also worth noting was England's 1929 *Blackmail*, the first successful European talking movie, directed by 29-year-old **Alfred Hitchcock**.

It would still take some time for sound movies to become the standard. Many smaller and rural movie houses couldn't afford the equipment. Producing them was also more complicated and expensive, and involved problems such as noisy cameras and arc lights, and keeping actors within range of a microphone. And projection rates had to be standardized over the sometimes haphazard rates of silent films.

In the 1930s as these problems were being addressed, sound-on-film also became the standard as Warner Brothers switched to it from sound-on-disk, as did any other remaining studios.

But clearly these problems were all overcome, and sound quality in movies increased dramatically over the next several decades to the point that several awards categories are now specifically for movie audio and music.

Speakers

Electronic speakers do the opposite of what microphones do, they convert electric impulses into sound waves.

The first speakers were in the earliest telephones in the 1860s and '70s. Most speakers today are based on the Dynamic design patented by Chester Rice and Edward Kellogg in 1924.

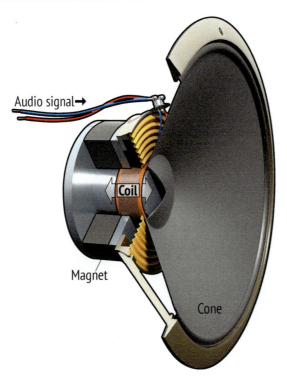

Audio signal→

Coil

Magnet

Cone

Dynamic (moving coil) speaker

This speaker works on the same principle as a dynamic microphone, but in reverse.

• The audio signal electrifies the coil wrapped around the central post

• This creates a magnetic field around the coil

• The coil's field is repelled by a stationary magnet behind it, causing the coil to slide forward

• As the audio signal varies in strength, the coil slides forward and back, causing the cone to vibrate and create sound waves.

Audio and video tape

Recording with electric microphones significantly improved sound quality, but the process in its early years had a major drawback: The output was engraved directly into a record disk, so if there was a mistake during the session, it usually had to be done over again from the beginning. It was possible to splice together several recordings by playing them on a phonograph in sequence into a microphone to create a new disk, but that resulted in a decrease in sound quality. What was missing was an editable recording medium.

Magnetic wire

The concept of recording magnetic patterns originated in the 19th century. It was proposed by American **Oberlin Smith** in 1888, and first successfully done by Danish inventor **Valdemar Poulsen**, who patented the **Telegraphone** in 1898. It captured varying patterns of magnetism on a length of wire, which could be used to record and play back sound. Poulsen tried to market the device for use as anything from a telephone answering machine to a dictation device, but was unsuccessful. The patent, however, was passed along through a succession of companies, including the Marconi Radio Company in England, which in the 1930s found a market with radio stations for a device based on the patent, using a narrow steel tape rather than wire. Among the customers were the BBC and the CBC.

Magnetic tape

Tape recorders capture audio input by magnetically altering the orientation of metallic particles in the tape. The recording can then be played back or erased for a new recording.

Audio reel-to-reel tape deck. Video recorders work on the same principles.

In a typical recorder, a roller called a capstan pulls the tape across three heads that each perform a different function.

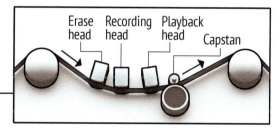

The tape is composed of a plastic strip with metallic particles, commonly iron oxide, embedded in it. The recording head creates a magnetic field that aligns the particles according to the audio input signal. The playback head reads the particle pattern to play back the audio.

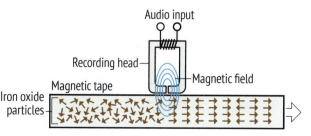

Magnetic tape

In 1929 German **Fritz Pfleumer** patented a magnetic tape using iron oxide bound to a strip of paper. The German electric equipment company AEG developed it into the **Magnetophone**, and in partnership with the German chemical company **BASF** (Badische Anilin und Soda Fabrik, German for *Baden Aniline and Soda Factory*), in 1935 created the first celluloid magnetic tape (technically cellulose acetate bound with iron oxide). BASF would later become one of the world's leading manufacturers of magnetic tape.

The Magnetophone, using the celluloid tape, was the most advanced tape recorder of its time, and the Germans held this superiority till the end of World War II. The Allies apparently only became aware of the device when it was captured late in the war.

The German patents were seized by the US following the war, which allowed a US company, **Ampex**, to begin making tape recorders and tape.

In the late 1940s US entertainer **Bing Crosby**, who had a radio show, was shown the tape recorder by **John Mullin**, the US soldier who had captured the German equipment. Soon Crosby began using the recorder to produce his radio show. The resulting publicity created high demand for Ampex equipment, and from this point on magnetic tape became the standard medium for producing both audio and video content.

The advantages of the tape were significant. It was inexpensive and easy to use, and editable. One could record over previous recordings or just portions of them, and it was possible to splice together different sections of tape.

Several large international companies became major suppliers of tape and equipment: **3M** in the US, **Phillips** in The Netherlands, **Sony** in Japan, and a reformed BASF in Germany. Various consumer products used the tape, including in 1979 the **Sony Walkman**, the first personal music player that played compact cassettes, and in the 1980s **VCRs**, or video cassette recorders, that allowed viewers to record and play back TV programs.

Compact cassette   Thegreenj / Creative Commons

1979 Sony Walkman   Dave L. Jones / Binarysequence

The age of electronic communication

In the industrialized parts of the world, the difference in societal structures from the early 19th century to the beginning of the digital era toward the end of the 20th century can only be described as the largest and most rapid shift in history. And certainly one of the largest influences was the change in communication, in how people received news, information and entertainment.

Even the difference between the start and end of the 20th century was pronounced. In 1900 the telephone and movies were just getting started, and radio and TV were yet to arrive. People were just beginning to own their own cameras, and seeing photos in print was still a novelty. It could still take days to receive news from beyond one's local area. By the 1990s, in contrast, the great majority of households had at least one TV with access to hundreds of channels, probably along with a video cassette recorder, and radios were small, portable and ubiquitous—nearly every car had one—which were already being displaced by newer media in the form of personal music players.

This was the result of the relentless technological innovations that were unleashed by the industrial revolutions and which accelerated throughout the Modern Era. Of course, technology had other profound effects, primarily in the use of electricity for manufacturing and lighting, and of the internal combustion engine for transportation. At the beginning of the 20th century the horse was still the principal means of local transportation for most people. By the middle of the century it was common for a First World family to own a motor vehicle, and within a few decades most adults owned one.

These changes were most profound in the Western First World, and most pronounced after World War II came to an end in 1945. While industrialized nations rebuilt quickly and prospered, impoverished states were left behind, stymied by lack of investment in the technology that created prosperity elsewhere. By the end of the century wealth disparities across the globe were deeper than ever.

But communication was more democratic. Radio and TV became common in even the poorest countries. Access to media content was determined not by a nation's wealth but by its political system. Whereas in Western Europe and North America there was little or no censorship, in repressive states such as those in the Soviet Union broadcast news and commentary were strictly controlled.

Radio by the 1930s was common in large parts of the world; anyone could build an inexpensive crystal set from a kit, and stations were broadcasting across most countries. It rapidly became a primary source of news and entertainment in most households. In the US, television arrived faster than any communication platform in human history: Nine percent of households had a TV set in 1950, 90 percent had one just twelve years later. And the trend was similar in most Western countries, but even in the poorest regions of the planet television still arrived. It would have been difficult in the year 2000 to find an inhabited spot on Earth where television wasn't accessible.

Broadcast radio and TV created shared experiences among people, capable of bridging societies and cultures. The lunar landing by US astronauts in 1969 was likely the most watched broadcast and the

Television ownership in the US
1950-2000

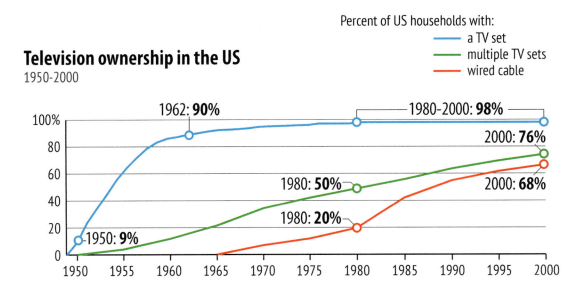

1962: **90%**

1980-2000: **98%**

2000: **76%**

1980: **50%**

2000: **68%**

1980: **20%**

1950: **9%**

Hours of television watched per day in the US
Hours per household, 1950-2000

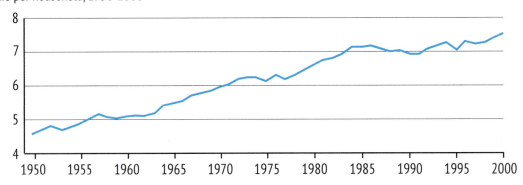

US average weekly movie attendance
Percentage of population, 1930-2000

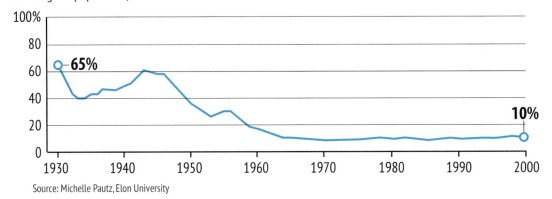

65%

10%

Source: Michelle Pautz, Elon University

most shared experience across the planet in history. And in many other instances the entire globe was now seeing historical events unfold in close to real time, such as the terrorist attacks on the US in 2001, known as 911.

The new media had cross-platform effects and influences. Television reduced audiences for movies and radio, and both radio and TV provided news faster than print media. When US President Kennedy was assassinated in 1963, the world heard about it first through broadcast reports. But it didn't have an overly negative impact on print. In Dallas there were lines several blocks long after the assassination to get a copy of the *Dallas Morning News*. The newspaper industry in fact continued to have healthy growth throughout the 1900s, as did magazines and books. It wasn't until the arrival of the World Wide Web that print news media started to decline.

Music sales in the form of records and tapes benefited immensely from radio, which was the best advertisement a performer could ask for, and was in fact essential exposure. And in the 1980s the sale and rental of movies on magnetic tape and then later on compact disks gave rise to an entire retail industry. Like print, these industries only declined with the advent of the Web.

TV had the biggest impact on radio and movies. Prior to TV there were radio dramas and entertainment shows; those lost their audiences to TV, and radio mostly turned to music programming along with some talk shows. Movies took the biggest hit, with dramatic declines in the number of people who attended movies on a regular basis. Nevertheless, the industry survived and has remained popular and profitable, in part by adapting to cable and the Web.

Accelerated global population growth, from 2 billion people in 1930 to over 6 billion in 2000, has offset some of the film industry's setbacks by expanding into international markets. Globalization has in fact created more demand for content in all media forms.

Competition for audience share forced content producers to improve quality. Movie studios invested heavily in their productions, especially in special effects, in order to compete with TV. Newspapers in the 1990s were much better designed, with color and visuals, than the drab, text-heavy papers at the beginning of the century. And TV competed with itself, as cable gave access to hundreds of new channels to challenge the established networks.

The most significant effect was that people became accustomed to having access to multiple types of media, and started consuming significantly more of it. In 2000 the average US household watched about three more hours of TV per day than it did in 1950. And transistors made it possible to build portable devices such as radios and tape players, in particular the Sony Walkman, making music in particular a more personal experience and thus changing people's media habits.

Increased media consumption influenced culture, especially as film, TV and music started finding larger international markets. Movies and TV influenced everything from fashion to language to political views. Hollywood has given the US outsized influence on other countries' cultures, but foreign films and media have found their way into every country, including the US. Electronic media have generated cross-cultural exchanges around the world.

This has been accelerated in the 21st century by the Internet, which has made access to film, video and music much easier across the globe.

The Digital Age

There were three developments that dramatically changed communication by the end of the 20th century: personal computers, digitized data, and the Internet.

Computers weren't intended to be communication machines. Their original purpose was no more complicated than their name, which was to compute, to perform intricate mathematical calculations that were difficult and time consuming. And that's all they were used for at first. But as they became compact and affordable enough for business use and for the general public, they gained capabilities in processing and displaying text, audio and video.

As electronics became ubiquitous in the second half of the 20th century, the way that information was recorded and stored was changed from analog to digital. This gradually happened to all forms of information, including text, audio, photography and video, which changed the way that information was created and then broadcast or transmitted over fiber optic networks.

And then came the Internet, which connected computers with each other no matter where they were in the world, and allowed users to send messages and content to each other.

In the last decade of the century the World Wide Web came into existence, and began to disrupt the systems by which every type of content—text, images, audio, video, movies—was distributed.

The result of these developments has been dramatic. In the first two decades of the 21st century, the Web has changed the way we communicate, with profound social, economic and political effects.

Computers

The first calculating machines were made centuries before the current era. They were, of course, entirely mechanical, electronic ones only appearing in the 20th century.

The earliest known arithmatic device, the **abacus,** was invented about 2,500 years ago. The oldest known mechanical calculating machine, the **Antikythera mechanism**, was recovered from a Greek shipwreck in 1901, and has been dated to some time between 2,200 and 2,000 years ago. Consisting of 37 bronze gears, it appears to have been used for astronomical calculations.

In 1642 CE, French mathematician **Blaise Pascal** invented the Pascaline, a calculator capable of decimal-level functions. In 1671 **Gottfried Wilhelm Leibniz**, a German, invented a calculator that could do square roots. Leibniz also came up with the concept of binary code.

These devices are not considered true computers, which require a set of encoded instructions that control their operation rather than being operated directly by a person. English mathematician **Charles Babbage** is credited with designing the first true computer in the mid-19th century. He actually made two machines. The first was the **Difference Engine**, a calculator, completed in 1832. He then drew plans for the **Analytical Engine** in 1856. It had an input mechanism, memory and a processor, and output its results through a printing mechanism, yet was completely mechanical. But he never completed its construction. Based on his drawings, one was built by Swedish printer George Scheutz in 1854, which was subsequently used by both the British and US governments. In the 1990s a reproduction of Babbage's Difference Engine was built by the Science Museum in London.

Electronic computers

In 1937 **Howard H. Aiken**, a Harvard graduate student, designed the **Harvard Mark I**, and IBM built it in the early 1940s. It was 51 feet long and weighed close to five tons, and required 530 miles of electric wire. It contained data in its memory with which it could perform almost any calculation. Commands were entered with punch tape, and the output was typed automatically by two typewriters. It was referred to as an automatic calculator, or more precisely the Automatic Sequence Controlled Calculator, or ASCC. The term computer wouldn't come into common use until 1945.

In England at a top-secret British military project in Bletchley Park, the **Colossus Mark I** went into operation in late 1943. It was a digital computer with 2,000 vacuum tubes that was programmed by switches rather than through stored data. An improved Mark 2 was built in 1944, and in

The recovered remains of the **Antikythera mechanism**, an ancient Greek calculating machine, are more than 2,000 years old.

the end ten of the machines were built. They were successfully used to decipher German code during World War II, providing valuable military information to the Allies. Difficult to program for other functions, the machines were retired after the war.

At the same time in Germany, engineer **Konrad Zuse** built the **Z3**, an electronic binary code computer that could be reprogrammed. Following the end of the war, IBM licensed his patents.

The machines up to now functioned partly with mechanical components. The first fully electronic computer was **ENIAC**, the Electronic Numerical Integrator And Computer, designed by **John Mauchly** and **J. Presper Eckert** and built between 1943 and 1945. It was even more of a behemoth than the Mark I, 80 feet in length, weighing 30 tons and containing 18,000 vacuum tubes. It performed calculations 1,000 times faster than previous machines. It was used by the US Army Ordnance Corps for munitions development, and for the development of the hydrogen bomb at Los Alamos National Laboratory.

Microprocessors and mainframes

With the arrival of transistors and integrated circuits in the 1960s and '70s, enormous machines such as ENIAC became obsolete. In 1968 Robert Noyce's Fairchild Semiconductor company developed the first **microprocessor chip**, a single chip that performed all the central operations of a computer, also called a central processing unit or **CPU**. These would become the heart of not only personal computers but of all digital devices to come.

Before PCs arrived, cabinet-size mainframe computers became standard use in business and research institutions, and in many cases are still in use for large operations. The servers at Google's facilities can be classified as mainframes. The sub-

category of super computers applies to the elite and most powerful machines. In 2020 the fastest machine was the **Fujitsu Fugaku** in Kobe, Japan, capable of 415 petaflops per second, a measure of the number of floating point calculations it can do in a second.

The first personal computer

In 1974 Fairchild released the **8080** chip, which was used by some of the first micro-computers. One of those was the **Altair 8800**, the first commercially successful personal computer. It was built by **MITS** (Micro Instrumentation and Telemetry Systems), founded by **Ed Roberts** and **Forrest Mims** in 1969.

The Altair went on the market in 1975, for sale as a mail-order kit for $397 (a little over $2,000 in 2020). It sold well above expectations, primarily to hobbyists.

The Altair was programmed by toggle switches and the output was through indicator lights, both of which were on the front panel. Separate hardware was needed to connect it to a printer.

Michael Holley / Creative Commons

The Altair 8800 Computer with an 8-inch floppy disk drive. This was the first commercially successful personal computer, which used the first Microsoft operating system.

1975: Founding of Microsoft

An ad for the Altair kit in the January issue of *Popular Electronics* caught the attention of aspiring programmers **Bill Gates** and **Paul Allen**, who offered to make an operating system for the Altair. MITS agreed, and the result was called Altair BASIC. Based on this success Gates and Allen founded **Microsoft**, which they originally spelled 'Micro-Soft', intended to stand for 'Microcomputer Software.'

And so the era of small computers made by big companies began.

1976: Founding of Apple

The Altair's success inspired dozens of entrepreneurs to enter the new personal computer market. Two of these were **Steve Jobs** and **Steve Wozniak**, who had met in 1971. Jobs was working at the Atari game company and Wozniak was at Hewlett-Packard, and both belonged to a computer hobbyist group in Menlo Park, near Palo Alto in California, where they first saw an Altair computer in 1975.

Wozniak set about building his own computer with what materials he had, using a 6502 microprocessor made by Mos Technology instead of the 8080 chip. His significant innovation was to add a keyboard for input and a TV for a monitor. He had built the prototype for the **Apple I**, which

Arnold Reinhold / Creative Commons

The Apple I was sold as a circuit board without a case. The buyer had to connect it to a keyboard and TV.

itself would become the prototype for future personal computers.

As Wozniak has recounted the story, at the time he didn't have ambitions of selling his new device. It was Jobs who saw its market potential. Jobs sold his VW Microbus to raise cash and Wozniak sold an expensive calculator, and with a third partner, Ronald Wayne, they founded **Apple Computer Inc.** in 1976.

Neither founder ever provided a firm explanation for the name choice. Jobs said that it occurred to him after spending time at an apple orchard, and that they simply couldn't come up with a better name.

The Apple I went on sale in July 1976 for $666.66, a number arrived at not for religious implications but as a result of a one-third markup from their wholesale price of $500.

Financing was precarious at first. No bank wanted to extend them credit, and they didn't have sufficient cash to pay for parts. Jobs managed to get an agreement with a local retailer, the Byte Shop in Mountain View, to take 50 computers, and with that agreement was able to obtain a small loan. At this point the third partner, Ronald Wayne, dropped out.

Wozniak made all 50 of the machines by hand with help from friends and relatives working at a kitchen table, and Jobs delivered them to the Byte Shop.

Two hundred of the machines were made over the next year, and all but 25 sold within ten months. Any that still exist today are highly valued collector's items. A few have been sold at auction for hundreds of thousands of dollars. A rare working version was bought in 2014 by the Henry Ford Museum in Michigan for $905,000.

1977: The Apple II

Based on the success of the Apple I, the Apple II was launched in 1977, this time manufactured in a molded plastic case with built-in keyboard. This was the first Apple product marketed to the public rather than hobbyists. The Apple I required expertise to assemble, program and run it; this machine only required knowledge of some basic keyboard commands.

It competed against two other computers with the same goal, the **Commodore PET 2001** and the **TRS-80**, all with similar design and features. The Apple's advantage was the ability to display color on a monitor, albeit limited to 16 colors if the resolution was 48 by 48 pixels, or six colors at 280 x 192 pixels. This is when Apple began using its multi-color logo.

The Apple II went on the market in June 1977. Programs had to be installed from an audio cassette recorder, which is also how data was saved (this was before floppy disks). Only upper case text could be typed and displayed. Price depended on how much memory was included, ranging from $1,298 for 4 kB to $2,638 for 48 kB, the maximum (about $5,500 and $11,000 in 2020 dollars).

The steep price didn't help sales. What boosted the Apple II was a new kind of software, **VisiCalc**, coded by **Dan Bricklin**, a Harvard Business School student, in 1979. It was the first spreadsheet for personal computers, and justified the cost of the computer for business use.

Apple logo, 1977

What also made the Apple II popular was its elegant functionality, and expansion slots that allowed third party manufacturers to sell components for it. Close to 16 million units were manufactured until it was discontinued in 1993.

1981: The IBM PC

IBM up to this time was only making mainframe computers. In 1980 they began development on their first PC, and a year later released the **5150**, built largely with outside vendor parts including the Intel 8080 CPU chip, and using PC DOS, an operating system from Microsoft. It cost $1,565.

Benefiting from a better marketing system through third-party vendors and with greater software and peripherals support than Apple had, the 5150 and succeeding PC models rapidly dominated sales for both business and home use through the 1980s. Their use of DOS also led to Microsoft's dominance in software.

The Apple II came in a molded case with built-in keyboard, and two game paddles. The monitor and cassette recorder were extra.

The recorder was used to load software and save data before floppy disk drives became available. In 1978 Apple introduced an external 5.25-inch floppy disk drive called the Disk II, designed by Steve Wozniak.

FozzTexx / Creative Commons

The Graphical User Interface

Apple went public in 1980 on the success of the Apple II. But even though it had a keyboard and could display colors, it was not like contemporary computers. It and the IBM PC were text based: They operated by line commands that had to be typed in to perform functions. There was no mouse. And the display didn't show images and graphics as modern users are accustomed to.

Jobs had heard of an innovation at Xerox called the **Graphical User Interface**, or GUI.

The two key features of the GUI are first, a visual display with windows and icons representing folders and documents, and second, an input device such as a mouse that moves a cursor across the display and opens or launches documents and applications by clicking on them.

This interface made computers easy to use compared to line-command systems. It made for a much more visual and auditory experience, with the capacity to display photos and graphics, to play video and audio, and to control the design and visual appearance of documents. It also made it a more interactive experience with features like drop-down menus, resizable and scrollable windows, and boxes with clickable options and fillable fields.

Jobs traded a hundred shares of Apple stock with Xerox in exchange for allowing him and a few employees to spend three days at PARC, Xerox's research facility that had developed the GUI.

Based on that experience Apple started work on two products, the **Lisa** and the **Macintosh**, both implementing a GUI with a mouse. The Lisa made it to market first in 1983, but its high price and sparse selection of available software resulted in poor sales.

In January of 1984 Apple introduced the first Macintosh with a dramatic and memorable Superbowl ad that made allusions to George Orwell's novel *1984*, and the machine went on the market at a cost of $2,495, which now included everything needed to operate it including monitor, keyboard and mouse.

But only 70,000 units were sold by May, far below projections and failing to challenge IBM's dominance in the market. One problem was a lack of compatible software, which developers had to rewrite to function with the new interface.

Gradually software became available for the Mac and sales improved. A version of Microsoft Word became available for it in 1985. But it was becoming clear that Apple wouldn't be competitive in office sales.

Internal conflicts in Apple's corporate structure ultimately caused Wozniak to leave in 1985, and with Mac sales initially sluggish, the board ousted Jobs. Apple's two founders were no longer in the company.

But the Macintosh became the model for future personal computers, with a GUI and mouse. Its basic design was how all PCs were subsequently designed, even as they became faster and more powerful, and added features such as internal hard drives and color displays.

Microsoft followed in 1985 with the first version of **Windows**, and IBM and other manufacturers adopted it, building PCs modeled after the Macintosh.

Public interest in computers grew as the public learned of their capabilities beyond business uses, and the GUI made it easy for anyone to operate a PC. Software that took advantage of the GUI helped sales, particularly games and graphic design applications, which helped Mac sales, as designers saw its potential.

Macintosh 128K

Although not the first GUI personal computer on the market, this was the first commercially successful one. Apple released it in January 1984 at the price of $2,495 (equivalent to about $6,100 in 2020).

The 128K refers to its memory: 128,000 bytes. It was followed less than a year later by the Mac Plus, which featured 512K of memory.

The Macintosh interface from the 1980s, with a window, icons for files and a menu bar at the top. The System disk holds the operating system needed to start up the computer.

Origins of the GUI

1963 Sketchpad, a graphical computer-aided design program developed by **Ivan Sutherland**, is sometimes cited as the first GUI. It allowed a user to draw on the computer display with a light pen, and for the computer to save the drawings as objects, so that they could be displayed again and edited.

Sutherland was a pioneer in the field of computer graphics, doing groundwork in 3D modeling, CAD (Computer Aided Design), and virtual reality.

1968 The first mouse was demonstrated by **Douglas Engelbart** at the Stanford Research Institute in Menlo Park, California. Engelbart had built a prototype in 1964 as part of a study comparing different input devices: light pens, joysticks and mice. The study showed that a mouse was the most efficient.

1973 A functional GUI interface was demonstrated at a Xerox facility called **PARC** (Palo Alto Research Center). The project, led by **Alan Kay**, unveiled the **Xerox Alto**, the first mouse-operated GUI computer with windows, menus, radio buttons and check boxes.

But the Alto was never commercially released. It was only used internally at the Center.

1979 The first GUI computer to be commercially sold was the **PERQ Workstation** from Three Rivers Computer Corporation. Its design was similar to the Xerox Alto. But Three Rivers went out of business in 1986, unable to compete with larger corporations such as Sun Microsystems and Silicon Graphics.

1981 Finally Xerox released a GUI computer, the **8010 Information System** (also known as the **Star**), based on the Alto. But Xerox had lost the innovation edge by then, and at $16,000 ($44,000 in 2020) and difficult to upgrade, it was a tough sell. Many Xerox engineers left at that time to go work for Apple.

1983 **Apple Computer** releases its first GUI machine, the **Lisa**. It featured drop-down menus, icons for every file in the system, a trash can, drag-and-drop functionality and window controls. But at $10,000 ($25,000 in 2020) and with a lack of compatible software, it wasn't successful.

1984 Apple's **Macintosh 128K**, released in January with a memorable Superbowl ad, cost a fourth of the Lisa's price and had more software. It became the first commercially successful GUI computer, and changed the market for PCs. It had the same features as the Lisa, including a one-button mouse. One of the factors in its success was a simplified mouse designed by **Jim Yurchenco** of **Ideo**, that cost much less to manufacture.

The 128K referred to its memory: 128,000 bytes of RAM. It had no hard drive.

Nine months later Apple released the **Mac Plus**, with 512K of memory.

1985 **Microsoft**, under **Bill Gates**, released **Windows 1.0**. By the 1990s Windows dominated market share, having largely captured the business office sector with inexpensive PCs running Microsoft Office.

Macintosh 128K—key components

Display

Grayscale CRT (cathode ray tube) with a diagonal measure of 9 inches and a resolution of 512 x 342 pixels. This works out to 72 pixels per inch, which became the standard resolution for CRT monitors.

The display has a depth of 1 bit, meaning that each pixel can only have one of two values, white or black, that is, fully lit or dark. Images are formed by patterns of black and white pixels.

Analog board: Controls video and audio. This was one of the first PCs with sound capabilities.

Motherboard

Holds essential electronic components such as the CPU and memory chips.

Note: Not all internal components are shown.

Disk drive

This early Mac had no hard drive, so all data had to be loaded into the memory chips from floppy disks. To start the Mac, a disk with the operating system is inserted into the drive and its data copied to the memory chips before the machine can start up.

Then each application has to be copied from another floppy to the memory chips before it can be run. And then all documents have to be copied to a floppy to save them. Once the Mac is turned off, all the data in the memory chips is erased.

Motherboard

This board contains the essential components for the computer to function.

① Microprocessor

This is the heart of the computer, called the Central Processing Unit, or CPU. The Macintosh 128K has a Motorola MC68000G8 chip. The 68,000 is the number of transistors.

Ports

For connecting the mouse and peripherals such as printers.

② Memory chips

16 memory storage chips, each with a capacity of 64,000 bits, for a total of 128 kB. Also referred to as **DRAM**, or Dynamic Random Access Memory. This is where applications store data temporarily while they're performing operations.

③ ROM chips

Read Only Memory chips contain permanent data that the Mac needs for the most basic operations, such as starting up.

④ Disk controller

Known as the "Integrated Woz Machine", Apple co-founder Steve Wozniak designed a simplified controller for the floppy drive that only required a single chip.

Software

MacWrite, a word processor, and **MacPaint**, a simple graphics application, came with the Mac, along with **Puzzle**, the first computer game played with a mouse.

Also available was **Microsoft Word**, the first version of which had been released in October 1983 for other platforms.

More software soon followed for graphics and publication design, for business use, and for entertainment.

The Macintosh design became the blueprint for all personal computers with graphical user interfaces, although subsequent models of both Macs and Microsoft-based PCs quickly separated the monitor from the box containing the motherboard, and added internal hard drives.

The 1998 iMac G3, designed by **Jonathan Ive**, reverted to an all-in-one design, which has become the standard configuration for Apple's consumer PCs, although in 2002, with the G4, the design switched to a flat panel on a stand, and in 2006 the Intel version switched to an all metal case.

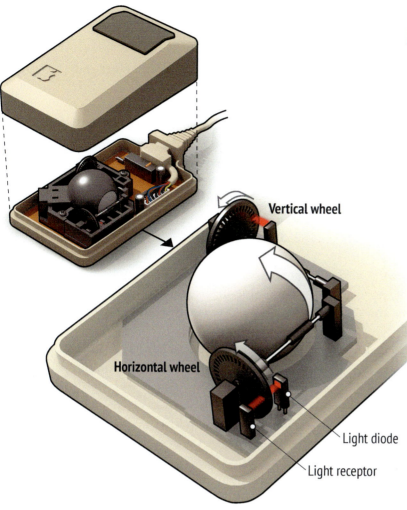

Mouse

Mechanical mouse

The first generation of mice were called mechanical mice. How they work:

• When the mouse is moved, a rubber ball inside it rolls.

• The ball turns two wheels, one for horizontal and one for vertical movement of the cursor.

• The wheels have a series of slots in them. A diode shines a beam of light through the slots to a receptor on the other side of each wheel.

• When each wheel turns, the light beam gets repeatedly interrupted. The computer counts the number of interruptions, and moves the cursor on the screen that many units (a set number of pixels, depending on tracking speed).

The Apple mouse shown here is the simplified design by **Jim Yurchenco** of **Ideo**, that cost much less to manufacture than previous designs.

Vertical wheel

Horizontal wheel

Light diode

Light receptor

Optical mouse

The first optical mice were invented in 1960, but didn't become commercially available until 1999. Since then they have mostly replaced mechanical mice. How they work:

• An LED light shines a light beam through a prism, which aims it at the surface underneath the mouse.

• The light beam bounces off the surface and back up to a light detector in the mouse.

• The light detector captures thousands of images a second, and compares differences between them. Changes in the image pattern are used to calculate movement, which is used by the computer to move the cursor on the screen.

Scroll wheel

Right button switch

Light detector

Prism

LED light

PC vs Mac

Since the mid-1980s, the two desktop/laptop operating systems that have dominated the market are Microsoft Windows and Apple's Macintosh OS. Windows is the most common. In 2018, over 88 percent of PCs had some version of Windows, while nine percent had the Macintosh OS.

The two companies are not very comparable, however. Apple is primarily a hardware company that makes the operating system software for its own devices, while Microsoft is primarily a software company whose programs are used by other PC manufacturers.

The two operating systems share many features. In fact, Apple sued Microsoft for copyright infringement following the release of Windows 1.0, but lost. The courts found that the "look and feel" of an interface was not subject to copyright.

There are several other operating systems, including Linux and Google Chrome, but they only have minor market shares.

Microsoft

It was founded in 1975 by friends since childhood **Bill Gates** and **Paul Allen**. After their first product, the Altair operating system, they bought 86-DOS, another operating system, from a company called Seattle Computer Products, rebranded it as MS-DOS and licensed it to IBM for use in their PCs. This was their first major product, and led to Microsoft's dominance in operating system software.

Microsoft's first version of **Excel** came out in 1982, first called Multiplan. The primary competition in spreadsheets at the time was **Lotus 1-2-3**. Excel wouldn't outcompete Lotus until 1988.

The first version of **Word** was released in 1983. The two most popular word processors then were **WordPerfect** and **WordStar**.

In 1985 the first version of Windows was released, built on top of MS-DOS. The company also went public that year.

In 1990 **Microsoft Office** was released, bundling Word and Excel. The upgrade of Windows to version 3 helped make Word and Excel the most popular business applications.

In 1994 Microsoft's legal troubles began as they were investigated for exacting license fees from PC manufacturers even if they weren't using the company's products. They would be further investigated in later years by the US Department of Justice for bundling software with their OS, particularly their Web browser **Explorer**, making it difficult for users to install competing software. The suit was eventually settled when Microsoft agreed to unbundle the different components.

In 2000 Gates handed over leadership of the company to Steve Ballmer, who would himself step down in 2014, replaced by Satya Nadella. Subsequently Microsoft diversified to a small degree into hardware with phones, tablets and the Xbox game station.

The company has remained dominant in its primary products of Windows and Office, with little chance of losing that status. Some criticisms of Microsoft are that it has never produced truly original products: MS-DOS was bought, Windows was copied from Apple, and Explorer was copied from Netscape, the first popular Web browser, subsequently sinking Netscape by making Explorer a part of the operating system. Several upgrades of Windows suffered from major bugs, incompatibility and sluggish performance.

Some vendors have complained of bullying tactics. But the company's success and market dominance are undeniable. In 2020 it was ranked 21st in the Fortune 500 list of US industrial firms, and had 144,000 employees.

Apple

Founded in 1976 by **Steve Jobs** and **Steve Wozniak**, the company established itself as a leader in innovative design of computer hardware and software with the Apple I and II in 1976 and 1977 and the full line of Macintoshes from 1984 to the present. The company went public in 1980. In 1985 they released the first laser printer aimed at the public, the **LaserWriter**. But in that same year internal conflicts caused Wozniak to quit and Jobs to be forced out by the board of directors, putting John Sculley in charge.

Apple continued largely on the popularity of the Macintosh within the creative and education communities, but was never able to compete with IBM and Microsoft for the office market. A slow decline ensued through the 1990s as Apple underwent several leadership changes, even at one point experimenting with leasing their operating system to other manufacturers, and then reversing that decision a few years later. The company had not come up with a successful new product since Jobs' ouster. By the late '90s it seemed increasingly likely that the company would fail.

After leaving Apple, Jobs took over the animation studio **Pixar** from Lucas Films, having sold all but one share of his Apple stock, and founded **NeXT**, which made an innovative Unix-based computer for high-end markets. In 1997, Apple understood it needed a new operating system and new leadership, and offered to buy **NeXTSTEP**, the NeXT OS. In the process, Apple hired Jobs back as CEO, at first on an interim

basis. That same year Apple launched the online Apple Store, selling its products directly to the public.

Under Jobs' leadership, Apple was revitalized. A succession of successful products with innovative designs followed, most notably the translucent, brightly colored all-in-one **iMacs**, **Power Macs G3** and **G4**, and their first consumer laptop, the **iBook**.

In 2001 **OS X**, based on NeXTSTEP's Unix framework, was launched. And the first walk-in retail **Apple Stores** were opened that year.

Also in 2001 Apple unveiled the first **iPod** digital music player, marking the company's expansion into a range of consumer electronics. In 2003 they opened the online **iTunes** store.

Over the next two decades Apple surged in popularity with innovative and attractively designed products, most notably the **iPhone** in 2007, the **iPad** in 2010 and the **Apple Watch** in 2014. Macintoshes diversified into iMacs, Mac Pros and several laptops, going through several design changes but by now characterized by their aluminum alloy bodies with the monochrome Apple logo. The iPhone became their most profitable product.

In 2011 Jobs stepped down and **Tim Cook** took his place. There had been reports for several years about Jobs' declining health. He had in fact been diagnosed with pancreatic cancer in 2003, and died from complications of it on October 5, 2011, at the age of 56.

Apple surpassed Microsoft in market value in 2011. In 2020 it was ranked fourth on the Fortune 500 list, a spot lower than the previous year due to Amazon's rise. It had 137,000 employees, many working at its futuristic circular office building in Cupertino, California.

Steve Jobs 1955-2011

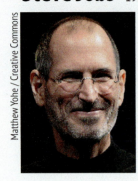

Matthew Yohe / Creative Commons

Steven Paul Jobs was born in San Francisco in 1955, adopted by a local family at birth and grew up in the Bay Area. As a boy he gained an interest in electronics from his adoptive father. He lacked direction in his early adulthood, dropping out of college in his first year, working for the Atari game company for a few months, and traveling in India. His interest in electronics kept him in contact with his high school friend Steve Wozniak. After Wozniak designed the Apple I they founded Apple Computer in 1976 and turned it into a successful corporation over the next decade. But by 1985 both had left, Wozniak voluntarily and Jobs ousted by the board of directors.

Jobs started another computer development company, NeXT, that same year, and in 1986 he took charge of Pixar in cooperation with LucasFilm, which would produce a line of successful 3D animated feature films such as *Toy Story*. Apple purchased NeXT in 1997, which led to Jobs returning as the CEO, where he remained for the rest of his life, leading Apple in the development of a line of highly successful products over the next decade, from the iMac to the iPhone. In 2003 he was diagnosed with pancreatic cancer, which led to his death on October 5, 2011. Jobs was almost universally described as a difficult and demanding boss, but his singular vision led to the populatization of GUI computers and touchscreen smartphones, which have had transformative impacts on communication and on the larger culture.

Bill Gates 1955-

DFID / Creative Commons

William Gates III was born in and grew up in Seattle. In grade school he became interested in programming and met Paul Allen, with whom he began to cooperate on software projects. In 1973 Gates enrolled in Harvard, but dropped out in 1975, the year that the MITS Altair 8800 was released. Gates and Allen wrote an operating system for it. With that success, the two formed 'Micro-Soft'. In 1976 they registered the name as Microsoft, and in 1979 opened their first headquarters in Bellevue, Washington. In 1980 IBM asked Microsoft to develop a PC operating system. Gates and Allen licensed one from Seattle Computer Products and adapted it for the IBM PC. This would be the basis for the first version of MS DOS, which Microsoft licensed to IBM and subsequently to other PC manufacturers. With its near-universal market adoption, Microsoft became the dominant supplier of operating systems for most PCs, as well as in office software with Word and Excel.

Microsoft was incorporated in 1981 with Gates as president and chairman. Allen left the company in 1983 due to illness and a falling out with Gates. Gates actively participated in software developing until the 1990s. In 1998 Microsoft became engaged in antitrust litigation and was found guilty of violating the Sherman Antitrust Act based on actions approved by Gates involving software bundling, but it had little long-term impact on Gates' or the company's fortunes. In 2006 Gates, by now one of the world's wealthiest persons, started delegating his responsibilities and in 2014 stepped down as Microsoft chairman. He has since devoted his time to philanthropy along with his wife. The Bill and Melinda Gates Foundation is one of the world's best endowed charitable organizations with programs across the globe. The couple have pledged to donate 95 percent of their wealth to charity over time.

Digital progress

The GUI changed the role of computers. It introduced the concept of desktop publishing and the digital design and pagination of print publications, replacing the paste-up process. It gave users the ability to not only play video, audio and games but to create and develop them on a personal computer.

And it laid the groundwork for the World Wide Web, first by providing the interface needed for the Web's visual experience, and second by increasing public interest in owning a personal computer. At the time of the Macintosh's first release, the number of households in industrialized nations with a PC was about eight percent; within ten years, that number had tripled to 24 percent. By 2020, the vast majority of households had at least one PC, whether Windows or Mac, and several mobile devices, each with its own GUI of some design.

Early PCs such as the IBM 5150 and the Macintosh established the basic hardware design of PCs with a CPU, memory chips, removable media such as floppy disks, and some sort of permanent data storage (although the first Mac didn't have one, internal hard drives subsequently became standard). Although the basic components didn't change, their functionality and capacities grew exponentially, fueled by increasing market demand and the resulting competition between manufacturers.

Moore's Law

In 1975, **Gordon Moore**, who had co-founded Fairchild Electronics and Intel with Robert Noyce, made a prediction that the density of transistors on a microchip would double every two years, while the cost of manufacturing the chip would drop by half, and that this growth would continue exponentially.

This turned out to be an accurate prediction up to about 2010, after which the trend has slowed. And at a certain point it won't be possible to pack any more transistors into a smaller space because the heat they generate would become too great. This limit is expected to be reached some time in the 2020s, assuming a solution to the dilemma isn't found.

The reason for the exponential growth in transistor density is that they have become vanishingly small. Their sizes are measured in **nanometers**, each of which is one billionth of a meter. A human hair is about 100,000 nanometers wide. In 2020 commercially produced transistors were typically about seven nanometers long, although experimental ones have been made as small as one nanometer. By comparison, a DNA molecule is about two nanometers wide.

A new production method, called 3D, positions each transistor vertically instead of flat, so that it extends up from the board. These can be as thin as 2.5 nanometers, although they are over 200 nanometers tall.

The accuracy of Moore's prediction resulted in dramatically faster and more powerful machines every few years. Also, data storage capacities increased almost as fast while similarly dropping in price.

As a result manufacturers have been able to market new machines that are much better than the ones from just a few years ago, incentivizing the public to upgrade on a regular schedule.

The trend has also made it possible to build smaller and more portable devices: laptops, smartphones and tablets. For these, battery technology also needed to increase substantially, which it did through new types, particularly lithium-ion batteries.

Number of transistors in computer CPUs, 1970-2020

The first transistor radio, in the 1950s, had four. In 1971 Intel's first CPU, or central processing unit, had 2,250. In 2020, 49 years later, a record 54 billion transistors had been achieved in a Nvidia CPU.
Other types of chips have even larger numbers. Samsung's 2020 eUFS V-NAND flash memory chip held the record with 2 trillion floating-gate transistors. Apple's 2020 iPhone 12 has 11.8 billion transistors on its A14 chip.

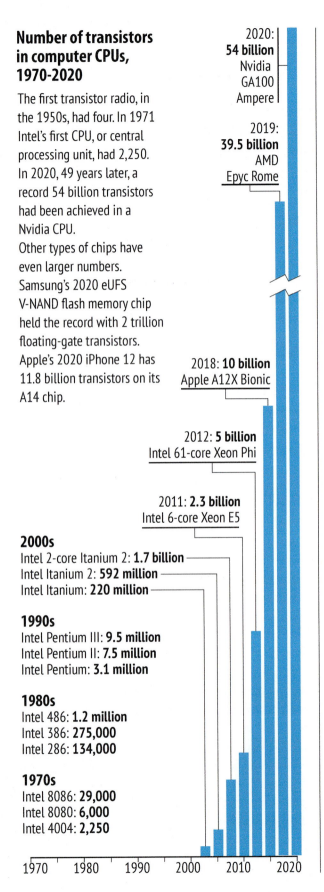

2020: **54 billion** Nvidia GA100 Ampere

2019: **39.5 billion** AMD Epyc Rome

2018: **10 billion** Apple A12X Bionic

2012: **5 billion** Intel 61-core Xeon Phi

2011: **2.3 billion** Intel 6-core Xeon E5

2000s
Intel 2-core Itanium 2: **1.7 billion**
Intel Itanium 2: **592 million**
Intel Itanium: **220 million**

1990s
Intel Pentium III: **9.5 million**
Intel Pentium II: **7.5 million**
Intel Pentium: **3.1 million**

1980s
Intel 486: **1.2 million**
Intel 386: **275,000**
Intel 286: **134,000**

1970s
Intel 8086: **29,000**
Intel 8080: **6,000**
Intel 4004: **2,250**

1970   1980   1990   2000   2010   2020

Data storage

There are two ways that data is stored in a computer: temporary and permanent. The temporary storage is done with RAM chips (Random Access Memory), which the CPU uses as it works. When the computer is turned off this data is lost. There are also chips called ROM (Read Only Memory) which contain basic information, mostly used during start-up, and whose data doesn't get changed except during upgrades.

Data that is created while using the computer gets saved onto two types of devices, magnetic disk drives and solid state circuit devices commonly called flash drives, and more recently SSDs, for Solid State Drives.

Removable 5.25-inch floppy disks came into common use starting in 1976. In the 1980s PCs used 3.5-inch floppies which held 800 kilobytes, and later 1.2 megabytes. Since then there have been dozens of external media, gradually increasing in capacity. From the 1990s to the 2010s capacity for both internal hard drives and external media grew from tens of megabytes to terabytes (one million megabytes).

Hard drives

IBM made the first magnetic hard drive in 1953 at their San Jose research facility, and began offering it commercially in 1957. The change in capacity between then and today is as dramatic as Moore's Law. That first drive consisted of fifty 24-inch platters with a total capacity of 3.75 megabytes. By current standards it was slow: It took the read/write head close to a second to access a sector in order to start its operation. IBM charged customers $640 a month per megabyte to store data.

By contrast, a two-terabyte drive, which

Platter

Read/write head

Actuator

Magnetic hard drive (with top cover removed): Inside a sealed case are one or more magnetic platters, typically 3.5- or 2.5-inch in diameter, that spin at up to 7,200 rpm, while binary data is read from and written to their surfaces through the swiveling actuator head. The surface of each platter is divided into distinct sectors, each holding a set amount of data.

Solid state drive: Essentially a large integrated circuit, it has the advantage of having no moving parts, and transfers data much more rapidly than magnetic disk drives. It consists of billions of transistors, each capable of storing a binary value of 0 or 1. These are called floating-gate transistors, which have the capability of retaining a charge even when the device containing them is turned off.

can hold more than a million times the data as IBM's first drive, cost about $60 retail in 2020.

One of the first PCs with an included hard drive was the 1983 IBM PC XT, which came with a 10 MB drive. The first Macintoshes to come with an internal hard drive option were the 1987 Macintosh SE, which looked nearly identical to the Mac Plus, and the Macintosh II, released the same year, which came with a 20 MB internal hard drive.

A standard hard drive size became 3.5 inches for desktops and 2.5 inches for laptops. By 1990 drives were still measured in tens of megabytes. By 1999 typical sizes were up to 340 MB. Capacities reached into gigabytes in the 2000s, and finally terabytes in the 2010s.

SSDs

Attempts to create solid state memory technology started as early as the 1950s, and some devices were developed in the 1970s for supercomputers, but until recently were too expensive for PC use. Small USB flash drives came on the market starting in 2000. SSD drives of sufficient capacity to replace hard drives started becoming available in the 2010s. Apple offered an SSD option with the 2008 MacBook Air, which then became standard in 2010. SSDs transfer data much more quickly than hard drives, are more compact, and are generally more reliable.

A wide range of storage devices from removable flash drives to memory cards started becoming available in the early 2000s. They're essential for most mobile devices, from cameras to smartphones.

Displays

Cathode ray tubes, or CRTs, were the common displays for PCs as well as televisions in the 1980s and '90s. They were not an option for laptops and mobile devices, however, as well as the wide range of electronics with displays of some sort, from digital cameras to appliances of all kinds. For this, flat panel technology was needed, which came in the form of LCDs.

LCD screens

Liquid Crystal Displays use arrays of crystals in a flat panel to modify light being projected from behind them in order to create images. Crystals are types of organic molecules that only allow light to pass through them when they are oriented in a specific direction. By controlling their orientation, they can be used to create images on a screen.

Light modulating properties of some crystals have been documented since the 1800s. Austrian chemist **Friedrich Reinitzer** documented them in 1888 in cholesterol extracted from carrots. The first functioning crystal display was invented by a team at RCA Labs led by **George Heilmeier** from 1964 to 1968. Inventor **James Fergason** patented the technology necessary for the first LCD consumer products. His company, the International Liquid Crystal Company, made the first LCD watch in 1972. The technology was soon in use for other small electronic devices such as calculators.

In the 1980s LCD video displays were developed, opening up the possibilities of laptop computers and other mobile devices such as phones. Color LCDs came next, in the form of small, handheld TVs. Seiko and Epson were the first companies to offer them, with screens only a few inches wide.

In 1988 the Sharp corporation released a 14-inch color TV, marking the beginning of full-size LCD TVs and computer monitors. They didn't become competitive in price or quality with CRTs until the 2000s. But by 2007 more LCD TVs were sold than CRTs as their quality surpassed CRTs.

LED displays are essentially LCDs. The acronym stands for Light Emitting Diode. An LED display simply uses LEDs as the source of backlighting. A normal LCD display uses CCFLs (cold cathode fluorescent lamps) for backlighting, which is a type of fluorescent lighting that emits light without producing heat. Smartphones, including iPhones, typically use LEDs due to their more compact size and better energy efficiency.

LCD and LED displays were an essential development for all mobile devices, from laptops to phones. Besides the obvious fact that a CRT can't be thin, LEDs are lighter, use less energy, and provide sharper images than CRTs.

U1Quattro / Creative Commons

First LCD displays
One of the first uses of LCDs was for watches. Shown here is a Casio multi-function watch from 1987.
in 1972 The Hamilton Watch Company offered the first digital watch on the market, the Pulsar Time Computer, for $2,100, equivalent to almost $13,000 in 2020. Within a decade digital watches were selling for less than $10.

LCD screens

Liquid Crystal Displays use the properties of certain molecules, called crystals, to control light. As with all digital displays, it generates images through rows of pixels by modifying the brightness and color of each pixel.

Modifying pixel brightness

Light from the back of the display must pass through two layers of polarizing film, between which the crystals channel the light or block it, depending on their orientation. This is how the brightness of each pixel is controlled.

1 In an LED monitor, light from a row of LEDs, light emitting diodes, is redirected, diffused and augmented by several layers of translucent sheets to make an even panel of backlighting.

2 In front of the backlighting, two polarized sheets are positioned at right angles to each other. Ordinarily this causes the front sheet to block any light from getting through.

3 Crystals are sandwiched between the polarized sheets. They only allow light to pass through their width, not their length. They are arranged in spirals, which twist light beams 90 degrees, allowing them to pass through the front polarized sheet, lighting up pixels in the front panel of the display.

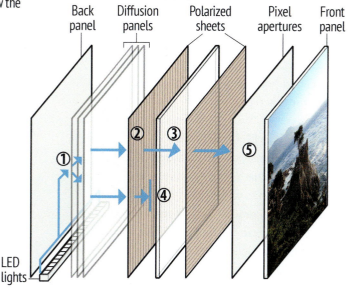

Back panel | Diffusion panels | Polarized sheets | Pixel apertures | Front panel

LED lights

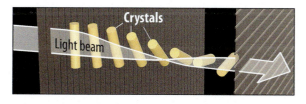

Crystals
Light beam

4 But when an electric charge is applied to the crystals, they turn sideways, preventing any light from reaching the front panel.
This can be used to turn individual pixels on and off, and to make them brighter or dimmer.

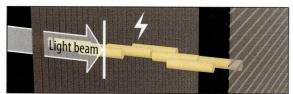

Light beam

Colorizing the pixels

5 In the front glass is a layer with rows of apertures, one for each pixel. Each has three color panes, red, green and blue. Each pane has its own transistor. The transistor for each pane controls how much light passes through it based on video information sent to it.

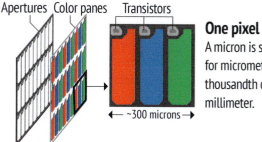

Apertures Color panes Transistors

~300 microns

One pixel
A micron is short for micrometer, a thousandth of a millimeter.

The amount of light passing through each pane allows the RGB color value for each pixel to be created.
Similar to CRTs, the pixels are arranged in rows, with each row being lit in sequence, typically at 400 hertz.

Touchscreen mobile devices

Smartphones and tablets resulted from a confluence of technologies: mobile phones and cellular networks, more powerful and compact microchips and other components, better batteries, and LCD touchscreens.

Mobile phones could start sending texts with the arrival of the 2G network in 1991, and gained limited Internet connectivity in 1998 with the launch of 3G, but the speed was still slow and the phones' processing power and memory were limited. They also needed better interfaces, either keyboards or touchscreens.

Touchscreen technology

There are a variety of types of touchscreens. The most common ones are **resistive**, which has two conductive layers that generate an electric signal when pressed together, and **capacitive**, which detects the electric field in a person's fingertip. Resistive screens are common in public devices such as grocery store self checkout counters; capacitive, which are more intricate, are more often used in personal devices such as smartphones.

The first touchscreen was made in the 1970s by **Frank Beck** and **Bent Stumpe** at the CERN research facility (the European Organization for Nuclear Research; in French: Conseil Européen pour la Recherche Nucléaire). A team at the University of Illinois also developed a touchscreen for use with a computer-assisted instruction system called Plato.

In 1983 Hewlett-Packard released a touchscreen computer, the HP150. It worked through infrared sensors arranged around the edge of a 9-inch CRT screen. From this point numerous companies started researching touchscreen technology for a multitude of uses, from game consoles to aircraft flight controls. Software development also expanded for use in touchscreen devices.

Personal Digital Assistants, or PDAs, came out in 1993 with the **Apple Newton** and the **IBM Simon**, often cited as the first smartphone. They could send and receive phone calls, faxes and email, and had an array of applications including address book, calendar, calculator and notepad. But the Simon was bulky and its battery only lasted an hour. The Newton was discontinued by Jobs when he returned to Apple in 1998. Other PDAs such as the Blackberry and the Palm Treo had keyboard input rather than touchscreens.

A variety of flip and compact phones gained rapid market acceptance in the later 1990s, mostly operated through physical buttons rather than touchscreens. The first one with a capacitive touchscreen was the **LG Prada** in 1997.

The first **iPhone** came out in 2007, with a touchscreen interface and full Internet connectivity, which improved in 2008 with a 3G-compliant model.

The first Android phone, the **T-Mobile G1**, appeared in 2008, but had a keyboard and trackball like a Blackberry.

Also in 2008, Apple opened the App Store and Google the Android Market, later renamed the Google Play Store. This marked the beginning of downloadable apps for smartphones, expanding their capabilities.

In 2010 Samsung released the first **Galaxy S**, a touchscreen phone, that became the most popular Android smartphone.

Also in 2010 Apple released the first **iPad**. There had been earlier tablets, noteably Microsoft's Tablet PC, but they had limited market success. Microsoft's later **Surface** tablet has been more successful. There are also a number of tablet readers such as Amazon's Fire and Kindle.

Touchscreens

There are several ways that touchscreen devices work, but all the methods involve a way to get input from touching an LCD-illuminated surface with a finger or a stylus in order to operate the device.

Resistive

This is the simplest and most economical method. A typical use is for point-of-sale devices such as self-checkout registers, or for appliances that have simple control panels. It has the advantage that a stylus can be used, but lacks the precision for use with high resolution displays.

Two transparent layers carrying conductive charges are in front of an LCD screen, and separated from each other by an air space. The top layer is flexible, and when pressed, comes in contact with the second layer, completing a circuit between the two. The location of the point of contact is sent to the device's CPU.

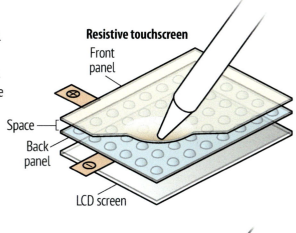

Resistive touchscreen
Front panel
Space
Back panel
LCD screen

Capacitance

Capacitors are devices or circuits that hold a constant electric charge. In a touchscreen, an electric grid generates an electromagnetic field across the screen that is always on. A person's finger has a slight electric charge as well, and when the screen is touched, it will interrupt the grid's field. The point of interruption is then calculated and sent to the device's CPU.
There are two methods: mutual and self capacitance.

Mutual capacitance: Two transparent layers have conductive lines embedded in them. The top layer contains driving lines, in which a constant electrostatic charge is maintained. The layer below that contains sensing lines. A finger touch causes a small disruption to the electric field in the driving lines, which is detected in the sensing lines. The point of contact is relayed to the device's CPU.

Self capacitance: Instead of driving and sensing lines, this method uses a sheet of electrodes arrayed in a grid pattern to generate the field and detect finger touches.

Most smartphones and tablets use one or the other capacitative method, which are both compatible with high resolution LED screens.

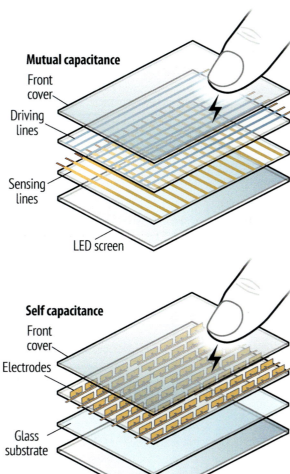

Mutual capacitance
Front cover
Driving lines
Sensing lines
LED screen

Self capacitance
Front cover
Electrodes
Glass substrate
LED screen

Touchscreen smartphones

The first iPhone was released by Apple in 2007, and became, if not the first, then the most successful touchscreen device: One million were sold within 74 days. With its success, the era of smartphones went mainstream, devices that are fully Internet connected, have video-capable cameras, play music, and almost incidentally are telephones. Apple developed an operating system specifically for it, iPhone OS.

Google-based Android smartphones have been the most popular worldwide since their release in 2008, with 2 billion in use in 2020, compared to 900 million iPhone users. However, the Android market share is divided among several phone makers, with Samsung having held the lead for a number of years.

2007
iPhone 1
Memory: 4 / 8 GB
Screen: 320 x 480 pixels
CPU: 70 million transistors
Camera: 2 megapixels

iPhone 1 components

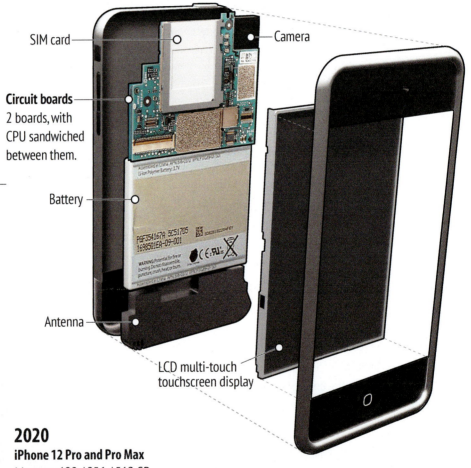

SIM card

Camera

Circuit boards
2 boards, with CPU sandwiched between them.

Battery

Antenna

LCD multi-touch touchscreen display

2020
iPhone 12 Pro and Pro Max
Memory: 128 / 256 / 512 GB
Screen: 1170 x 2532 / 1284 x 2778 pixels
CPU: 11.8 billion transistors
Camera: Three in back and one in front, 12 megapixels each

Digital data

Computers run on binary code, which consists of only two digits—zeros and ones—because it's an ideal code for electric circuits. The most basic thing to do with a current is to turn it on and off. If 'off' is zero and 'on' is one, then you can codify data as a pattern of zeros and ones by rapidly turning a circuit on and off. In a sense, it's similar to Morse code, except that computers can process code much faster.

The code is simple. For numbers, 000 represents the integer zero, one is 001, two is 010, three is 011, four is 100, and five is 101. And the code continues in this manner.

Each alphabet character also has its own code as well, for example, the letter A is 01000001, and B is 01000010.

The basic binary unit is called a **bit**, which is a zero or a one. The code shown above for the letters has eight bits, which is called a **byte**. Digital storage is listed in multiples of bytes: a **kilobyte** is a 1,024 bytes (8,192 bits), a **megabyte** is a 1,024 kilobytes (1,024 times 1,024, or more than a million bytes), and so on. Data processing and transmitting is measured in kilobytes or megabytes, or even gigabytes, per second.

Software

When you build a machine to perform cognitive functions on its own, then you're going to need a language to communicate with it. Computers are supposed to take problems and figure out answers through a logical set of steps. In fact, Apple calls the main circuit board in its computers the 'logic board.'

We solve problems by applying logic to facts that we learn or already know. Similarly, computers need two things, sets of data, and instructions on what to do with that data.

Memory

This is why computers need memory, to store both data and instructions. The most basic instructions are usually stored permanently in a Read Only Memory, or **ROM**, chip, with simple code for starting up and initiating basic functions. The code to make the computer fully functional is called the Operating System, or **OS**. On startup, the OS has to be loaded into Random Access Memory chips, or **RAM**. These chips don't store data permanently, they get erased

Claude Shannon 1916-2001

Claude Shannon's 1948 paper, "*A Mathematical Theory of Communication*", written while working at Bell Labs, is considered the foundational document that launched the Information Age.

In it he introduced the concept of using binary code, and the idea of the bit as the fundamental unit of information. This began the path away from analog data, consisting of waves and pulses, to digital data consisting of ones and zeros. His proposals helped the evolution of computers from mechanical devices to fully electronic ones that used binary code to calculate and store data. Often referred to as 'The Father of the Information Age,' Shannon was also a prolific inventor of quirky devices, including a rocket-powered frisbee and a machine whose only purpose was to turn itself off. He enjoyed juggling and unicycle riding.

when the computer is turned off, or if it crashes. Before computers had hard drives, the OS had to be loaded from a tape drive or a floppy disk every time the computer was turned on; now, the OS is loaded into RAM from an internal drive.

Next, specific applications, or programs, have to be loaded into RAM, which is what happens when you launch a program. They then interact with the OS and use it to perform specific functions. The communication between programs and the OS is called the Application Programming Interface, or **API**, which is a protocol for synchronizing the programs. The API acts as an interpreter between programs and the OS.

Once all the programming information is loaded into the memory chips, then the microprocessor, or CPU, can access that information to perform commands from the user. As it works it temporarily stores results in the RAM chips. The results are only saved permanently with a save command, which writes the data to the internal hard drive or an external drive.

Interfaces

The first electronic computers such as ENIAC received their data and instructions through paper tape or, most commonly, punch cards. This was a laborious process requiring manually typing the data on a keyboard machine that punched a sequence of holes in each card. The result would be a stack of cards, which were then fed into the computer through a card reader, one by one. The computer would then deliver its results through dot matrix printers or teletype machines, on paper.

Punch cards predate computers by centuries. The first ones were used in the early 1700s for textile looms to mechanically create patterns in fabric. In the 1890s **Herman Hollerith**, the founder of IBM, developed a recording system for the US census using punch cards.

Punch cards became obsolete in the 1970s with the combined developments of memory chips, keyboard inputs and data storage on magnetic disks.

Programming languages

The first computers were programmed through switch positions or with punch tape or cards, which meant that binary code was being entered directly. This was arduous and risky, as a single error usually meant starting over from the beginning. It also meant that the process was not saved, but had to be repeated every time that a calculation was run.

Storing a program in electronic memory was done for the first time in 1948 at The University of Manchester in England, on a computer called the **Manchester Baby**. This was the first computer that had something equivalent to dynamic memory,

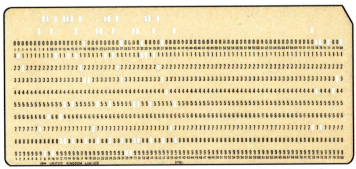

A typical punchcard.

Pete Birkinshaw / Creative Commons

and on which was demonstrated the concept of a computer program, code that could be stored and run more than once.

Programming languages came into existence starting in the 1950s. One of the first, **Fortran**, was created by IBM for science and engineering. **Cobol** (common business-oriented language), was written for business use by a team that included one of the first female programmers, Jean Sammet. **BASIC** (Beginners' All-purpose Symbolic Instruction Code) was designed to be easy to use in fields other than math and science.

These languages made it possible to use computers without writing custom code for each purpose. They are still in wide use today. BASIC became especially useful with the emergence of microcomputers, which needed lean coding for their limited computing capabilities. In 1991 Microsoft made a version called **Visual Basic** that is in common use today. More recent languages include **Pascal** and **C**, and **Unix**, on which the Macintosh OS X is based.

These languages are used to write both operating systems and programs for specific uses, such as Word or Photoshop, different versions of which have to be coded for different platforms: There are Windows and Mac versions of Word, for example.

Women in programming

Women throughout history have often been excluded from science and engineering endeavors, a problem which still persists in the 21st century. Several women were still able to make contributions to mathematics and computer programming. Of note:

Antoine Claudet

Ada Lovelace 1815-1852

Daughter of poet and politician Lord Byron, she was a mathematician who is often credited as the author of the first computer program, written for Charles Babbage's Analytical machine, with whom she collaborated. Surviving notes of hers contain an algorithm intended for the machine. Even though it was never implemented, the notes provide evidence of her logical solutions to making a computer work.

Jean Sammet 1928-2017

Sammet started her career as a programmer in the 1950s when the concept of computer programs was new. Her most significant contribution was in helping to create the programming language COBOL in 1959. She was one of a team of six that wrote the protocol for the language, which subsequently became one of the most used computer languages for handling business data. In 1961 she went to work for IBM, where she stayed for three decades.

Katherine Johnson 1918-2020

Johnson worked as a mathematician for NASA at the Langley Research Center, doing calculations for navigation of spacecraft. She calculated by hand the trajectory of the first manned space launch, and gained the respect of astronauts in the program for her abilities. She also did calculations for the first lunar landing, and later for shuttle missions. In 2015 President Obama awarded her the Presidential Medal of Freedom, and she was portrayed in the film 'Hidden Figures' in 2016. As an African American woman, she helped break down barriers for both women and minorities in science and technology.

Analog to digital

The term analog generally applies to things that have been produced physically or mechanically, such as grooves in vinyl records or photos developed in a darkroom. Analog data is continuous, for example, sound is transmitted by waves of varying strength, which are translated to an electric current by varying the current's strength: the louder the sound, the bigger the wave, the stronger the current.

Converting an analog sound wave to digital is done by assigning digital values to different points on the wave to represent different current strengths. So instead of being continuous it is better visualized as a series of stair steps. The quality will depend on how many data points, or steps, there are.

Analog photos and video consist of variations in value and intensity of colors: Value is a measure of light to dark, intensity is bright to dull. To digitize them they are converted to patterns of small dots called **pixels**. Each pixel is assigned a color value code. There are several color codes; the most common is called a **hex code**, which consists of six numbers and/ or letters. For example, a red with a little blue in it is #ff0024, whereas pure red light is #ff0000. In digital graphics applications, colors can also be defined by the amount of red, green and blue light in it, each of which is measured on a scale between 0 and 255. So, the #ff0024 color in RGB is 255/0/36. There are several other color models used in digital applications but they are less common.

The quality of audio and video depends on the number of data points and the number of pixels: the more the higher the quality. There is a tradeoff between quality and file size which usually has to be taken into consideration for processing, transmission and storage. A photo two thousand pixels wide and a thousand pixels in height has a total of two million pixels, which could be several megabytes in size (it depends on how many different colors there are). In the early days of computers processing and storing a file that size would have been challenging, as would sending it over the first network connections. The first hard drives were less than five megabytes in capacity, so data had to be as lean as possible, even sometimes at the sacrifice of quality.

Digital audio

Sound was one of the first media to be digitized, beginning in the 1970s. At first the binary code was recorded on magnetic tape, using the same tape head technology that was used for recording video. Since this preceded widespread ownership of personal computers and digital music devices, it was only used for professional studio recording and broadcasting. Digital recordings had a few advantages: They had less background noise, and didn't degrade through repeated playback as happened on

Analog to digital audio

Physical sound is manifested in continuous waves of varying length and amplitude, or strength. To digitize it, points along the wave are assigned a digital value in an attempt to approximate the shape of the waves.

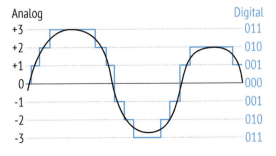

analog devices. It also made tasks such as editing and splicing easier.

CDs, or compact discs, were invented in 1979, and the first consumer CD players appeared in the early 1980s. The first was the **Sony CDP-101**, a stereo-component sized CD player first released in Japan in 1982. The next year it was released worldwide as the **Philips CD100**. The **Sony D-5/D-50 Discman**, the first portable player, was released in 1984. It was later rebranded as the Sony Walkman, taking the name of the company's earlier compact cassette tape player.

At the same time, ownership of personal computers was rising, providing another means of playing digital music. By the early 1990s sales of music CDs had surpassed those of compact cassettes and vinyl records.

With the arrival of the World Wide Web, it became possible to download and play digital music files on a computer without the need for any physical medium.

In 1997 the first **MP3 player**, the **MPMan F10**, was released by a South Korean company, **SaeHan Information Systems**. MP3 is a common audio coding standard that was released in 1994. The MPMan introduced to the public for the first time a portable music player with songs downloaded from a computer. It used flash memory for storage. There soon followed a number of similar commercial players from a variety of manufacturers.

In 2001 Apple released its first **iPod**. It was in fact a miniature computer with a hard drive, with an innovative circular control panel. Apple made several variations of the iPod over the next decade, including the mini, the nano and the shuffle. The full-size versions could also be used as an external storage device for digital files.

iPods popularized this category of device. They accounted for 90 percent of the market for hard-drive music players, and 70 percent of all players during the 2000s. iPods did, however, cause a crisis in the music industry, as sales of music media such as CDs dropped, and unlicensed copies of songs proliferated. The industry has since been forced to turn to online sales through Apple's own iTunes store or through licensing with online music services which rely on

1984 Sony Discman D50. Bamman / Creative Commons

1997 MPMan MP3 player. Michele M. F. / Creative Commons

2001 Apple iPod MP3 player.   Apple

customer subscriptions. It has not wholly recovered.

In the 2010s iPods began being displaced by iPhones and other smartphones which have the same music playing capabilities. In 2020 Apple was still offering an iPod, the Touch, but it is a minor part of the company's overall sales.

Digital text

A standard binary code for text was proposed in the US in 1963, called **ASCII** (American Standard Code for Information Interchange), which assigned a binary code to each of 128 characters, including upper and lower case letters, numbers and punctuation marks. It didn't achieve universal use until IBM adopted it for their personal computers. Different countries made minor variations of it.

In the 1980s a more universal code was proposed, called **Unicode**. It solved a few limitations with ASCII and greatly expanded the character set, and is widely used today.

Word processing: Electric typewriters first appeared in the 1910s and 1920s,

eventually leading to the most successful models by **Remington** and **IBM**, particularly the latter's Selectric model.

IBM coined the term 'word processor' in the late 1960s with the release of their **MT/ST** typewriter. It had some automated capabilities using commands from a magnetic tape, allowing it to type out form letters and the like. The tapes were later replaced with magnetic cards.

In the 1970s several companies released word processors featuring CRT screens which displayed text being entered. A model by **Wang Laboratories** was particularly successful, and resembled in most ways an early personal computer. By the mid-1970s the machines being marketed were true micro-computers, using integrated circuits and a digital operating system, and the first 5¼-inch floppy disks, which had come on the market in 1976 from IBM.

Also in 1976 Apple began selling its first personal computer, the Apple I, launching the PC industry. In 1981 IBM offered the first PCs running Microsoft's MS-DOS. These machines did everything word processors did at more affordable prices. As a result, the concept of word processing went from machines to software.

A few early word processing applications appeared in the 1970s, first **Electric Pencil** from Michael Shrayer Software in 1976, and then **Wordstar** in 1978, which enjoyed brief success. **Satellite Software International** released **WordPerfect** in 1982, designed for use with MS-DOS, to which Wordstar had failed to adapt, and capture the market. In 1983 Microsoft released its first version of **Word**. When Microsoft introduced its first Windows operating system in 1985, WordPerfect was unable to make a successful transfer, and Word became the dominant application on the market, a position it has enjoyed ever since on both PCs and Macintoshes, although there are numerous other word processing applications for both platforms.

Digital print design

Manual paste-up of phototypeset columns of text on paper was still how print products were designed in the 1980s. But when the Mac came out with its graphical user interface, designers saw the potential of doing their work on a PC.

Steve Jobs had understood the value of typography, and the Macintosh was designed to accomodate that, with the ability to use digital versions of typefaces.

The **Adobe** corporation was launched in 1982 by **John Warnock** and **Charles Geschke**, who had been working at the Xerox PARC lab. They wrote **Postscript** code, which translates a digitally designed document into data that allows a printer to accurately reproduce the document. Postscript has been the foundation of digital printing technology. Its code precisely describes all the features of typefaces that comply with it, including character shapes and spacing, so that print output matches the digital display.

Jobs first attempted to buy Adobe, but the offer was declined. Instead Apple licensed Postscript for use in its computers, which was one of the reasons print designers were attracted to the Macintosh for their work.

In 1985 Adobe began work on **Illustrator**, a vector drawing program, and released its first version in 1988, called Illustrator 88. With Adobe's purchase of Photoshop and its release in 1990, Adobe was offering some of the most popular design applications.

The **Aldus** company released **Pagemaker** in 1985, the first widely used publication design application for the Macintosh. Aldus

also released a competing application to Illustrator, **Freehand**.

The **Quark** company released **Xpress** in 1987, which provided more precise page design and typographic control for print documents than Pagemaker. It quickly became the industry standard, a position it held through the 1990s.

Lacking its own page design application, Adobe acquired Pagemaker when it merged with Aldus in 1994, but couldn't dislodge Quark Xpress from its dominant position until it released **InDesign** in 1999, with comparable features to Xpress. In 2002, when Apple released OS X, Quark failed to make Xpress compatible with the new operating system, giving InDesign an opening to capture the market, which it did very quickly and decisively within a few years.

Adobe also acquired Freehand when it purchased the Macromedia company in 2005, which had acquired the vector application during the Adobe-Aldus merger in 1994. Adobe subsequently shelved Freehand.

By this time Adobe held a near monopoly on industry-standard design applications with Photoshop, Illustrator and InDesign, a position it continued to fortify with the addition of a range of other applications, expanding into Web design and video editing. In 2002 it began bundling all its applications as a single purchase called the **Creative Suite**. This continued until 2013 when it switched to an online subscription model and renamed it the **Creative Cloud**. Access to it, which by 2020 included more than 20 different applications, has required a monthly fee since then, as well as Internet connectivity.

By the early 2000s digital print design had mostly replaced paste-up. It was now possible to design print publications on a desktop computer and make printing plates from the digital documents. Furthermore, the sophistication of graphics applications made it easier to do creative designs.

Digital design has also vastly expanded the number of available typefaces. Whereas in the analog world one had to manually switch entire sets of type slugs, or matrices in a Linotype machine, or font disks in a phototypesetter, not just for a different typeface but for each size, on a computer it's a simple matter of installing digital versions and choosing them from a menu. Whether that has contributed to better quality design is debatable in some cases.

Photos and video

Digital images consist of rows of pixels. Software for displaying and modifying them first came out in the 1980s along with the first Macs and PCs that had graphical user interfaces, meaning that photos could be displayed on their screens. The first Mac came with two graphics applications, **MacPaint** and **MacDraw**. MacPaint displayed images through different values of grayscale pixels, and had tools such as virtual paintbrushes with which one could create images composed of lighter and darker pixels (the first Macs and PCs only had grayscale monitors). This is called a **Bitmap** or **Raster** application. MacDraw had tools that created anchor points which were connected to each other with lines, creating shapes which could be filled with different levels of gray. This is called a **Vector** application.

The first version of Microsoft Windows, released in 1985, came with **Paint**, a counterpart to MacPaint.

In 1987 both Macs and PCs started supporting color monitors. That year **Photoshop** was created by brothers **Thomas** and **John Knoll**, on a Macintosh Plus. In 1988 Adobe bought a distribution license from them, and in 1990 Photoshop 1.0 was released for the Macintosh.

A Windows version came in 1993. It has become the industry standard for processing digital and scanned photos for both print and Web use.

Scanners: Image scanners are devices to convert physical objects such as prints of photos into digital data. The first one was made in 1957 at the US National Bureau of Standards by a team led by **Russell A. Kirsch**. It was a drum scanner originally intended to convert print data sheets into digital data. It worked with photosensors that detected lighter or darker parts of an image and assigned them a digital value. Kirsch used it to make the first ever scan of a photo, one of his three-month-old son, resulting in a grayscale digital image 176 pixels wide. Computers at the time didn't have displays, but they were able to see the scan results through a CRT oscilloscope connected to a computer.

Drum scanners were used at first by commercial photo labs as they were preferable for scanning film negatives. But in the 1980s flatbed scanners started

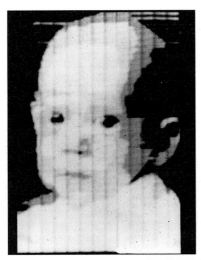

Russell A. Kirsch / NIST

A digital scan of a photo, one of the first ever, from 1957 done at the US National Bureau of Standards, of team leader Russell A. Kirsch's infant son.

coming on the market, and by the 1990s were of sufficiently good quality to make most drum scanners obsolete, and soon were reasonably priced enough to become consumer products.

Digital cameras: These didn't enter the consumer market until the 1990s. The technology for making digital photos wasn't the problem, it was making a small and lightweight camera with sufficient data storage, processing power and battery life at an affordable price.

NASA started using digital cameras in their space probes in the 1960s. The first photos of the moon's surface were sent back to Earth as digital data and enhanced on computers, in a project to make a complete map of the moon's surface. The US government also used digital imaging in its spy satellites. Development of the technology for these uses helped improve digital photography.

Cameras with some electronic features appeared as early as the 1970s, but still relied on film for stills and magnetic tape for video.

Converting light into digital data is done with a **CCD**, a charged coupled device, or a **CMOS**, a complementary metal oxide semiconductor. CCDs were invented by **Willard Boyle** and **George E. Smith** at Bell Labs in the 1960s. These integrated circuits use arrays of light-sensitive diodes to convert light into static charges that are then converted into digital values. A CCD only captures and stores light energy as an electric charge, whereas a CMOS also does the conversion to digital data.

The basis for CCD technology is **Albert Einstein's** 1905 discovery of the photoelectric effect, in which he showed that light energy striking a surface caused electrons to be knocked loose, which could be converted into electrical energy. This is the principle behind all digital cameras (and solar energy panels).

In 1983 Sony released the first consumer camcorder, the **Betamovie BMC-100P**, combining a video camera with a video cassette recorder into one device, using CCD technology. Quickly other manufacturers followed suit.

Digital cameras

A CCD or a CMOS is an integrated circuit consisting of an array of photodiodes, which are transistors connected to light-sensitive materials, and capacitors, which hold a static charge, linked together in a circuit.

When the camera shutter is opened and light strikes each photodiode, energy is captured and built up in its coupled capacitor until the shutter is closed.

The charge's relative strength is then converted into a digital value, which determines the color of a pixel in the resulting image.

All digital cameras work this way, whether full-size SLRs or cell phones. Quality is determined by the amount of pixels, and sensitivity and size of photodiodes.

Lens

CMOS chip

Photodiodes

Cell for one pixel

Filters divide light into red, green and blue wavelengths.

The amount of each wavelength is recorded, and converted to a digital value.

77 95 50

When the image is viewed, the pixel will be displayed according to the digital value.

In 1986 Kodak created a mega-pixel sensor capable of recording 1.4 million pixels, enough to produce a 5 x 7-inch print. In 1991 the company released the first digital single lens reflex camera, or DSLR, the **DCS-100**, using a 1.3-megapixel sensor mounted inside a Nikon F3 SLR in place of the film roll. It came with an external 200-megabyte hard drive on which to store the photos, which could hold about 160 shots, but had to be carried separately. With a $20,000 sticker price, the intended market was photojournalists with the hope that news operations would cover the expense. Many did.

Digital cameras more affordable to the public arrived in 1994 with the **Apple QuickTake 100**, in 1995 with the **Kodak DC40** and the **Casio QV-11**, and in 1996 with the **Sony Cyber-Shot**. These came with a cable allowing the camera to be connected to a computer in order to download the photos.

Over the next couple of decades pixel and storage capacity went up as cost came down, resulting in a wide range of high-quality digital cameras and making film obsolete except for some high-end professional use. And eventually cameras became small enough to fit inside other devices such as smartphones.

The same technology resulted in digital video cameras that no longer used magnetic tape, as data storage capabilities increased enough to handle the much larger files that video produces. This made video editing easier, and specialty software has proliferated for this purpose, from professional applications such as Adobe's **Premiere Pro** and Apple's **Final Cut Pro**, to a wide range of low-cost to free applications.

Most modern digital cameras, and even smartphones, can now shoot both still and video images, and have sufficient data storage capacity.

Digital movies

Commercial film has been the last medium to convert completely to digital. As briefly discussed in the chapter on photography and film, the transition has been incremental due to two factors. One is the expense for theaters, since a digital projector costs as much as $150,000. The other is resistance from some in the industry, particularly directors who feel that traditional film retains a visual quality that cannot be reproduced digitally. This sentiment is also shared by some professionals and enthusiasts in still photography, as well as in audio recording and playback.

But major film studios are slowly moving to digital. Several of them, notably **Paramount Studios**, no longer produce any movies on film.

A more noticeable impact that digital technology has had on movies is with special effects and animation. Up until the 1980s most special effects were created through analog methods, with models and painted backdrops. The earliest but very limited use of **CGI**, or Computer Generated Imagery, was in the 1958 Hitchcock movie *Vertigo*, to create animated patterns. Its use was limited for the next two decades. In the 1980s there was a series of breakthrough films, such as *Tron* in 1982, in which a significant part of the movie was computer generated. In the 1990s, with new software and increased processing power, effects became highly realistic, as with *Jurassic Park*'s CGI dinosaurs, and animation seamless, as in Steve Jobs' **Pixar Studios** movies such as *Toy Story*.

From that point on CGI became both common and increasingly sophisticated, and cost-effective enough for television series as well as movies, to the point of being taken for granted today.

The Internet

The terms Internet and Web are often used interchangeably, but they're not the same. The Internet is the infrastructure: all the cables and servers and other hardware that allow communication between digital devices. The Web is the data that gets transmitted over the Internet. And it took a while to develop and build that infrastructure before the Web as we know it could begin.

Origins of the Internet

Research and development of the Internet was largely funded by the US Department of Defense at first, through the Defense Advanced Research Projects Agency (DARPA, later shortened to ARPA), which had been created by US President Eisenhower in 1958 in the early years of the Cold War between the US and the Soviet Union. In that year the Soviets launched the first satellite, Sputnik, which caused alarm in the US military establishment. There was also concern following the 1962 Cuban missile crisis that the military's communication systems were vulnerable, especially in the event of a nuclear attack.

The Internet was first proposed in 1962 by **J.C.R. Licklider**, an MIT researcher at DARPA. His concept, which he called the 'Galactic Network,' was a proposal for computers to exchange messages over the existing telephone network.

In 1965 an experimental connection was tried over the phone between computers in Massachusetts and in California. The experiment highlighted a problem. Phone calls are closed circuits between two phones, during which no one else can contact either participant. It would be too limiting for a computer network if for each message a single circuit connection had to be made between the sender and recipient, the message delivered, and then the circuit disconnected, as happens with a phone call.

So a different method was devised, called **packet switching**, in which messages would be broken up into small packets, each of which would travel separately, and be reassembled at the recipient's end. This would allow multiple documents and data to all travel at the same time, and for a computer to receive multiple documents at any time while maintaining a constant network connection.

The packet switching concept was conceived by several groups at nearly the same time, at MIT (Massachusetts Institute of Technology), at RAND (Research And Development), a government-funded think tank for military planning, and at the United Kingdom's NPL (National Physical Laboratory).

ARPANET is launched

The next experiment took place in September of 1969 between computers at UCLA and Stanford universities, both in California, resulting in a successful message exchange using packet switching. Two more universities, UC Santa Barbara and Utah, were added to the network, and the Internet was born. The network was named ARPANET.

More connections, called nodes, were added, typically at research institutions with mainframes, as this was still years before personal computers would arrive.

In 1971 the first email was sent by **Ray Tomlinson**, who established the convention of the @ between the user name and the name of the computer storing the message.

In 1972 the first public demonstration of ARPANET took place at a computer conference in Washington DC.

Several problems remained to be solved as ARPANET grew. Technically it was a broad network connecting local networks, each of which had protocols different from each other, making it difficult to communicate with a user in a different network. A universal system was necessary, which became known as the Internet Protocol, or **IP address**, a string of numbers assigned to each connected computer. Transmission Control Protocol, or **TCP**, which is the system that controls how packets are delivered, was improved with the addition of IP addresses. In 1983 the combined system, **TCP/IP**, became the accepted way that ARPANET was organized.

But it was difficult to remember IP addresses, being just numbers, so by 1984 the Domain Name System, or **DNS**, was established, which provided a unique name for each address. Now a computer address whose IP was 12.345.678.99 could also be found by a name such as www.mysite.com, now commonly called a domain name.

Expansion

In the 1970s the only people using ARPANET were working in research institutions and in the military, fulfilling its original purpose. In 1975 there were still only 57 nodes. But even by then the military had growing concerns about who had access. There was no real control. When personal computers became available in the late 1970s, the number of connections greatly increased.

Public awareness, and the military's fears, were heightened with the 1983 movie *War Games*, in which a teenager is able to connect to the NORAD super computer and almost start World War III.

In response the Department of Defense split the network into two parts, ARPANET for researchers and MILNET for the military, with restricted access to the latter. Governmental control of ARPANET shifted largely to the National Science Foundation, which had its own network, NSFNET, leaving a separate network for academia, CSNET. Commercial use wasn't allowed, and if one weren't in research and academia, access was limited.

But public interest in email was growing, which led to the first commercial email systems in the late 1980s. At this point the Internet was still a loose connection between both government and corporate networks. Several companies including IBM and MCI wanted to expand their business capabilities over the national network, and formed a corporation to sell corporate

A bulletin board service from the 1980s and early 1990s. Entirely text-based, it could be navigated with keyboard commands. The first BBS's appeared before graphical user interfaces and computer mice were available.

Internet access, and reached an agreement with the NSF to do this. Several Internet service providers then formed a network called **CIX**, Commercial Internet Exchange. As other ISPs joined CIX, it became the central point through which all data was transferred, effectively unifying all the networks into one. CIX is now referred to as 'the backbone of the Internet.' Now both business and non-profit organizations were using the same network, laying the groundwork for commercialization of the Internet. And with CIX the public would now have access to the Internet, through the service providers.

In 1990 ARPANET was officially decommissioned and the government relinquished control, leaving it in the public domain. But getting online and finding anything of use was still difficult, and mostly limited to those with the technical knowledge to do so. There were no websites as we know them today, no easy-to-use software, and no standardized way to format information.

BBS's

In 1990 Internet options were mostly limited to email and to **BBS's**, or Bulletin Board Services, which were rudimentary text-based websites where one could read and post messages and exchange documents and photos.

The first BBS was created by two computer enthusiasts in 1978, **Ward Christensen** and **Randy Suess**, in Chicago during a blizzard, to allow their computer club to meet online. The software they wrote, CBBS, became widely used, resulting in a proliferation of BBS's on the Internet.

HTML

In 1989 **Tim Berners-Lee**, a scientist at CERN, the French nuclear research agency (where the first touchscreen was invented in the 1970s), proposed making a universal code for documents posted on the Internet, and in 1990 he created **HTML**, or Hyper Text Markup Language. It was a simple way to codify any document so that it

HTML

Tim Berners Lee's code, Hypertext Markup Language, is the standard code used to format content on the Web.

It is very simple at its most basic level. In writing the code, blocks of text are enclosed inside of tags, like this:

```
<h1>Headline</h1>
<p>This is a block of text in a paragraph.</p>
```

A hyperlink looks like this:

```
<p>This is a link to a document:
<a href="http://doc1.html">Document 1</a></p>
```

And this line adds an image:

```
<img src="tomato.jpg" alt="tomatoes photo" />
```

Modern Web design is much more complicated, however, and involves several other coding languages to add styles and interactive functionality.

This is what it will look like in a Web browser:

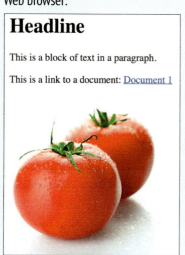

Headline

This is a block of text in a paragraph.

This is a link to a document: Document 1

could then be displayed through the use of an application called a **browser**.

Berners-Lee had already created a prototype of the code in 1980 called ENQUIRE, with which he demonstrated **hypertext**, which embeds in a section of text links to other text or documents. This became an important component of HTML, allowing documents to be linked to each other.

His proposal wasn't the only one, others had been proposed. But Berners-Lee made HTML free for anyone to use, leading to its widespread adoption. He also created a simple browser for it, but it only worked on the operating system for Steve Jobs' new computer company, NeXT.

Web browsers

HTML was gaining acceptance as the standard code for online documents, but was still lacking an application to display it. This was provided by two graduate students at the University of Illinois Urbana-Champaign, **Marc Andreessen** and **Eric Bina**. In 1993 they published **Mosaic**, the first widely used Web browser for both Mac and Windows. There were earlier browsers including ViolaWWW and Cello, but Mosaic was the first to allow images to be shown in the same window as text.

With this confluence of HTML, a browser and public access to the Internet, the **World Wide Web** could be said to have been born. But it still wasn't easy to access. Windows still didn't support TCP/IP, and accessing an ISP was complicated. And once online, there wasn't anywhere near the wealth of content that we now enjoy. But many people were not discouraged. Mosaic was free, and within months of its release more than 5,000 copies were being downloaded every month. Within a year the rate had risen to 50,000 copies a month. The Web had quickly become popular.

Andreesen and Bina quickly saw the market possibilities of their invention, and in 1994 released the first commercial browser, **Netscape Navigator**. It made it easier to access and use the Web, and quickly dominated the market. When it went public in 1995 it quickly reached a billion dollars in valuation.

Microsoft had lagged in adapting to the Web, but set about obtaining their own browser. Called **Internet Explorer**, its code was purchased from another company, **Spyglass**. It was released along with their OS upgrade, Windows 95, first as a free add-on, and then controversially bundled with the OS, so that it was automatically installed on every Windows machine. Further, it was the default browser, and it was difficult to install a different one.

Netscape and Spyglass sued Microsoft, and the US Department of Justice took up the case on antitrust grounds. The case was finally resolved in 1999, finding Microsoft guilty of acting as an illegal monopoly. But by then it was too late. Explorer was the dominant browser due to Windows' dominance of the PC market, and Netscape never recovered.

Netscape ceased operations in 2007. But by then Andreeson had already publicly released Navigator's source code, which was used by **Mozilla**, a not-for-profit organization, to create the **Firefox** browser.

The modern Web

In the meantime the Web was expanding and getting populated with new sites at a multiplying rate, while at the same time the number of users was growing rapidly. Commerce was now okay, and it became obligatory for every business to have its own site. And advertising started appearing: In 1994 the first banner ads appeared, for Zima and for AT&T, and Pizza Hut started taking orders online.

Key dates in Internet history

1969: ARPANET begins.

1972: First public demonstration of ARPANET.

1983: TCP/IP address system established.

1984: Domain name system established.

1987: Number of hosts surpasses 10,000.

1989: Number of hosts surpasses 100,000.

1990: ARPANET ends, World Wide Web begins with the creation of HTML.

1992: Number of hosts surpasses 1 million.

1993: Mosaic web browser released.

1994: Netscape Navigator is released. Yahoo! search engine is launched. Amazon Books is launched.

1995: Microsoft releases Internet Explorer. Dial-up service providers start: America Online, Compuserv, Prodigy. eBay is launched.

1997: Google search engine is launched.

1998: 2 millionth domain name is registered.

2000: 7% of people worldwide and 43% in US use the Internet.

2003: iTunes and Safari are released.

2004: Facebook is launched.

2005: YouTube is launched.

2006: Twitter is launched. More than 439 million computers have an IP address worldwide. 92 million websites worldwide.

2007: Apple releases first iPhone. iTunes downloads surpass 1 billion. Google becomes most visited website.

2008: First Android phone is released. Apple opens App store, Google opens Android Market.

2009: 24% of people worldwide and 75% in US use the Internet.

2010: Apple releases first iPad. Instagram is launched.

2019: 54% of people worldwide and 89% in US use the Internet.

Tim Berners-Lee 1955-

Berners-Lee is often credited as the 'inventor of the Web' for having in 1990 created HTML, the standard code used for Web documents and to create websites.

He is a professorial research fellow in the Computer Science Department at the University of Oxford, director of the World Wide Web Consortium (known as W3C), director of the World Wide Web Foundation, president and founder of the Open Data Institute in London, and is involved in a number of other Web-related organizations.

Berners-Lee was born in London and graduated from Oxford in 1976. He worked at CERN in 1980, where he designed a precursor to HTML called ENQUIRE, in which he demonstrated the use of hypertext, a key component of HTML. He returned to CERN in 1984, and in 1989 made his proposal for HTML, completing it in late 1990. Using the code, he created the world's first website, which can still be seen at:

http://info.cern.ch/hypertext/WWW/TheProject.html

He also created the first web browser.

In 2004 he was knighted by Queen Elizabeth II. He has received honorary degrees from Manchester, Harvard and Yale. He leads the Solid (Social Linked Data) project, which aims to improve data privacy and ownership on the Web.

Internet hardware

For most people accessing the Internet in its early days could only be done through a **modem** connected to a phone line.

A type of modem was in use as early as the 1920s to send telegrams over phone lines. A teletype machine would print out the message. The first commercial modem for computers came out in 1962, the **Bell 103** made by AT&T. It had a transmission rate of 300 bits per second, which, when considering that each character in a word needs eight bits, amounted to roughly seven or eight average words per second, or a painfully slow 450 words in a minute.

Dale Heatherington and **Dennis Hayes** made the first modem for use with PCs in 1977. They founded **Hayes Microcomputer Products**, which became the leading seller of PC modems through the 1980s. They made a modem board that could be installed in the Apple II, boosting Apple sales and making it a popular choice for BBS hosts and users.

Modem speeds fortunately increased by 1990, reaching 9,600 bps, then 14,400 in 1991, and doubling that by 1994. The top speed of 56k was reached in 1996. This was adequate for text, but for photos and graphics was still slow. In addition, dial-up modems tied up a phone line, which was inconvenient and could result in long distance fees if there was not a local number available for an ISP.

High-speed Internet

Cable TV had been available in the US since as early as 1948. By the 1980s more than half of all households in the US subscribed to a cable provider.

In the 1990s upgrades to the network with fiber optic and coaxial cables allowed cable providers, which now came to be called **ISPs**, or Internet Service Providers, to start offering high-speed Internet access. Bundled services of TV, Internet and phone became common, and as subscriptions rose, more people could now discard their dial-up modems and enjoy substantially faster Internet speeds.

In 2020 there were over 100 million broadband Internet subscribers in the US, but there are still rural areas that the cable network doesn't reach. In most of the industrialized world, high-speed Internet access through fiber optic cables is common.

Using the Internet

In order to get on the Internet and find information, for example in a Google search, certain hardware and software requirements must be met.

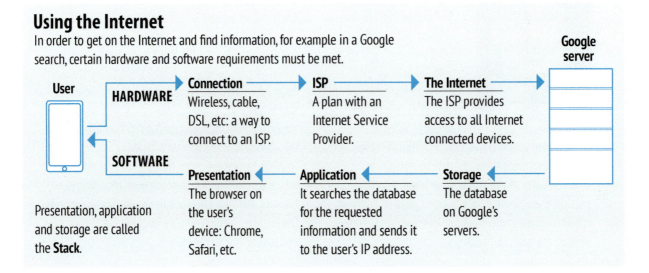

User

HARDWARE

SOFTWARE

Presentation, application and storage are called the **Stack**.

Connection — Wireless, cable, DSL, etc: a way to connect to an ISP.

ISP — A plan with an Internet Service Provider.

The Internet — The ISP provides access to all Internet connected devices.

Google server

Presentation — The browser on the user's device: Chrome, Safari, etc.

Application — It searches the database for the requested information and sends it to the user's IP address.

Storage — The database on Google's servers.

The digital transformation

In the Digital Age, virtually all communication involves computers. Clearly the Internet does, but so do all other platforms, since almost all information has been digitized and turned into binary code. Even print is overwhelmingly designed on computers, and printing plates are made from digital data before being placed in presses, which are controlled by computers, which are also used at every step in press operation, inventory and distribution. There are still a few pockets of the industry where analog technology is used such as phototypesetters and manual paste-up, but that is increasingly rare.

This transformation happened in a few decades, beginning in the 1970s and '80s as computers became practical and affordable for business use, and in the 1990s as public access to the Web increased interest in computers for personal use, and consumer products such as digital cameras started to become available.

As more people started using the Web, companies that would become dominant in their markets made their first appearances: Amazon, Google, Yahoo, Facebook, Twitter. In the first decades of the 21st century social media would become a preferred destination for the majority of Web users.

All of this was only possible because of several key technological innovations:

1950s: Transistors and integrated circuits were the necessary first step before portable electronics, personal computers and smartphones could be possible.

1969: Packet switching technology made the start of the Internet possible.

1970s: The first personal computers, such as the Altair and the Apple II, made home ownership of a computer possible.

1984: The Macintosh with a graphical user interface made PCs easy and fun to use, and allowed both production and consumption of every kind of media.

1989: The Motorola MicroTAK, the first pocket-size mobile flip phone, started the trend of mobile phone use in the 1990s.

1990: The World Wide Web began with the release of the Internet into the public domain, and the introduction of HTML code, which standardized Web documents and sites.

1993: The first widely used Web browser, Mosaic, followed by Netscape Navigator and Microsoft Explorer, made Web use easier, more visual, and interactive.

1998: The introduction of the 3G network gave mobile phones Internet access.

2004: Facebook was launched, popularizing the use of social media platforms.

2005: YouTube was launched, popularizing the posting and watching of personal videos online.

2006: Twitter was launched.

2007: The first iPhone was released, popularizing smartphones, which increased the popularity of social media and increased Web use among the public. One no longer needed to sit in front of a desktop or laptop computer in order to access the Web.
In the same year, Google became the most visited website, becoming the primary reference source for most people.

In the developed world of the 21st century, the Internet has increasingly influenced virtually every aspect of people's lives as it has become most people's primary source of information and communication. As a result the balance of power in everything from retail to politics to news and entertainment has shifted dramatically. A comparison between pre- and post-Web times in any field would likely reveal dramatic changes. Some examples:

• **News:** Traditional news media, both in print and broadcast, has continued to lose audience to the Internet, in particular to social media such as Facebook. Most people are more likely to learn about breaking news from social media postings than from any other source, even though the post probably links to a news media website.

• **Entertainment:** TV shows, movies, sporting events and music are increasingly being accessed online, as over-air and cable broadcast is being supplanted by Internet streaming and subscription services. And an increasing amount of content prepared solely for online access has begun to capture public attention, such as on YouTube channels.

• **Politics:** Social messaging and online content have shown the power to decide political elections, and in general to shape the public's opinions on any topic. To be successful, political campaigns increasingly rely on social media and online messaging.

• **Commerce:** An increasingly large amount of commerce has shifted to online transactions, fueling the dominance of retailers such as Amazon while causing the decline of brick-and-mortar stores. The vast majority of retail and service

establishments have found it necessary to have an online presence and to be able to conduct transactions online. Banking and financial transactions also are increasingly conducted online. A side effect has been the increasing use of credit card and debit transactions instead of through paper money and coins.

• **Education:** Classroom instruction is beginning to shift online, particularly in higher education. Some universities are offering online degree programs, as well as MOOCs, Massive Open Online Courses, online lectures available for free to anyone. Also, commercial subscription websites offer instructional videos in a wide range of technical areas. For that matter, anyone looking to do any number of activities from learning to play a musical instrument to doing car repairs can probably find instructions posted by other people on YouTube or elsewhere online.

• **Social interactions:** People's social lives are increasingly being organized and conducted online through meetup groups and dating apps, while at the same time an increasing amount of many people's interactions are taking place on social media platforms such as Facebook and Twitter.

It would in fact be difficult to name a single field, from industrial design and production to scientific research, from agriculture to commercial transport, that doesn't rely on computers, digital data and Internet connectivity.

For those young enough to have been born into the Digital Age, all of these topics might seem obvious and a description of everyday life, but in each case it is a dramatic change from how things were done before the advent of the Web. The digital revolution is the latest in a string

Percentage of people worldwide using the Internet, 2001-2019

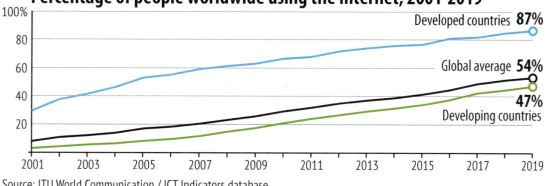

Developed countries **87%**

Global average **54%**

47%
Developing countries

Source: ITU World Communication / ICT Indicators database

Number of people using the Internet by region, 2019

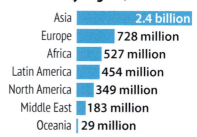

Region	
Asia	**2.4 billion**
Europe	**728 million**
Africa	**527 million**
Latin America	**454 million**
North America	**349 million**
Middle East	**183 million**
Oceania	**29 million**

Latin America includes South and Central America and the Caribbean

Source: Internet World Stats: March 2019

Facebook users, 2008-2019

Number of monthly active Facebook users, in billions

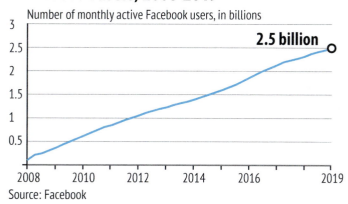

2.5 billion

Source: Facebook

---

of marked social upheavals that were first sparked by the industrial revolutions, all of which have brought about significant changes in society and culture. By many metrics this latest revolution appears to be unfolding the most rapidly, and in some ways is the most dramatic in history.

As with many revolutions, the disruptions have had negative consequences as well. The ease with which anyone can post information on the Web has taken away editorial control from established media operations, resulting in the dissemination of false and misleading information, which is contributing to the political and social polarization of society. Also, people's private data, gathered by a wide range of industries, has been repeatedly breached, raising concerns about privacy.

And there is an unanticipated problem that will occur in the future: Digital storage of data is inherently fragile. There is no practical way to store electronic data for hundreds, much less thousands of years: Magnetic media and static storage devices lose their charges in a few decades, and CDs, which use dye, fade equally as fast. Also, software to read the data becomes obsolete just as fast. Unlike with Mesopotamian clay tablets which are still intact after five millenia, it's possible that we will leave no trace of our lives for future historians.

But the Internet and the digital world is difficult for any government or entity to control, as hard as some have tried.

Conclusion

We have now covered five and a half thousand years of technology, from the simplest writing media to the most complex digital devices in current use: from clay tablets to smartphones.

In those places where writing first appeared at the beginning of recorded history, the most advanced form of communication has now taken hold. China, with almost a fifth of the World's population, had more than 850 million Internet users in 2020, more than half of all users on Earth. India was second, with 560 million users. Egypt and Iraq (formerly Mesopotamia) are considered part of the developing world, and have lower percentages of Internet use, but still in 2020 there were almost 50 million people online in Egypt and 21 million in Iraq, roughly half of each country's population.

This is the trend in almost every country, with worldwide connectivity reaching more than half of humanity by the second decade of the 21st Century, a trend that will likely keep growing at a rapid pace. Barring some unforseen change of circumstances, it appears that virtually the entire human race will soon be digitally connected.

Many of the topics covered in this book might seem mundane and not terribly relevant to the contemporary world. Who needs to know about the origins of Proto-Sinaitic or Cyrillic languages, or how Gutenberg made type slugs, or how vacuum tubes work? But all of these minutiae are not isolated historical details. Mankind wasn't going to go straight from cave paintings to the Internet, all the intermediate technological steps that we've covered were needed to arrive at the forms of communication that are currently shaping our contemporary world. Here are the key moments in our timeline:

Pre- and early history: All of our current political and societal structures have their roots in the earliest permanent settlements and the establishment of the first cities. This is where people first learned how to co-exist in urban settings, create the legal systems required to do so, and establish commerce and trade. It also created the need for written language, which would have been necessary for governing and trade.

Writing: The way that written language evolved influenced how communication technology was developed. The jump from logosyllabic and pictographic writing systems to alphabetic ones in the West proved to be advantageous in the development of printing systems, and is likely one of the factors that led to moveable type presses having a stronger impact in Europe than in Asia.

It's also important to understand the different writing systems around the world, their cultural roots, and what issues this raises in a modern global economy. And it's important to recognize how foundational these centuries- and millenia-old writing systems still are to modern communication.

Paper and printing: Paper was a significant advancement in communication, providing a convenient, portable and relatively inexpensive medium. It was also a necessary development for printing presses, which require standard sizes and weights of paper in order to function.

Moveable type presses were, of course, a revolutionary invention, making possible for the first time mass communication, which in turn led to significant societal shifts as literacy rates rose and information became more accessible to larger segments of the population. Ink on paper became the dominant platform for communication across the world from the 15th through the 20th centuries.

Industrial Age technologies: Advances in energy, metals, plastics and chemistry were necessary for every modern communication technology, from industrial printing to electronics. Electricity is central to all modern technology and is arguably the most transformative development in human existence since the control of fire some two million years ago. In order to understand how modern communication works, a basic knowledge of electricity is necessary, and how it is used in electronic devices.

Photography: Being able to capture reality at a moment in time, and to preserve it in a reproduceable image, provided a new way to communicate information besides text, and in a more authoritative manner than with illustrations. Still photography also provided the technology to make movies, leading to the film industry, followed by TV content and videos, which have all had significant influences on cultural and social norms.

Technology has also made it practical and affordable for anyone to make their own photos and videos, which now populate social media platforms.

Electronics: From the first speculations about the nature of electricity and its relationship to magnetism, to the discoveries of the wave-like nature of electromagnetic energy, to the inventions for which it was harnessed is a remarkable story. Electricity radically changed communication with the appearance of broadcast and recorded media, making information more immediate and accessible to the world in ways that print could not accommodate. And electronics laid the foundation for digital media.

The Digital Age: Digital media were developed out of analog electronics. Media content that is created on computers is often a virtual version of its analog form: Digital print design is a virtual equivalent of a paste-up board and drafting table, Photoshop is a virtual darkroom, and digital audio files are virtual vinyl records and magnetic tape in the same way that digital videos are virtual film. So there is nothing new about the media forms, what is different is how they are made, using digital tools instead of analog or physical ones. These new tools, however, did expand the possibilities of what could be created while also making it easier to create sophisticated content, and making the process affordable and accessible to more people.

The Internet is a new and radical idea, although it still uses analog metaphors: Web pages for example, and is mostly used to deliver the same content that was printed on paper: words and pictures. Its major impact is in convenience and accessibility, not in a major shift in the content itself but in ease of production and distribution: One doesn't need to own a printing press anymore, just the rights to a website, or even just a social media account. A news story on a website is little different in form and content from a news story printed in a newspaper, it's simply easier to access, at least in those parts of the world that have the Internet. But because both production and access are so much easier, it has enabled many more people to publish their own content, with little or none of the editorial checks that a news organization provides. One could cynically say that what the Internet provides is considerably more quantity without noticeable improvement in quality, but there is something to be said in favor of the ease of obtaining the wealth of information that the Internet provides.

As our theme has been throughout this book, it is only possible to get a comprehensive view of how communication has arrived at its current state by understanding all the previous developments, from the evolution of writing systems to the first forms of mass communication to the industrial revolutions to the invention of electronics. There is a thread running throughout the entirety of recorded history, as each new medium was built upon previous ones, usually to address its predecessors' shortcomings.

Paper replaced clay tablets and bamboo, which were cumbersome and difficult to store and transport, and papyrus, which was labor-intensive to make and hard to preserve. Printing presses replaced ink-and-quill hand-written copies. The telegraph could send a message nearly instantaneously over long distances while mailing a letter could take weeks or months. The telephone didn't need to be decoded by a trained operator. The radio didn't need telephone wires, and could be heard by broad audiences instead of just one person.

Photography created images more quickly and economically than illustrations, and more true to life. Moving pictures could tell stories. Television was more versatile and convenient than going to a movie theater, and delivered much more content, including movies.

Magnetic tape was reusable and more versatile and economical than vinyl records. Video tape had the same advantages over celluloid film.

Digital media made production of all previous media types, from print to audio to video, easier while providing greater versatility, efficiency and capabilities.

And the Internet provided far greater convenience and capacity for delivering all forms of content, while adding interactivity and the ability for anyone to self-publish.

Each new step in technology came about through the work of some inventor, or more often, the sequential work of several inventors, who saw the possibility of improving on what existed. Through most of history these were independent entrepreneurs, often pursuing their fortune, sometimes putting their economic futures on the line.

But even with a successful invention, fame and fortune were not guaranteed. Gutenberg lost his press to an investor when he couldn't pay his debts. Nicolas-Louis Robert, the maker of the first paper machine, never saw a profit from it. Friedrich Koenig, inventor of the first steam-powered press, suffered through patent disputes and infringements and died before enjoying financial reward. William Bullock, inventor of the web-fed rotary press, was killed by his own machine shortly after its implementation.

Nicéphore Niépce, the first photographer, died before his discovery could be commercialized. Similarly, Louis Le Prince, the maker of the first movie camera, disappeared mysteriously after boarding a train in 1890, leaving his device an unrealized curiosity. Perhaps the most tragic story is that of Nikola Tesla, who gave us our electrical power system and some key inventions necessary for radio, dying alone and in debt in a New York hotel room paid for by the man he made wealthy, George Westinghouse.

Others saw fame and financial success: Ottmar Mergenthaler, inventor of the Linotype, Thomas Edison for a lengthy list of inventions, Alexander Graham Bell for the telephone, George Eastman, founder of Kodak, Robert Noyce, developer of integrated circuits and cofounder of Intel.

History gets complicated and is unfortunately hazy at times. T'sai Lun is often given credit for the invention of paper in 190 CE, but scraps of paper have been found that are centuries older. It's possible that Lorens Coster invented the moveable type press and not Gutenberg. For that matter, Bi Sheng invented moveable type four centuries before Gutenberg, and the first metal-type printing took place in Korea before him as well.

Johann Philipp Reis made a functional telephone a decade before Bell, who might have stolen his version from Elisha Gray. It's possible that the only reason for Bell's success was in being first to the patent office.

We likely will never know the true history behind these events.

And then there are those who saw commercial possibilities in others' work and seized it. Guglielmo Marconi cobbled his radio together with the inventions of others, including Tesla's coil, and used it to establish his broadcast operations, while managing to co-opt Tesla's US patents along the way. Bill Gates didn't write Microsoft's first version of MS-DOS, it was acquired from another company. A lot of Microsoft's products for that matter have been imitations of existing applications: Windows copied a lot of the Macintosh OS features, as did Internet Explorer with Netscape. Steve Jobs wasn't a programmer or designer at all, the Apple I and II were created by Steve Wozniak, and the graphical user interface used for the Macintosh was invented at Bell Labs.

But perhaps these individuals deserve credit for being visionaries. Certainly Apple wouldn't exist without Jobs' seeing the commercial possibilities in Wozniak's work, and even if it had, the company likely would have folded before coming up with the succession of "i" products that Jobs envisioned: the iMac, iPod, iPhone and iPad. And Gates led Microsoft in dominating the business office PC market by making inexpensive desktop computers possible, which helped to popularize PCs with the public, a necessary step in the popularization of the Web.

One unfortunate historical trend reveals a social injustice: Almost all the inventors in the West who are given credit for significant inventions and discoveries from the 15th to the 20th centuries are white men. This is

iPhone 12. Smartphones incorporate almost all previous media in one way or another. Besides being telephones, they are computers, web browsers, cameras, music players and writing tablets that communicate through radio waves. They also incorporate the oldest and most fundamental aspect of communication, written language.

a cultural artifact: Women and minorities in most cultures, unless they were of nobility or of high social stature, were excluded from the education and financial backing needed to pursue such endeavors. This type of discrimination has still not been entirely addressed even into the first decades of the 21st century. There remains evidence of sexism in particular running through the engineering communities of Silicon Valley, and only within the last several decades have women and minorities been encouraged to pursue science and technology careers in most of the world. In the US, prior to the Civil Rights Act of 1968, blacks and other minorities were almost entirely excluded from higher education programs in the sciences.

So the history is messy, incomplete and rife with injustices. But in spite of that, technology has progressed, mostly driven by capitalist forces of supply and demand, with transformative inventions appearing at ever faster intervals, from millennia to centuries to decades.

Smartphones and tablets are the culmination and melding of almost all previously separate methods of communication. They combine the camera for both still photos and video, telephone, music player, ebook reader, writing tablet and Web browser, along with all the additional capabilities that can be added through the 2.8 million apps in the Google Play Store and 2.2 million apps in the Apple App Store, all in a pocket-size device that operates by radio waves. But the way most people use them still relies on the most ancient of codes, written language. They are the modern equivalent of clay tablets, papyrus scrolls, bamboo slips and sheets of paper, infinitely more complex but still largely used for the same purposes, to record and communicate information. Because of these devices' ubiquity there is probably now more written communication done in a single year than in all of previous history combined.

A few visionaries as far back as the 19th century predicted something like the Internet. Mark Twain had a device called a Telectroscope in an 1898 story, that displayed events from around the world in real time. Numerous science fiction writers had some version of it: George Orwell, Ray Bradbury, Isaac Asimov. Marshall McCluhan described it accurately in 1962.

So what can we predict of the future from this point in time?

The current trend indicates that the Internet will soon reach the remaining portion of the human population still lacking it, and that it will be the conduit of all media and communication. As smartphones have already done, media will merge through multimedia devices.

The print industry is still healthy, in spite of the decline of newspapers and magazines. Google Books has catalogued nearly 130 million book titles printed in the modern era, with an estimated 2.2 million new books printed each year across the globe. And a wide variety of other printed material are produced for numerous purposes and audiences. But Google itself has been busy scanning and digitizing its book catalog (inciting a number of lawsuits surrounding copyrights), and increasingly books are being made available in digital form to be read on electronic devices, as are newspapers and magazines.

If these trends continue, then the use of printing presses and radio and TV broadcast towers will become, if not obsolete, then niche products, while increasingly powerful wireless and satellite networks will provide near-universal Internet access, which will be the source and depository of most communication and information.

Moore's Law, the prediction that transistor density on integrated chips will double every two years, will probably hit a wall by the mid-2020s, but new types of computers might appear, including ones based on quantum theory, that could be orders of magnitude more capable. Given mankind's demonstrated ingenuity, it's a safe bet that digital devices will continue to gain in power and capability.

It's an open question as to how much of our daily lives will start taking place in virtual spaces, but that technology already exists and continues to increase in sophistication. It's possible that many future interactions, both professional and social, will be done in this manner, which, after all, is a staple in science fiction movies. Whether that would have cultural effects is also hard to predict, except that it could eliminate geographical barriers, and might lead to a more centralized world economy, and similarly a more global cultural experience.

New forms of communication have historically both advanced civilization while also disrupting existing social orders. We are already witnessing the disruption that the Internet causes, which is sometimes unsettling, and unprecedented in history in its speed and in the number of industries and cultural institutions that have been affected. It would be difficult to identify a facet of human activity that has not been touched.

While displacing traditional media forms, the Internet has, as a positive outcome, democratized communication and the ability to publish and disseminate content of all types by anyone. It has opened up vast catalogs of information on any topic, now accessible literally at

Changing media habits in the US

Media habits in the US are good indicators of shifts in media consumption in most industrialized countries. The most obvious, of course, is a decline in newspapers and a sharp increase in Internet use. But also television watching has declined since its peak in 2009, a trend that is expected to continue. Print and broadcast will likely continue to decline in spite of population increase.

US Internet usage

Percent of population and number of users, 1990-2019

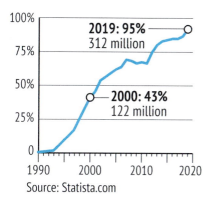

2019: 95% 312 million

2000: 43% 122 million

Source: Statista.com

Hours of television watched per day in the US

Hours per household, 1950-2019

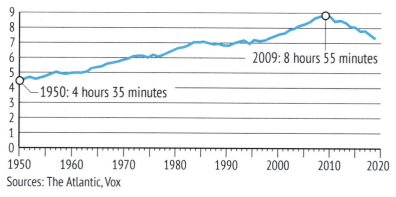

2009: 8 hours 55 minutes

1950: 4 hours 35 minutes

Sources: The Atlantic, Vox

US newspaper circulation

1940-2018

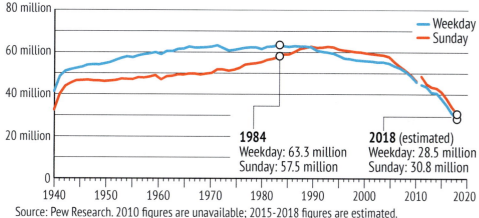

— Weekday
— Sunday

1984
Weekday: 63.3 million
Sunday: 57.5 million

2018 (estimated)
Weekday: 28.5 million
Sunday: 30.8 million

Source: Pew Research. 2010 figures are unavailable; 2015-2018 figures are estimated.

US population

1940-2018

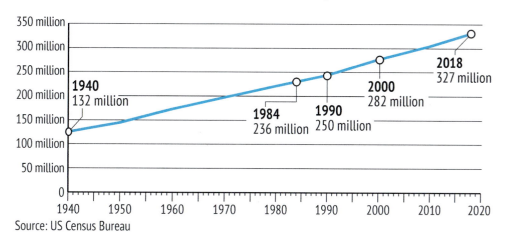

1940
132 million

1984
236 million

1990
250 million

2000
282 million

2018
327 million

Source: US Census Bureau

one's fingertips. It has increased access to entertainment and the ability to participate in geographically widespread groups, allowing interaction with people whose paths one would not have previously crossed, while also maintaining and strengthening social bonds with family and friends. And it has made shopping and business transactions more convenient.

But the Internet has also caused problems likely not anticipated by its creators. With the flood of new content came a dramatic increase in unverified and outright false information, particularly in science and politics, leading to societal fragmentation as people gravitate to the narratives they find most appealing, resulting in unresolvable confrontation and political paralysis as previously trusted institutions are villified and denounced.

It has impacted creative industries such as movies, music, professional photography, literature and graphic illustration by allowing the theft and unlicensed distribution of such work. Music was already being illicitly copied with the invention of audio tape, but it

usually only involved one or two copies at a time. Trying to control unauthorized reproductions on the Internet is a herculean task for music producers and movie studios, and virtually impossible for smaller content producers.

It continues to impact retail industries as shopping is increasingly being done online, to the advantage of large corporations over small businesses.

And it has given unparalleled power to a small number of companies that have become the conduits of information. Although there were roughly 189 million active websites (and more than 1.2 billion registered domain names) in 2020, the vast majority of traffic only visits a handful of them, principally search engines Google and Yahoo in the West and Baidu in Asia, social media sites such as Facebook, where advertising is now gravitating, and large retailers and resellers including Amazon and eBay in the West and Alibaba in Asia.

These companies depend on the acquisition of data about their users, control of which is key to their continued

Internet websites

Registered domain names and active sites, worldwide

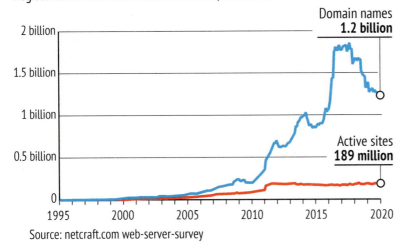

Source: netcraft.com web-server-survey

Most visited websites

Worldwide in 2020

1 Google.com

2 YouTube.com

3 Facebook.com

4 Twitter.com

5 Instagram.com

6 Baidu.com

7 Wikipedia.org

8 Yahoo.com

9 Yandex.ru

10 Amazon.com

Source: Similarweb.com

dominance. As a result many of them now operate in an interconnected web of their own, which is difficult for ordinary people to avoid being a part of. In July 2020 reporter Kashmir Hill wrote in *The New York Times* of an experiment in which she tried to remove all interactions with Amazon, Facebook, Google, Apple and Microsoft from her day-to-day life. She found it very difficult, as she discovered all the ways that these companies control online interactions: For example, besides having a virtual monopoly on online searches, Google provides fonts and ads for many other sites. They also monopolize maps, which is essential to services such as Uber and Lyft, as well as any site that needs to offer location information. Amazon controls a large segment of online transactions, fulfilling them for other parties, while also hosting a large amount of Web content on its servers. Facebook similarly controls the majority of social media interactions; opting out of it can leave one socially isolated. And Apple's iOS and Google's Android operating systems overwhelmingly dominate the smartphone market.

Hill came to the conclusion that these companies are the de facto backbone of the Internet. If one wants to use the Internet, there is little choice but to use their services, but even if one wasn't interested there seems to be little choice, as these companies control so many parts of the economy in the emerging digital world.

This represents a historic shift in economic and political power that took place in just a few decades beginning in the late 1990s. Throughout most of human history, limitations in communication methods allowed governments to control information. The printing press complicated that, but books could be banned and presses shut down. Broadcast media opened more avenues, but could still be censored and blocked.

A quote often credited to the linguist Noam Chomsky, and sometimes to the Nazi Joseph Goebbels, is that he who controls the media controls the minds of the public. But the Internet has proven to be much harder for anyone to control. Some countries try. China employs a vast apparatus to censor Internet traffic, but must expend considerable resources to do so, with only partial success.

The shift in media control from governments to a few global corporations is unprecedented, indicating that we are entering a new era in human history. How political, economic and social structures adapt to this new framework remains to be seen, and the large question about how to control false information on the Web is still unanswered.

It's probably safe, however, to predict that technology will keep advancing, and barring cataclysmic events in the future, it will allow ever more sophisticated levels of communication among us. For these are the two characteristics that define humanity: the ability to share complex, empirical and abstract thoughts with each other, and the ability to build remarkable machines with which to do so.

Index

Bibliography and Sources

Overview

Population growth

History Database of the Global Environment:
themasites.pbl.nl/tridion/en/themasites/hyde

Hyperbolic Growth of the World Population in the Past
12,000 Years. Ron W. Nielsen, Environmental Futures Research
Institute, Griffith University, Australia 2019

Netherlands Environmental Assessment Agency: History
Database of the Global Environment

World Population links

Worldbank.org

Ourworldindata.org

Montgomery, Keith, University of Wisconsin-Marathon County

United Nations

Worldometers.info

Weforum.org

Prehistory

Human evolution

Sapiens: A Brief History of Humankind. Yuval Noah Harari,
HarperCollins 2011

ancient.eu/Paleolithic

exploratorium.edu/evidence/lowbandwidth /INT_hominid_
timeline.html

humanorigins.si.edu

ibtimes.co.in/177000-year-old-jawbone-fossil-discovered-israel-
oldest-human-remains-found-outside-africa-758401

nature.com/news/oldest-homo-sapiens-fossil-claim-rewrites-
our-species-history-1.22114

news.nationalgeographic.com/2018/01/oldest-human-outside-
africa-discovered-fossil-jaw-israel-science

newscientist.com/article/dn9989-timeline-human-evolution

proof-of-evolution.com/human-evolution-timeline.html

sciencealert.com/did-homo-sapiens-kill-off-all-the-other-humans

theatlantic.com/magazine/archive/2019/03/how-humans-
tamed-themselves/580447

Speech

Why Are so Many Languages Spoken in Some Places and so
Few in Others? Marco Túlio Pacheco Coelho and Michael Gavin,
The Conversation Aug. 15, 2019

nature.com/articles/s41559-019-0903-5

phys.org/news/2019-05-language-comprehension-vocal-
production.html

theatlantic.com/science/archive/2018/06/toolmaking-
language-brain/562385

theatlantic.com/science/archive/2019/12/when-did-ancient-
humans-start-speak/603484

Oldest markings

livescience.com/48991-homo-erectus-shell-tools.html

nature.com/news/homo-erectus-made-world-s-oldest-doodle-
500-000-years-ago-1.16477

Cave art

smithsonianmag.com/history/journey-oldest-cave-paintings-
world-180957685/

U-Th dating of carbonate crusts reveals Neandertal origin of
Iberian cave art. D. L. Hoffmann et. al.:
science.sciencemag.org/content/359/6378/912?iss=6378

webexhibits.org/pigments/intro/early.html

Indonesia: advances.sciencemag.org/content/7/3/eabd4648

Neanderthals

aeon.co/essays/to-know-ourselves-we-must-first-know-the-neanderthals

nytimes.com/2019/07/10/science/skull-neanderthal-human-europe-greece.html

sciencemag.org/news/2016/09/neandertals-made-their-own-jewelry-new-method-confirms

Figurative art

nature.com/articles/s41586-019-1806-y

Oldest ceramic figure: pubmed.ncbi.nlm.nih.gov/17806391

science.sciencemag.org/content/336/6089/1696

visual-arts-cork.com/prehistoric/venus-of-berekhat-ram.htm

visual-arts-cork.com/prehistoric/venus-of-tan-tan.htm

Counting

bbc.com/future/story/20121128-animals-that-can-count

en.m.wikipedia.org/wiki/History_of_ancient_numeral_systems

newscientist.com/article/mg20227131-600-animals-that-count-how-numeracy-evolved

newscientist.com/gallery/mg20227131600-animals-that-count

Migration

nature.com/articles/d41586-019-02589-2

nytimes.com/2016/09/22/science/ancient-dna-human-history.html

smithsonianmag.com/history/the-great-human-migration-13561

smithsonianmag.com/history/the-seeds-of-civilization-78015429

Early history

First cities

Emergence and Change in Early Urban Societies. Edited by Linda Manzanilla, Universidad Nacional Autónoma de México, Springer-Verlag US 1997

Emergence and Change in Early Urban Societies. Edited by Linda Manzanilla, Springer 1997

sciencemag.org/news/2017/03/when-did-humans-settle-down-house-mouse-may-have-answer

smithsonianmag.com/history/gobekli-tepe-the-worlds-first-temple-83613665/

smithsonianmag.com/history/the-seeds-of-civilization-78015429

Mesopotamia

The Babylonians—An Introduction. Gwendolyn Leick, Routledge 2002

ancient.eu/article/37/the-sumerians-of-mesopotamia/

britishmuseum.org/explore/themes/writing/literacy.aspx

Egypt

history.com/topics/ancient-history/ancient-egypt

India

ancient.eu/Brahmi_Script/

ancient.eu/Indus_Script/

nature.com/news/ancient-civilization-cracking-the-indus-script-1.18587

China

ancient.eu/Chinese_Writing/

thoughtco.com/yellow-river-in-chinas-history-195222

Money

ancient.eu/coinage

telegraph.co.uk/finance/businessclub/money/11174013/The-history-of-money-from-barter-to-bitcoin.html

Writing

First writing

Oxford Companion to Archaeology. Edited by Brian M. Fagan, Oxford University Press 1996

ancient-origins.net/news-history-archaeology/8000-year-old-slab-holds-oldest-writing-ever-discovered-or-does-it-009675

archaeology.org/issues/213-1605/features/4326-cuneiform-the-world-s-oldest-writing

Writing evolution

Alphabet: The History, Evolution, and Design of the Letters We Use Today. A. Haley, Watson-Guptill 1995

The Alphabetic Labyrinth: The Letters in History and Imagination. J. Drucker, Thames & Hudson 1995

The Blackwell Encyclopedia of Writing Systems. F. Coulmas, Blackwell: Oxford 1999

The Cambridge Ancient History (3rd ed. 1970) pp. 43–44. I. E. S. Edwards, C. J. Gadd, N. G. L. Hammond, Cambridge University Press

Letter Perfect: The Marvelous History of the Alphabet from A to Z. D. Sacks, Broadway Books 2003

The Story of Writing. A. Robinson, London: Thames & Hudson 2007

Writing Systems: A Linguistic Introduction. Geoffrey Sampson, Stanford University Press 2011

hgage0912-good.blogspot.com/2010/09/origins-of-abc.html

mnstate.edu/houtsli/tesl551/Writing/page4.htm

nytimes.com/2016/11/15/science/cuneiform-tablet-cookies.html

sciencephoto.com/media/111032/view/evolution-of-cuneiform-writing

sites.utexas.edu/dsb/tokens/the-evolution-of-writing

Mesopotamia

Cuneiform. Irving L. Finkel, British Museum Press 2001

ancient.eu/article/37/the-sumerians-of-mesopotamia

ancientmesopotamians.com/ancient-mesopotamia-writing-system.html

ancientscripts.com/cuneiform.html

bcmuseum.blogspot.com/2017/06/sumerian-cuneiform-around-world-from-80.html

britishmuseum.org/explore/themes/writing/literacy.aspx

dvp-cuneiform.blogspot.com

edsitement.neh.gov/lesson-plan/cuneiform-writing-system-ancient-mesopotamia-emergence-and-evolution

historyextra.com/period/ancient-egypt/cuneiform-6-things-you-probably-didnt-know-about-the-worlds-oldest-writing-system

historyonthenet.com/the-epic-of-gilgamesh

international.loc.gov/intldl/cuneihtml/about.html

members.bib-arch.org/biblical-archaeology-review/31/2/10

metmuseum.org/toah/hd/wrtg/hd_wrtg.htm

omniglot.com/writing/sumerian.htm

pages.mtu.edu/~scmarkve/2910Su11/WrSys/evolofcuneiform3100-600BC.htm

theintegralschoolblog.org/2016/10/29/cuneiform-script

udel.edu/~dlarsen/ling203/Slides/Writing.pdf

Cylinder seals
ancient.eu/article/846/cylinder-seals-in-ancient-mesopotamia---their-hist

crystalinks.com/sumercylinderseals.html

johnsteins.com/woodblock-printing.html

historyonthenet.com/mesopotamian-cylinder-seals

teachmiddleeast.lib.uchicago.edu/historical-perspectives/the-question-of-identity/before-islam-mesopotamia/image-resource-bank/image-15.html

Brick stamps
Written on Mud: Brick Inscriptions from Mesopotamia. H. Hameeuw, E. Gorris, J. Tavernier, Centre Assyriologicue Georges Dossin 2015

Egyptian
Egyptian Grammar: Being an Introduction to the Study of Hieroglyphs pp. 438–548. 3rd Ed. A.H. Gardiner, Griffith Institute, Oxford 1957

afrostyly.com/gardiner/list/p/

egyptianhieroglyphs.net/gardiners-sign-list/fish-and-parts-of-fish

egyptianhieroglyphics.net/hieratic-and-demotic-script/

discoveringegypt.com/egyptian-hieroglyphic-writing/egyptian-hieroglyphic-alphabet/

omniglot.com/writing/egyptian.htm

penn.museum/blog/museum/somethings-fishy-in-the-palace-of-merneptah-graffiti-in-ancient-egypt

penn.museum/cgi/hieroglyphsrealphp?name=fish&inscribe=insrcibe

Papyrus, Parchment
cornell.edu/culconservation/2015/04/03/parchment-making/

lib.umich.edu/papyrology-collection/how-ancient-papyrus-was-made

metmuseum.org/toah/hd/papy/hd_papy.htm

Ink
ancientegypt.co.uk/writing/explore/scribe.html

brooklynmuseum.org/community/blogosphere/2010/09/22/pigments-and-inks-typically-used-on-papyrus

colourlex.com/project/egyptian-blue

geology.com/minerals/realgar-orpiment.shtml

newsweek.com/ancient-egypt-papyrus-ink-metal-copper-scroll-713434

theweek.co.uk/innovation-at-work/63310/the-history-of-ink

visual-arts-cork.com/artist-paints/egyptian-colour-palette.htm

zmescience.com/science/copper-traces-egypt-inks

Proto-sinaitic
Alphabets, Texts and Artifacts in the Ancient Near East. Various authors. Van Dieren Editeur. 2016.

The Alphabet: Its Rise and Development from the Sinai Inscriptions. Martin Sprengling. U. of Chicago Press, 1931

Colorful Chart Reveals Evolution of English Alphabet From Egyptian Hieroglyphics. Emma Taggart, 2019: mymodernmet.com

Proto-Sinaitic – Progenitor of the Alphabet. Frank Simons. University of Birmingham, 2011

ancientscripts.com/protosinaitic.html

earlysemitic.weebly.com/proto-semitic-alphabet.html

medium.com/the-purple-people/the-true-story-of-the-alphabet-e291e29f288f

Greece
ancient.eu/Linear_B_Script

ancient.eu/Polis

ancient-greece.org/history.html

ancient-greece.org/resources/timeline.html

carolandray.plus.com/Eteocretan/archaic_alpha.html

greek-language.com/History.html

greekreporter.com/2015/10/22/9-greek-cities-among-europes-15-oldest

nationalgeographic.com/news/2011/03/110330-oldest-writing-europe-tablet-greece-science-mycenae-greek

omniglot.com/writing/greek.htm

owlcation.com/humanities/Hellenistic-versus-Hellenic-Civilization-The-istic-ic-difference

Rosetta Stone
britishmuseum.org/collection/object/Y_EA24

history.com/news/what-is-the-rosetta-stone

Latin alphabet
The Alphabet's Brilliant Conquest: How letters spread from ancient Canaan to your computer. Daniel Kenis, 2016. Medium.com

latinata.com/LatinPronunciationAndWriting.pdf

omniglot.com/writing/latin.htm

Writing systems

In the Beginning: A Short History of the Hebrew Language. Joel Hoffman, NYU Press, 2004

ancient.eu/Chinese_Writing

ancientscripts.com/arabic.html

ancientscripts.com/armenian.html

ancientscripts.com/ethiopic.html

arc-japanese-translation.com/chinese/04tidbits.html

britannica.com/topic/Ethiopic-alphabet

britannica.com/topic/Japanese-language

korean-arts.com/about/korean%20alphabet.htm

linguistics.byu.edu/classes/Ling450ch/reports/japanese.htm

metmuseum.org/learn/educators/curriculum-resources/art-of-the-islamic-world/unit-two/origins-and-characteristics-of-the-arabic-alphabet

npr.org/templates/story/story.php?storyId=6077734

nytimes.com/2006/09/15/science/15writing.html

omniglot.com/writing/armenian.htm

omniglot.com/writing/devanagari.htm

omniglot.com/writing/ethiopic.htm

qfi.org/blog/history-of-the-arabic-alphabet

sciencemag.org/news/2002/12/roots-mesoamerican-writing

thoughtco.com/yellow-river-in-chinas-history-195222

wikipedia.org/wiki/List_of_writing_systems

yeskorean.com/learn-korean/lesson-1-the-korean-alphabet-is-24-letters/

Paper

Papermaking

Papermaking. The History and Technique of and Ancient Craft. Dard Hunter, Dover Publications, 1943 reprinted 1978

Paper: Paging Through History. Mark Kurlansky, W. W. Norton & Company, New York, London, 2016

European Papermaking Techniques 1300-1800. Paper through Time: Nondestructive Analysis of 14th- through 19th-Century Papers. T. Barrett, The University of Iowa 2012

Early European Papers / Contemporary Conservation Papers. Timothy Barrett, The Paper Conservator 13 Part I, 7–27, 1989. paper.lib.uiowa.edu/european.php

The Dictionary of Paper, including pulp, paperboard, paper properties and related papermaking terms, 3rd ed. American Paper and Pulp Association 1965.

A Brief History of Paper. Fuller, Neathery Batsell. STLCC.edu, 2002

The Lost Language of Symbolism. Harold Bayley, Citadel Press 1909 (1970)

The Story of Papermaking. Edwin Stutermeister, R.R. Bowker Company 1954

Who was the Inventor of Rag-paper? A. F. Rudolf Hoernle, Journal of the Royal Asiatic Society of Great Britain and Ireland Art. XXII, p. 663, 1903

A chronology of paper and papermaking. Joel Munsell, Albany, J. Munsell 1864. archive.org/details/chronologyofpape00muns

Paper Basics: Forestry, Manufacture, Selection, Purchasing, Mathematics and Metrics, Recycling. David Saltman, Van Nastrand Reinhold Company 1978

Papermaking. Ralf Weidenmüller, John Kalish translator. Thorfinn International Marketing Consultants Inc. San Diego and Ralf E. Soderholm, London 1980

The Manufacture of Paper: Being a Description of the Various Processes for the Fabrication, Coloring, and Finishing of every Kind of Paper. Charles Thomas Davis, Arno Press 1886 reprinted 1972

Ink on Paper, A Handbook of the Graphic Arts. Edmund C. Arnold, Harper & Row 1963

Papermaking: The Historical Diffusion of an Ancient Technique. Jonathan M. Bloom, Springer 2017

atlas.lib.uiowa.edu

chinaonlinemuseum.com/painting-four-treasures.php

paper.lib.uiowa.edu/european.php

pulppapermill.com/sizing-agents/

users.stlcc.edu/nfuller/paper

uzbekjourneys.com/2011/09/samarkand-revival-of-papermaking.html

Paper mills

openluchtmuseum.nl

paperhistory.org/museums-nl.htm

verdoyer.fr/en/articles-regions/paper-mill-vaux-and-forges-savignac-ledrier

Earliest paper

Envisaging the City. David Buisseret, U. of Chicago Press 1998, p. 12.

schoyencollection.com/pre-gutenberg-printing

wikipedia.org/wiki/Missal_of_Silos

Waterwheel

Denis Diderot's Encyclopedie, 1767

plato.stanford.edu/entries/diderot

scihi.org/denis-diderot-encyclopedia

thoughtco.com/history-of-waterwheel-4077881

top-alternative-energy-sources.com/water-wheel-history.html

waterhistory.org/histories/waterwheels

wikipedia.org/wiki/List_of_ancient_watermills

China exploration

Ancient Chinese Explorers. Hadingham, Evan, PBS 2001:

pbs.org/wgbh/nova/article/ancient-chinese-explorers/

Block books

The Quincentennnial of Netherlandish Blockbooks. Allan H. Stevenson, British Museum Quarterly, Vol. 31, No. 3/4 Spring 1967

Printing

Earliest printing

A Chronology of Printing. Colin Clair, Cassell 1969

Handbook to Life in Ancient Mesopotamia 1st Edition. Stephen Bertman, Oxford University Press 2005

The Invention of Printing in China and its Spread Westward. Thomas Francis Carter, NY Columbia U. Press 1925

Paper and Printing in Ancient China. Berthold Laufer, Caxton Club 1931

Media

Aramaic and Figural Stamp Impressions on Bricks of the Sixth Century B.C. from Babylon. Joachim Marzahn, Benjamin Sass, Harrassowitz 2010

ancient.eu/article/846/cylinder-seals-in-ancient-mesopotamia---their-hist/

britannica.com/topic/sigillography#ref523745

cdli.ucla.edu/projects/seals/seals.html

funsci.com/fun3_en/tablets/tab.htm

inkston.com/stories/guides/chinese-inks

Pre-Gutenberg

The History of Pre-Gutenberg Woodblock and Movable Type Printing in Korea. Hye Ok Park, International Journal of Humanities and Social Science Vol. 4, No. 9(1), July 2014

The Shorter Science and Civilisation in China, Volume 4, p. 14. Needham, Joseph, Cambridge University Press 1994

historyofinformation.com/expanded.php?id=1643

korea.prkorea.com/wordpress/?p=230

medium.com/@RossAlTejada/movable-type-the-very-first-printer-and-a-brief-look-at-its-history-4228bde57e9a

schoyencollection.com/pre-gutenberg-printing

Woodblock

Japanese Print-Making: A Handbook of Traditional & Modern Techniques. Toshi Yoshida and Rei Yuki, Charles E. Tuttle 1966

Japanese Woodblock Printing. Rebecca Salter, University of Hawaii Press 2002

artelino.com/articles/woodblock-print-kento.asp

druckstelle.info/en/holzschnitt_china.aspx

education.asianart.org/explore-resources/background-information/invention-woodblock-printing-tang-618%E2%80%93906-and-song-960%E2%80%931279

en.people.cn/n3/2019/0116/c90000-9538194-8.html

johnsteins.com/woodblock-printing.html

schoyencollection.com/pre-gutenberg-printing

unesco.org/courier/december-1978/200-years-gutenberg-master-printers-koryo

web.archive.org/web/20081120130752/http://www.ifla.org/IV/ifla62/62-yosz.htm

China

Chinese History: A New Manual. Wilkinson, Endymion. Harvard University Asia Center for the Harvard-Yenching Institute 2012

The Great Wall: China Against the World, 1000 BC - AD 2000. Julia Lovell, Grove Press 2007

The Woman Who Discovered Printing. Timothy Hugh-Barrett, Yale University Press 2008

Stone rubbing

britannica.com/art/rubbing

chinadaily.com.cn/culture/2016-08/01/content_26295399_6.htm

lib.berkeley.edu/EAL/stone/rubbings.html

library.harvard.edu/collections/chinese-rubbings-collection

Woodworking tools

A Carpenter's Chest: Tools of the 15th Century. Lord Findlaech mac Alasdair, The Oak, The Arts and Sciences Newsletter for the Kingdom of Atlantia, issue #12

paleotool.com/2014/08/08/carpenter-15th-century/

Writing tools

History of Drawing. Thomas Buser. historyofdrawing.com

medievalwriting.50megs.com/tools.htm

pencils.com/pencil-history

Intaglio

21stcenturyrenaissanceprintmaker.wordpress.com/2014/04/10/the-intaglio-studio-and-press

Gutenberg press

The Machine That Made Us. Patrick McGrady director, Wavelength Films, BBC 2008

Printing Presses: History and Development from the 15th Century to Modern Times. James Moran, University of California Press 1973

Great Inventions and Discoveries, pp. 27-28. Willis Duff Piercy, Charles E. Merrill Co. 1911

How the Printing Press Changed History. Nel Yomtov, Abdo Publishing, 2015

The Invention of Printing. Theodore Low De Vinne, Francis Hart & Co. 1876: https://archive.org/details/inventionofprint00deviuoft

Leaders of the Information Age. Edited by Clifford Thompson, The H.W. Wilson Company 2004

Printing Press. Gordon Alley-Young, Salem Press Encyclopedia 2015

gutenbergsapprentice.com/printing/early-printing-gallery-images

printmuseum.org

psymon.com/koster

Double press: crandallprintingmuseum.com

Type slugs
circuitousroot.com/artifice/letters/press/hand-casting/literature/index.html

hrc.utexas.edu/educator/modules/gutenberg/invention/printshop/

letterpresscommons.com/setting-type-by-hand

spiritcreative.wordpress.com/2010/06/26/the-letterpress-typesetting-printing-process

Bookmaking
The book: the life story of a technology pp 140–148. Nicole Howard, Greenwood Publishing Group 2005

atlasobscura.com/articles/medieval-luxury-books-pearls-jewels-gold-silver-manuscript-covers

Typography
A History of Graphic Design. Philip B. Meggs, John Wiley & Sons 1998

Exploring Typography. Tova Rabinowitz, Cengage Learning 2015

cjr.org/language_corner/points-picas-typography-print.php

designhistory.org/Type_milestones_pages/SansSerif.html

design.tutsplus.com/articles/the-rise-of-the-sans-serif--cms-33548

imagine-express.com/the-history-of-helvetica

typotheque.com/articles/a_brief_history_of_sans_serif_typefaces

Martin Luther
Brand Luther: How an Unheralded Monk Turned His Small Town into a Center of Publishing, Made Himself the Most Famous Man in Europe—and Started the Protestant Reformation. Andrew Pettegree, Penguin Press 2016

washingtonpost.com/opinions/the-power-of-luthers-printing-press/2015/12/18

Social impact
A Farewell to Alms: A Brief Economic History of the World. Gregory Clark, Princeton University Press 2009

The Better Angels of Our Nature: Why Violence Has Declined. Steven Pinker, Penguin Books 2012

The Distribution of Wealth: A Theory of Wages, Interest and Profits. John Bates Clark, The Macmillan Company 1908

Empathy and the Novel. Suzanne Keen, Oxford University Press; 1st edition 2010

Great Inventions and Discoveries pp. 30-31. Willis Duff Piercy, Charles E. Merrill Co. 1911.

Leonardo's Library: How a Renaissance Artist Discovered the Meaning of Books. Dr. Paula Findlen, Stanford U.

The Printing Press as an Agent of Change. Elizabeth L. Eisenstein, Cambridge University Press 1980

Industrial and Modern Ages

James Watt
bbc.co.uk/history/historic_figures/watt_james.shtml

Electricity
Nikola Tesla: The Extraordinary Life of a Modern Prometheus. Richard Gunderman, The Conversation Jan. 2018

americanhistory.si.edu/blog/rural-electrification

An introduction to electric motors. STMicroelectronics: st.com/en/motor-drivers.html

bbvaopenmind.com/en/science/leading-figures/lightning-and-sparks-did-benjamin-franklins-kite-actually-exist

en.wikipedia.org/wiki/List_of_Edison_patents

explainthatstuff.com/electricmotors.html

First practical electric motor: eti.kit.edu/english/1376.php

fi.edu/benjamin-franklin/kite-key-experiment

founders.archives.gov/documents/Franklin/01-04-02-0135

history.com/topics/inventions/thomas-edison

mentalfloss.com/article/66551/true-story-behind-ben-franklins-lightning-experiment

rigb.org/our-history/iconic-objects/iconic-objects-list/faraday-generator

rigb.org/our-history/iconic-objects/iconic-objects-list/faradays-motorand%20generator

smithsonianmag.com/history/the-rise-and-fall-of-nikola-tesla-and-his-tower-11074324/

thehistoricalarchive.com/happenings/57/the-history-of-electricity-a-timeline/

thoughtco.com/history-of-electricity-1989860

thoughtco.com/michael-faraday-inventor-4059933

Steel
The 'Copper Age'—A History of the Concept. Mark Pearce, Journal of World Prehistory Vol. 32, pages 229–250, 2019

History of Metal Casting. Dr. Altan Turkeli, Marmara University, Turkey

Copper Age, Bronze Age and Iron Age: factsanddetails.com/world/cat56/sub362/item1495.html

courses.lumenlearning.com/suny-hccc-worldhistory2/chapter/steel-production

industrialmetalcastings.com/history.html

thebalance.com/steel-history-2340172

worldsteel.org/media-centre/press-releases/2020/Global-crude-steel-output-increases-by-3.4--in-2019.html

Plastics
The Early History of Insulated Copper Wire. Allan A. Mills, Annals of Science Vol. 61, No. 4, 453-467, 2004

en.wikipedia.org/wiki/Gutta_Percha_Company

industrialrubbergoods.com/types-of-synthetic-rubber.html

plasticsmakeitpossible.com/whats-new-cool/fashion/styles-trends/bakelite-the-plastic-that-made-history

sciencehistory.org/the-history-and-future-of-plastics

tandfonline.com/doi/abs/10.1080/00033790110117476

Elements
Cyclopædia of Useful Arts, Mechanical and Chemical, Manufactures, Mining, and Engineering. Charles Tomlinson, G. Virtue & Co. 1854

bbc.com/future/article/20161017-your-old-phone-is-full-of-precious-metals

sciencenotes.org/printable-periodic-table

thoughtco.com/properties-basic-metals-element-group-606654

Social impact
A Farewell to Alms: A Brief Economic History of the World (The Princeton Economic History of the Western World). Gregory Clark, Princeton University Press 2009

Industrial printing

Paper
Delaware Papermakers and Papermaking 1787-1840. Harold B. Hancock, Aug. 1955

daviddarling.info/encyclopedia/P/paper.html

digital.hagley.org/MS1645_33#modal-close

gutenberg.org/files/58319/58319-h/58319-h.htm

hagley.org/research/digital-exhibits/tj-gilpin

historyofinformation.com/detail.php?id=4291

historyofpaper.net/paper-history/paper-machine-history

joemillerscompletejestbook.weebly.com/paper-manufacturer---innovation.html

osiskars.com/roberts-paper-machine

todayinsci.com/F/Fourdrinier_Henry/FourdrinierPapermakingMachine.htm

Industrial Age presses
A Catalogue of Nineteenth Century Printing Presses. Harold E. Sterne, Oak Knoll Press 2001

American Iron Hand Presses. Stephen O. Saxe and John Depol, Oak Knoll Press 1992

Frederick Koenig: Inventor of the Steam-printing Machine, pp. 274-319: Men of Invention and Industry. Samuel Smiles, Book Jungle 2008

History of the Platen Press. letterpresscommons.com/platen-press-history

Richard March Hoe and the Evolution of Past Printing Presses. Henry Lewis Bullen, The Inland Printer Vol. 69 April 1922 pp. 851-854. Inland Printer Company, Chicago

Richard Hoe: A powerful press opens mass media age. Frank Daniels III, The Tennessean, Sept. 14, 2012

The International Printing Museum, Carson CA. printmuseum.org/museum/collection

britannica.com/topic/printing-publishing/Koenigs-mechanical-press-early-19th-century#ref417302

historyofinformation.com/detail.php?entryid=501

historyofinformation.com/detail.php?id=3205

koenig-bauer.com/en

letterpresscommons.com/press/stanhope/

letterpressprinting.com.au/page58.htm

prepressure.com/printing/history/1850-1899

scihi.org/ruchard-march-hoe-rotary-printing-press/

tompainepress.blogspot.com/2011/05/visit-to-stanhope-press-at-ditchling.html

wikiwand.com/en/Rotary_printing_press

Linotype
Ottmar Mergenthaler: The Man and His Machine: A Biographical Appreciation of the Inventor on His Centennial. Basil Charles Kahan, Oak Knoll Press 1999

americanhistory.si.edu/blog/2009/04/printing-history-and-the-intertype-linotype-machine.html

atlasobscura.com/articles/m-h-type-foundry-san-francisco

bostonglobe.com/metro/2019/11/10/with-linotype-print-old-new-again/BEUHE9HdT28E6DkLr1JJoL/story.html

circuitousroot.com/artifice/letters/press/compline/technology/models/linotype-us/square-base/index.html

digitalcheck.com/phototypesetters-printing

invention.si.edu/simple-operation

letterpresscommons.com/linotypeandintertype

letterpresscommons.com/merganthaler-linotype

museum.syssrc.com/artifact/1300

printinghistory.org/linotype-baltimore

sites.google.com/a/umich.edu/from-tablet-to-tablet/final-projects/the-invention-of-the-linotype-machine-jienne-alhaideri-13

theatlantic.com/technology/archive/2011/05/celebrating-linotype-125-years-since-its-debut/238968

thehenryford.org/collections-and-research/digital-collections/artifact/288228

keyboard:
oztypewriter.blogspot.com/2015/10/etaoin-shrdlu-anyone.html

Monotype: letterpresscommons.com/monotype

Lithography
A History of Graphic Design. Philip B. Meggs, John Wiley & Sons 1998

Exploring Typography. Tova Rabinowitz, Cengage Learning 2015

Introduction to Photo-Offset Lithography. Kenneth F. Hird, Bennett Publishing Co. 1981

Offset Printing Technology. S. Arunjunai Valavan and G. Venkateswaran, Arasan Ganesan Polytechnic College, Sivakasi 2018

Understanding Photo Typesetting. Michael L. Kleper, North American Publishing Co. 1976

britannica.com/technology/lithography

blog.drupa.com/en/pioneers-of-printing-godefroy-engelmann-2

centrecolours.co.uk/a-printing-revolution-the-history-of-lithography

chromolithography: prepressure.com/printing/history

historyofinformation.com/detail.php?entryid=666

metmuseum.org/toah/hd/lith/hd_lith.htm

offsetpressman.blogspot.com/2011/09/short-history-of-offset-printing.html

offsetprintingtechnology.com/sub-categories/offset-lithography

si.edu/es/object/nmah_882246

whatislithoprinting.com/history.html

Color printing
atlasobscura.com/articles/color-printing-lithography

clubink.ca/blog/print/history-behind-cmyk-colour-model

loc.gov/item/74223678

printinghistory.org/category/seeing-color-printing-color

printinghistory.org/color-german-graphic-art-1487-1600

printinghistory.org/color-printing-fifteenth-nineteenth-centuries-survey

tedium.co/2017/04/18/color-printing-lithography-history

Oldest magazines
foliomag.com/how-america-s-oldest-magazines-are-modernizing-and-monetizing-their-archives

Color in newspapers
The Poynter Institute for Media Studies

Harvard University curator Melissa Banta: library.hbs.edu/hc/naai/05-challenge-of-color.html#fn9

cimages.me/content/when-did-newspapers-start-printing-color

harvardmagazine.com/2010/07/rise-of-color

historyofinformation.com/detail.php?id=3189

nytimes.com/1993/05/31/business/the-media-business-newspapers-adoption-of-color-nearly-complete.html

Phototypesetting
Fundamentals of Modern Photo-composition. John W Seybold, Seybold Publication 1979

Introduction to Photo-Offset Lithography. Kenneth F. Hird, Bennett Publishing 1981

Understanding Photo Typesetting. Michael L. Kleper, North American Publishing Co. 1976

99designs.com/blog/design-history-movements/history-of-digital-fonts

creativepro.com/scanning-around-gene-back-when-typesetting-was-craft

digitalcheck.com/phototypesetters-printing

historyofinformation.com/detail.php?entryid=867

kymsinformation.wordpress.com/2014/11/24/typesetting

thelawlers.com/Blognosticator/?p=961

Book publishing data
Inside Book Publishing 6th Edition. Giles Clark and Angus Phillips, Routledge 2019

Production of manuscripts and books from 500 to 1800: ourworldindata.org/books

Literacy rates
Central Intelligence Agency, The World Factbook

National Center of Education Statistics, National Assessment of Adult Literacy, accessed April 23, 2013

UNESCO, Compendium of statistics on illiteracy, various editions

UNESCO, Progress of Literacy in Various Countries, a Preliminary Statistical Study of Available Census Data since 1900, pdf 1953, accessed April 22, 2013

UNESCO World Illiteracy at Mid-Century, pdf 1957, accessed April 21, 2013

World Bank, World Development Indicators database

brewminate.com/the-growth-of-literacy-in-western-europe-from-1500-to-1800

data.worldbank.org/indicator/se.adt.litr.zs

hbs.edu/businesshistory/courses/resources/historical-data-visualization/Pages/details.aspx?data_id=31

jstor.org/stable/4285275?seq=1#page_scan_tab_contents

ourworldindata.org/literacy

medievalcolloquium.sewanee.edu/ask-a-medievalist/aam-columns/literacy.php

worldpopulationreview.com/countries/literacy-rate-by-country

Timeline
Printing 1770-1970: An Illustrated History of Its Development and Uses in England. Michael Twyman, British Library 1998

Printing Presses: History and Development from the 15th Century to Modern Times. James Moran, University of California Press, 1978

Printing Yesterday and Today. Harry Ransom Center, The University of Texas at Austin, 2018

Mechanick Exercises: Or, The Doctrine Of Handy-Works. Joseph Moxon 1703 (reprinted by The Toolemera Press 2016)

spokesman.com/stories/2020/jun/28/history-printing-press

Photography and film

Photography

The Focal Encyclopedia of Photography: Digital Imaging, Theory and Applications, History, and Science, edited by Michael R. Peres, Routledge, 2007

History and Evolution of Photography. Mark Osterman and Grant B. Romer, George Eastman House and International Museum of Photography and Film 2007

kottke.org/17/08/the-oldest-known-photo-of-a-us-president

photo-museum.org/photography-history

camera obscura

obscurajournal.com/history.php

physics.kenyon.edu/EarlyApparatus/Optics/Camera_Lucida/Camera_Lucida.html

physics.kenyon.edu/EarlyApparatus/Optics/Camera_Obscura/Camera_Obscura.html

Halftoning

Halftone. Dusan C. Stulik and Art Kaplan, The Getty Conservations Institute 2013

Photojournalism: The Professionals' Approach. Kenneth Kobre and Betsy Brill, Amsterdam: Focal 2004

loc.gov/rr/print/guide/port-2.html

sbmhist128.wordpress.com/2011/06/23/photography-in-newspapers

Cameras

americanhistory.si.edu/collections/search/object/nmah_760118

blog.scienceandmediamuseum.org.uk/the-vest-pocket-kodak-was-the-soldiers-camera

cs.montana.edu/paxton/145/spring2010/HarrisObernesser/html/slr.html

daily.jstor.org/how-the-brownie-camera-made-everyone-a-photographer

earlyphotography.co.uk/site/entry_C251.html

en.wikipedia.org/wiki/Kine_Exakta

en.wikipedia.org/wiki/Asahi_Pentax

klassik-cameras.de/SLR_History.html

fi.edu/history-resources/kodak-brownie-camera

lens.blogs.nytimes.com/2014/06/30/photos-world-war-i-images-museums-battle-great-war

mikeeckman.com/2019/05/kepplers-vault-38-herbert-huesgen-tourist-multiple

shutterbug.com/content/leica-i-camera-change-photography

thedarkroom.com/film-formats/35mm-film-format-135-film

theoldtimey.com/35mm-camera-history

thoughtco.com/brownie-camera-1779181

SLR

bhphotovideo.com/explora/content/who-brought-us-slr

cs.montana.edu/paxton/145/spring2010/HarrisObernesser/html/slr.html

klassik-cameras.de/SLR_History.html

pentaxforums.com/camerareviews/asahi-pentax-ap-tower-26.html

Color photo

blog.scienceandmediamuseum.org.uk/a-short-history-of-colour-photography

openculture.com/2016/08/the-very-first-color-photograph-1861.html

petapixel.com/2015/10/11/a-brief-history-of-color-photography-from-dream-to-reality

Film

blog.scienceandmediamuseum.org.uk/very-short-history-of-cinema

Infoculture, the Smithsonian Book of Information Age Inventions. Steven Lubar, Houghton Mifflin 1993

infostory.com/2013/10/17/edisons-first-movie-projector-a-phonograph-for-pictures

open.lib.umn.edu/mediaandculture/chapter/8-2-the-history-of-movies

popularmechanics.com/culture/movies/g1046/a-brief-history-of-the-movie-camera

web.archive.org/web/19991128020048/http://www.bbc.co.uk/education/local_heroes/biogs/biogleprince.shtml

willevb.wordpress.com/2014/02/26/motion-picture-cameras-from-film-to-digital-video

Kinetograph and kinetoscope

collection.sciencemuseumgroup.org.uk/objects/co8078749/edison-kinetoscope-kinetoscope

history.com/this-day-in-history/edison-patents-the-kinetograph

historyofinformation.com/detail.php?id=546

Museudelcinema: Virtual recreation of kinetoscope: youtube.com/watch?v=SRIjUYh3MEs

theasc.com/asc/asc-museum-kinetoscope

Cinematograph: Lumiere Brothers

Le Cinéma des Origines: Les Frères Lumière et leurs Opérateurs. Jacques Rittaud Hutinet, Edition du Champ Valon, France 1985

The Ciné Goes to Town: French Cinema 1896–1914. Richard Abel, University of California Press 1994

The Emergence of Cinema: The American Screen to 1907. Charles Musser, Charles Scribner's Sons 1990

The Rise of the Cinema in Great Britain. John Barnes, Bishopsgate Press 1983

americanhistory.si.edu/collections/search/object/nmah_759313 blog.scienceandmediamuseum.org.uk/autochromes-the-dawn-of-colour-photography

digitalcommons.chapman.edu/jonathan_silent_film/1681

history.com/news/the-lumiere-brothers-pioneers-of-cinema

scienceandmediamuseum.org.uk/objects-and-stories/robert-paul

Kinemacolor
Trewinnard Collection of Replica Pioneer Motion Picture Cameras

Bell & Howell
Bell & Howell Company: A 75-Year History. Jack Robinson, Bell & Howell 1982

chicagology.com/silentmovies/bellhowell2709

firstcinemakers.com/the-studio-standard

Film projector
engineerguy: how a film projector works

en.wikipedia.org/wiki/File:How_a_Film_Projector_Works.webm

en.wikipedia.org/wiki/Frame_rate

history.com/this-day-in-history/first-movie-projector-demonstrated-in-united-states

8mm camera
global.canon/en/c-museum/history/story04.html

Color film
cinema.ucla.edu/blogs/archival-spaces/2018/08/03/Barbara-Flueckiger-timeline-historical-film-colors

filmcolors.org

nydailynews.com/entertainment/tv-movies/first-ever-color-movie-found-britain-national-media-museum-bradford-article-1.1158971

provideocoalition.com/history-color-film-television

victorian-cinema.net/erturner

Technicolor
artsandculture.google.com/exhibit/technicolor/ZQIS8XV-3nr-Jg

digital-intermediate.co.uk/examples/3strip/technicolor.htm

eastman.org/technicolor/decades/1915-1935

facebook.com/Vox/videos/1248124632041803

museumofwesternfilmhistory.org/current-upcoming-exhibitions/current-exhibitions/142-resources/further-information-about-current-exhibits/57-technicolor

theatlantic.com/technology/archive/2015/02/technicolor-at-100/385039

70mm movies
comingsoon.net/movies/news/639493-whats-old-is-new-again-the-history-of-70mm-film#

indiewire.com/2017/07/70mm-film-history-dunkirk-christopher-nolan-2001-space-odyssey-kubrick-movies-shot-1201851885

3D film
ign.com/articles/2010/04/23/the-history-of-3d-movie-tech

The Vintage News, April 23, 2020

Best-selling movies
Apple, Charles: spokesman.com/stories/2020/jun/11/50-best-selling-movies-all-time-adjusted-inflation

imdb.com/list/ls053826112

Digital movies
newrepublic.com/article/119431/how-digital-cinema-took-over-35mm-film

qz.com/1026532/with-huge-tvs-replacings-screens-cinemas-are-becoming-giant-versions-of-your-living-room

Electronics

Documentary
Shock and Awe: The Story of Electricity. BBC 2011

Vacuum tube
electronics.howstuffworks.com/diode1.htm

electronics-notes.com/articles/electronic_components/valves-tubes/how-does-a-vacuum-tube-work-theory.php

engineering.com/story/vacuum-tubes-the-world-before-transistors

history-computer.com/ModernComputer/Basis/diode.html

pbs.org/transistor/science/events/vacuumt.html

Transistor
computerhistory.org/siliconengine/invention-of-the-point-contact-transistor

explainthatstuff.com/howtransistorswork.html

hackaday.com/2019/08/21/largest-chip-ever-holds-1-2-trillion-transistors

icinsights.com/news/bulletins/Transistor-Count-Trends-Continue-To-Track-With-Moores-Law

pbs.org/transistor/science/events/pointctrans.html

sjsu.edu/faculty/watkins/transist.htm

technologyreview.com/2016/10/07/157106/worlds-smallest-transistor-is-cool-but-wont-save-moores-law

wikiwand.com/en/Transistor_count

wordpress.haverford.edu/bitbybit/bit-by-bit-contents/chapter-eight/8-2-the-point-contact-transistor

Integrated circuit
anysilicon.com/history-integrated-circuit

falconerelectronics.com/history-of-circuit-boards

Symbols
electronicshub.org/symbols

rapidtables.com/electric/electrical_symbols.html

Telegraph

atlantic-cable.com/Books/Whitehouse/DDC/index.htm

elon.edu/e-web/predictions/150/1830.xhtml

history.com/topics/inventions/telegraph

members.kos.net/sdgagnon/te5.html

time.com/4307892/samuel-morse-telegraph-history

Last telegram:

cbsnews.com/news/last-telegram-ever-to-be-sent-july-14

theatlantic.com/technology/archive/2016/01/rip-stop-telegrams/425136

Telephone

arctos.com/dial

elon.edu/e-web/predictions/150/1870.xhtml

historydaily.org/alexander-graham-bell-facts-stories-trivia

loc.gov/static/programs/national-recording-preservation-board/documents/FIRST%20TRANSATLANTIC%20CALL.pdf

nationalitpa.com/history-of-telephone

oceanofk.org/telephone/html/part1.html

privateline.com/?page_id=193

smithsonianmag.com/history/first-and-last-pay-phone-180952727

techwalla.com/articles/history-of-the-rotary-phone

telegraph.co.uk/technology/connecting-britain/first-public-transatlantic-phone-service

wired.com/2011/09/att-conquered-20th-century

Mobile phone

foxnews.com/tech/the-first-mobile-phone-call-was-placed-40-years-ago-today

mobilephonehistory.co.uk/motorola/motorola_9800X.php

theatlantic.com/technology/archive/2013/04/the-first-mobile-phone-call-was-made-40-years-ago-today/274611

wikivisually.com/wiki/Motorola_MicroTAC

wikivisually.com/wiki/Motorola_MicroTAC#MicroTAC_9800X

Mobile network

cnet.com/news/cell-phone-industry-celebrates-its-25th-birthday

cnn.com/interactive/2020/03/business/what-is-5g/index.html

pcmag.com/news/what-is-5g

qz.com/1422569/the-first-commercial-cell-phone-call-was-made-35-years-ago-today

Frequency hopping

wirelesscommunication.nl/reference/chaptr05/spreadsp/fh.htm

Radio

James Clerk Maxwell:
biography.com/scientist/james-c-maxwell

physicsworld.com/a/james-clerk-maxwell-a-force-for-physics

Hertz:
aaas.org/heinrich-hertz-and-electromagnetic-radiation

famousscientists.org/heinrich-hertz/

micro.magnet.fsu.edu/optics/timeline/people/hertz.html

Oliver Lodge:
ethw.org/Oliver_Lodge

Tesla:
Nikola Tesla, My Inventions: The Autobiography of Nikola Tesla. Hart Brothers 1982

Tesla: Man Out of Time. Margaret Cheney, Touchstone 1981

Tesla, Marconi, and the Great Radio Controversy: Awarding Patent Damages without Chilling a Defendant's Incentive to Innovate. Christopher A. Harkins, Missouri Law Review Vol. 73, No. 3 Summer 2008

edn.com/tesla-gives-1st-public-demonstration-of-radio-march-1-1893

engadget.com/2014-01-19-nikola-teslas-remote-control-boat.html

stltoday.com/news/archives/1893-tesla-stuns-a-st-louis-crowd-with-his-first-demonstration-of-radio/article_49b2dbbe-5bc7-11ea-a174-d74d53c88bfb.html

Tesla coil:
griffithobservatory.org/exhibits/halloftheeye_teslacoil.html

livescience.com/46745-how-tesla-coil-works.html

teslasociety.com/teslacoil.htm

Ernst Alexanderson:
alexander.n.se/the-radio-station-saq-grimeton/the-alexanderson-transmitter/?lang=en

Reginald Fessenden:
autodesk.com/products/eagle/blog/father-radio-reginald-fessenden

interestingengineering.com/reginald-fessenden-the-father-of-radiotelephony

Recreation of the first radio broadcast, Derek Gunn:
youtube.com/watch?time_continue=547&v=mdSXNVbdu1Y&feature=emb_logo

Marconi:
history.com/this-day-in-history/marconi-sends-first-atlantic-wireless-transmission

theguardian.com/education/2001/dec/11/highereducation.news

pbs.org/wgbh/aso/databank/entries/dt01ma.html

patent dispute:
pbs.org/tesla/ll/ll_whoradio.html

theguardian.com/education/2001/dec/11/*Titanic*:
history.com/topics/early-20th-century-us/titanic
encyclopedia-titanica.org/titanic-survivors

Radio broadcasting

autodesk.com/products/eagle/blog/wireless-basics-radio-waves-work

chegg.com/homework-help/crystal-radio-set-phenomenon-resonance-makes-possible-listen-chapter-22-problem-79ap-solution-9781111794545-exc

cusustainableenergy.pbworks.com/w/page/7390350/Solarintro

dummies.com/programming/electronics/components/radio-electronics-transmitters-and-receivers

eh.net/encyclopedia/the-history-of-the-radio-industry-in-the-united-states-to-1940

electronicshub.org/modulation-and-different-types-of-modulation

encyclopedia.com/education/news-and-education-magazines/radio-1929-1941

fcc.gov/engineering-technology/policy-and-rules-division/general/radio-spectrum-allocation

home.bt.com/tech-gadgets/internet/retro-tech-the-transistor-radio-11363937910884

hyperphysics.phy-astr.gsu.edu/hbase/Audio/radio.html

lifewire.com/how-fm-radio-works-3135076

ofcom.org.uk

regencytr1.com

smithsonianmag.com/smithsonian-institution/the-transistor-radio-launches-the-portable-electronic-age-110761753

steampunk.wonderhowto.com/how-to/complete-guide-build-crystal-radio-plus-they-work-0141117

techwholesale.com/history-of-the-radio.html

teslauniverse.com/nikola-tesla/articles/teslas-dream-world-system-wireless-part-1

United States Frequency Allocations. US Dept. of Commerce/National Telecommunications and Information Administration/Office of Spectrum Management

unesco.org/new/en/unesco/events/prizes-and-celebrations/celebrations/international-days/world-radio-day-2013/statistics-on-radio

Television

bbc.co.uk/history/historic_figures/baird_logie.shtml

bebusinessed.com/history/history-of-the-television/

earlytelevision.org/color.html

electronics.howstuffworks.com/tv12.htm

library.duke.edu/specialcollections/scriptorium/adaccess/tv-history.html

Mechanical TV:
earlytelevision.org/mechanical_tv.html

Networks:
audienceservices.cbs.com/feedback/cbs_through_the_years/through_the_years.htm

britannica.com/topic/CBS-Corporation

en.wikipedia.org/wiki/American_Broadcasting_Company

en.wikipedia.org/wiki/PBS

nbcuniversal.com/history

newworldencyclopedia.org/entry/Columbia_Broadcasting_System

statista.com/statistics/189655/number-of-commercial-television-stations-in-the-us-since-1950

Audiences:
The Decline in Average Weekly Cinema Attendance: 1930 -2000. Michelle Pautz, Issues in Political Economy, 2002, Vol. 11

184.168.166.95/facts-stats.htm

americancentury.omeka.wlu.edu/items/show/136

livinghistoryfarm.org/farminginthe50s/life_17.html

marketingcharts.com/featured-24817

nytimes.com/2011/05/03/business/media/03television.html

nyu.edu/classes/stephens/History%20of%20Television%20page.htm

statista.com/statistics/186833/average-television-use-per-person-in-the-us-since-2002

theatlantic.com/business/archive/2014/05/global-mobile-media-smartphones-tv-maps/371760

theatlantic.com/technology/archive/2018/05/when-did-tv-watching-peak/561464

theguardian.com/tv-and-radio/2013/sep/07/history-television-seduced-the-world

vox.com/2018/6/8/17441288/internet-time-spent-tv-zenith-data-media

Cathode ray tube:
electronics.howstuffworks.com/tv3.htm

en.wikipedia.org/wiki/Cathode-ray_tube

hypebeast.com/2018/1/super-mario-the-slow-mo-guys-video

thoughtco.com/television-history-cathode-ray-tube-1991459

Communication

Satellite:
history.com/news/the-birth-of-satellite-tv-50-years-ago

space.com/16549-telstar-satellite-first-tv-signal-anniversary.html

Fiber optic cable:
City of Light: The Story of Fiber Optics. Jeff Hecht, Oxford University Press 2004

Fiber Optics Technician's Handbook. Jim Hayes, Delmar Publishers 2001

Fiber-Optic Technologies. Vivek Alwayn, Cisco Press 2004

en.wikipedia.org/wiki/Attenuation

jeffhecht.com/history.html

networkworld.com/article/2235353/the-incredible-international-submarine-cable-systems.html

tevelec.com/history

timbercon.com/resources/blog/history-of-fiber-optics

thoughtco.com/birth-of-fiber-optics-4091837

Audio

mclerranjournal.com/technology-1/2017/6/4/a-short-history-of-the-music-box

Vinyl

americanhistorynow.org/2014/01/27/the-history-of-vinyl

electrohome.com/vinyl-record-speeds-33-45-78-mean

Microphone

AH Electronics: youtube.com/watch?v=Pqw6NWPdlZQ

cuidevices.com/product-spotlight/electret-condenser-microphones

en.wikipedia.org/wiki/Shure

Speakers

blog.landr.com/how-do-speakers-work

edisontechcenter.org/speakers.html

explainthatstuff.com/loudspeakers.html

soundguys.com/how-speakers-work-29860

thoughtco.com/history-of-loudspeaker-4076782

Magnetic tape

artsites.ucsc.edu/EMS/music/equipment/analog_recorders/analog_recorders.html

edisontechcenter.org/MagRec.html

electrospectivemusic.com/1928-magnetic-tape

ethw.org/Magnetic_Tape

ethw.org/Telegraphone

hyperphysics.phy-astr.gsu.edu/hbase/Audio/tape2.html

reverb.com/news/how-does-magnetic-tape-work-the-basics

youtube.com/watch?v=FoO6kzd_Ars

Sony Walkman

newyorker.com/culture/cultural-comment/the-walkman-forty-years-on

Digital

Pre-digital

webdesignerdepot.com/2012/02/design-before-computers-ruled-the-universe

Babbage

cbi.umn.edu/about/babbage.html

computerhistory.org/babbage

smithsonianmag.com/history/what-a-difference-the-difference-engine-made-from-charles-babbages-calculator-emerged-todays-computer-109389254

Computers

How Computers Work: The Evolution of Technology, 10th Edition. Ron White, Que Publishing 2014

bletchleypark.org.uk/visit-us/the-national-museum-of-computing

columbia.edu/cu/computinghistory/mark1.html

Computer museum: museum.syssrc.com/home

computerhistory.org/revolution/birth-of-the-computer/4/78

computerhistory.org/timeline/computers

computerhope.com/history/monitor.htm

en.wikipedia.org/wiki/Micro_Instrumentation_and_Telemetry_Systems

explainthatstuff.com/historyofcomputers.html

factmyth.com/how-do-computers-work

home.bt.com/tech-gadgets/computing/retro-tech-the-ibm-5150-personal-computer-the-computer-that-changed-the-world-11363996701188

homepage.cs.uri.edu/faculty/wolfe/book/Readings/Reading04.htm

ibm.com/ibm/history/exhibits/markI/markI_intro.html

lowendmac.com/2014/personal-computer-history-the-first-25-years

oldcomputers.net/osborne-1.html

people.idsia.ch/~juergen/zuse.html

plato.stanford.edu/entries/leibniz

plato.stanford.edu/entries/pascal

sites.harvard.edu/~chsi/markone/about.html

wired.com/story/the-us-again-has-worlds-most-powerful-supercomputer

Xerox PARC

computerworld.com/article/2515874/computer-hardware/timeline--parc-milestones.html

computinghistory.org.uk/det/17020/ICL-PERQ-2-T1-Workstation

parc.com

thocp.net/hardware/xerox_star.htm

GUI

arstechnica.com/features/2005/05/gui

history-computer.com/ModernComputer/Software/Sketchpad.html

CPU chip

ARM PRocessor Evolution: Briining High Performance to Mobile Devices. Simon Segars EVP and GM, ARM 2011

wired.com/story/computex-2018-new-chips-qualcomm-amd-intel

Mouse

ideo.com/case-study/creating-the-first-usable-mouse

history-computer.com/ModernComputer/Basis/mouse.html

inc.com/betsy-mikel/the-designer-of-apples-first-mouse-displays-these-items-in-his-office-to-inspire-creativity.html

wired.com/2014/08/the-engineer-of-the-original-apple-mouse-talks-about-his-remarkable-career

First video game

popularmechanics.com/technology/g2711/most-popular-video-game-the-year-you-were-born

theawesomer.com/the-first-video-game/542459

Apple

cnet.com/pictures/the-complete-history-of-apples-ipod

fortune.com/company/apple

lifewire.com/history-ipod-classic-original-2000732

macworld.com/article/1163181/the-birth-of-the-ipod.html

macworld.co.uk/feature/apple/history-of-apple-steve-jobs-mac-3606104

moca.ncl.ac.uk/micros/index.htm#Macintosh

wired.com/story/apple-kills-itunes

Macintosh

9to5mac.com/2014/01/24/falling-in-love-with-the-macintosh-128k-back-in-1984

cnet.com/news/apples-original-mac-can-fetch-1598-on-ebay

cnet.com/news/the-macintosh-turns-30-going-the-distance

everymac.com/systems/apple/mac_classic/specs/mac_128k.html

ifixit.com/Teardown/Macintosh+128K+Teardown/21422

macworld.co.uk/feature/mac/mac-pro-vs-macintosh-128k-3597861

moca.ncl.ac.uk/micros/Macintosh.htm

support.apple.com/kb/SP186?locale=en_US

IBM

ibm.com/ibm/history/exhibits/pc25/pc25_birth.html

Microsoft

core.co.uk/blog/blog/history-microsoft-word

fortune.com/company/microsoft/fortune500

thoughtco.com/microsoft-history-of-a-computing-giant-1991140

Windows

computerhope.com/history/windows.htm

theguardian.com/technology/2014/oct/02/from-windows-1-to-windows-10-29-years-of-windows-evolution

theverge.com/2012/11/20/3671922/windows-1-0-microsoft-history-desktop-gracefully-failed

Hewlett-Packard

computerhistory.org/blog/50th-anniversary-of-the-hp-2116-minicomputer

en.wikipedia.org/wiki/HP_2100

hp9825.com/html/hp_2116.html

hpmuseum.net/display_item.php?hw=95

OS market share

https://netmarketshare.com/operating-system-market-share.aspx

Computer ownership

statista.com/statistics/184685/percentage-of-households-with-computer-in-the-united-states-since-1984

Moore's Law

appuals.com/largest-processor-ever-built-packs-1-2-trillion-transistors-leaves-top-end-intel-and-amd-cpus-and-gpus-behind

hackaday.com/2019/08/21/largest-chip-ever-holds-1-2-trillion-transistors

investopedia.com/terms/m/mooreslaw.asp

karlrupp.net/2018/02/42-years-of-microprocessor-trend-data

wiki2.org/en/Transistor_count

Transistor size

cmte.ieee.org/futuredirections/2019/03/13/tiniest-transistor-yet-2-5-nm

economist.com/science-and-technology/2020/07/18/a-new-material-helps-transistors-become-vanishingly-small

popularmechanics.com/technology/a23353/1nm-transistor-gate

Hard drive

backblaze.com/blog/history-hard-drives

computerhope.com/history/hdd.htm

pcworld.com/article/127105/article.html

thinkcomputers.org/the-history-of-the-hard-drive

SSD

arstechnica.com/information-technology/2012/06/inside-the-ssd-revolution-how-solid-state-disks-really-work/2

semiconductorstore.com/blog/2014/The-Development-and-History-of-Solid-State-Drives-SSDs/854

techwalla.com/articles/the-history-of-usb-flash-drives

Digital watch

pcmag.com/news/the-digital-watch-a-brief-history

wired.com/2015/03/tech-time-warp-week-1972-digital-watch-cost-car

LCD

Liquid Gold: The Story of Liquid Crystal Displays and the Creation of an Industry. Joseph A. Castellano, World Scientific Publishing Company 2005

cnet.com/news/led-vs-lcd-which-is-better

digitaltrends.com/home-theater/led-vs-lcd-tvs

eeexplore.ieee.org/document/6487587?reload=true

en.wikipedia.org/wiki/Liquid-crystal_display

en.wikipedia.org/wiki/File:Lcd-engineerguy.ogv

ethw.org/Milestones:Sharp_14-inch_Thin-Film-Transistor_Liquid-Crystal_Display_(TFT-LCD)_for_TV,_1988

Touchscreen

businessinsider.com/history-of-the-tablet-2013-5

Capacitive Sensing Made Easy, Part 1: An Introduction to Different Capacitive Sensing Technologies. Pushek Madaan and Priyadeep Kaur, Cypress Semiconductor Corp. 2012

electronics.howstuffworks.com/iphone2.htm

electronicproducts.com/touchscreens-large-and-small

en-touch.com/mutual-capacitance-vs-self-capacitance-touchscreen-technology en-touch.com/single-touch-vs-multi-touch-whats-the-difference

en.wikipedia.org/wiki/Apple_Newton

en.wikipedia.org/wiki/PLATO_(computer_system)

lorextechnology.com/self-serve/how-touch-screen-monitors-work/R-sc3100030

Touch Technology Brief: Projected Capacitive Technology. 3M Touch Systems, 3M Company 2013

wired.com/2013/08/remembering-the-apple-newtons-prophetic-failure-and-lasting-ideals/

Smartphone

businessinsider.com/worlds-first-smartphone-simon-launched-before-iphone-2015-6

nmsu.edu/~nex/ET255/final_project/f3

time.com/3137005/first-smartphone-ibm-simon

toucharcade.com/2008/07/07/under-the-hood-the-iphones-gaming-mettle

Smartphone usage

9to5mac.com/2020/01/28/apple-hits-1-5-billion-active-devices-with-80-of-recent-iphones-and-ipads-running-ios-13

gs.statcounter.com/os-market-share/mobile/worldwide

statista.com/statistics/271496/global-market-share-held-by-smartphone-vendors-since-4th-quarter-2009

theverge.com/2019/1/29/18202736/apple-devices-ios-earnings-q1-2019

Digital Data

Binary code:
convertbinary.com/alphabet

fortune.com/2016/04/30/google-claude-shannon-bit-inventor

purplemath.com/modules/numbbase.htm

ASCII:
ascii-world.wikidot.com/history

computinghistory.org.uk/det/5942/First-edition-of-the-ASCII-standard-was-published

differencebetween.net/technology/software-technology/difference-between-unicode-and-ascii

ethw.org/ASCII

historyofinformation.com/detail.php?id=803

API:
medium.com/@perrysetgo/what-exactly-is-an-api-69f36968a41f

mulesoft.com/resources/api/what-is-an-api

Programming

The Mathematical Theory of Communication. Claude E. Shannon, Warren Weaver, University of Illinois Press 1998

blogs.scientificamerican.com/cross-check/profile-of-claude-shannon-inventor-of-information-theory

fortune.com/2016/04/30/google-claude-shannon-bit-inventor

columbia.edu/cu/computinghistory/cards.html

computerhope.com/jargon/p/punccard.htm

Women in programming

insider.com/inventions-by-women-credited-to-men-2018-9

newyorker.com/tech/annals-of-technology/ada-lovelace-the-first-tech-visionary

npr.org/2020/02/24/517784975/katherine-johnson-nasa-mathematician-and-an-inspiration-for-hidden-figures-dies

nytimes.com/2017/06/04/technology/obituary-jean-sammet-software-designer-cobol.html

Digital audio

adorama.com/alc/analog-vs-digital-audio-whats-the-difference

blogs.scientificamerican.com/observations/which-sounds-better-analog-or-digital-music

chnm.gmu.edu/digitalhistory/digitizing/6.php

Digital camera

A Comprehensive Beginner's Guide to Photography, Second Edition. Scott G. Shelp, Selective Focus Press 2006

astropix.com/html/i_astrop/how.html

av.jpn.support.panasonic.com/support/global/cs/dsc/knowhow/knowhow27.html

en.wikipedia.org/wiki/CMOS

explainthatstuff.com/webcams.html

thephoblographer.com/2014/04/17/back-1991-nasa-used-hacked-nikon-f3-kodak-digital-back-space

thinklucid.com/tech-briefs/understanding-digital-image-sensors

thoughtco.com/history-of-the-digital-camera-4070938

zdnet.com/pictures/digital-photography-in-1991-photos/2

Word processor

computernostalgia.net/articles/HistoryofWordProcessors.htm

Digital prepress

prepressure.com/prepress/history

Digital design

arstechnica.com/information-technology/2014/01/quarkxpress-the-demise-of-a-design-desk-darling

ccjk.com/language-translation/quarkxpress-qxp-translation/history-of-quarkxpress

en.wikipedia.org/wiki/Adobe_Photoshop

siliconvalleyhistorical.org/adobe-corporation-history

Scanner

history-computer.com/ModernComputer/Basis/scanner.html

Camera phone

bhphotovideo.com/explora/photography/features/camera-phone-20-years-old

digitaltrends.com/mobile/camera-phone-history

tigermobiles.com/evolution/#fifthPhone

Digital movie

mentalfloss.com/article/55429/11-movies-shaped-digital-revolution

The Triumph of Digital Will Be the Death of Many Movies. Helen Alexander and Rhys Blakely, New Republic, Sept. 12, 2014

CGI

computeranimationhistory-cgi.jimdofree.com

vashivisuals.com/the-ultimate-history-of-cgi-movies

Quantum computing

sciencealert.com/new-chip-promises-to-bridge-the-gap-between-classical-and-quantum-computing

wired.com/story/wired-guide-to-quantum-computing

Internet

Internet history

darpa.mil

hpe.com/us/en/insights/articles/the-real-history-of-the-modern-internet-1801.html

internetsociety.org/internet/history-internet/brief-history-internet

spokesman.com/stories/2020/jun/22/history-world-wide-web

theconversation.com/au/topics/how-the-internet-was-born-32844

theconversation.com/how-the-internet-was-born-from-the-arpanet-to-the-internet-68072

Tim Berners-Lee

en.wikipedia.org/wiki/Solid_(web_decentralization_project)

en.wikipedia.org/wiki/Tim_Berners-Lee

w3.org/People/Berners-Lee

Predictions

paleofuture.gizmodo.com/early-predictions-of-the-internet-date-back-to-19th-cen-1831319970

webafrica.co.za/blog/general-knowledge/7-science-fiction-stories-that-predicted-the-internet-and-how-we-use-it

DNS

cloudns.net/blog/dns-history-creation-first

en.wikipedia.org/wiki/Domain_Name_System

URL

blog.cloudflare.com/the-history-of-the-url

personalpages.manchester.ac.uk/staff/m.dodge/cybergeography/atlas

Modems

en.wikipedia.org/wiki/Hayes_Microcomputer_Products

history-computer.com/ModernComputer/Basis/modem.html

whirlpool.net.au/wiki/d_u_m_h

First BBS

chinet.com/html/cbbs.html

en.wikipedia.org/wiki/CBBS

theatlantic.com/technology/archive/2016/11/the-lost-civilization-of-dial-up-bulletin-board-systems/506465

Browser

A Singular Moment in Time. T. Scott Plutchak, Journal of the Medical Library Association April 2004

mozilla.org/en-US

ncsa.illinois.edu/enabling/mosaic

zdnet.com/article/mosaics-birthday-25-years-of-the-modern-web

zdnet.com/article/the-beginning-of-the-peoples-web-20-years-of-netscape

User data

internetworldstats.com/stats.htm

internetworldstats.com/top20.htm

itu.int/en/ITU-D/Statistics/Pages/stat/default.aspx

itu.int/pub/D-IND-WTDR

ourworldindata.org/internet

statista.com/topics/1145/internet-usage-worldwide

statista.com/statistics/217348/us-broadband-internet-susbcribers-by-cable-provider

statista.com/statistics/264810/number-of-monthly-active-facebook-users-worldwide

statista.com/statistics/272014/global-social-networks-ranked-by-number-of-users

statista.com/statistics/617136/digital-population-worldwide

worldbank.org/indicator/IT.NET.USER.ZS

Cable

calcable.org/learn/history-of-cable

en.wikipedia.org/wiki/Internet_access

Websites

spokesman.com/stories/2020/apr/23/youtube-and-seven-internet-icons-their-beginnings

Online newspapers

content.time.com/time/business/article/0,8599,2045682,00.html

poynter.org/archive/2004/new-media-timeline-1980

poynter.org/reporting-editing/2014/today-in-media-history-compuserve-and-the-first-online-newspapers

twitter.com/JeremyLittau/status/1088503510184927233

Conclusion

tech giants

buzzfeednews.com/article/josephbernstein/in-the-2010s-decade-we-became-alienated-by-technology

nytimes.com/2020/07/31/technology/blocking-the-tech-giants.html

book publishing

datasets.socialhistory.org/dataset.xhtml

mashable.com/2010/08/05/number-of-books-in-the-world

ourworldindata.org/books

theifod.com/how-many-new-books-are-published-each-year-and-other-related-books-facts

Internet user data

alexa.com/topsites

fred.stlouisfed.org/series/ITNETUSERP2USA

freshysites.com/web-design-development/20-most-popular-websites-2020

gadgetsnow.com/slideshows/10-most-popular-websites-in-the-world/photolist/74077594.cms

hostingfacts.com/internet-facts-stats

internetlivestats.com/total-number-of-websites

netcraft.com/active-sites

moz.com/top500

news.netcraft.com/archives/category/web-server-survey

oberlo.com/statistics/most-visited-websites

siteefy.com/how-many-websites-are-there

statista.com/chart/19058/how-many-websites-are-there

statista.com/statistics/276445/number-of-internet-users-in-the-united-states

weforum.org/agenda/2019/09/chart-of-the-day-how-many-websites-are-there

Social change

Empathy and the Novel. Suzanne Keen, Oxford University Press 2010

How Was Life?: Global Well-being since 1820. J. van Zanden et al. OECD Publishing 2014

Leveling the Playing Field: The Democratization of Technology. Rod Scher, Rowman & Littlefield 2016

Revolutions in Communication: Media History from Gutenberg to the Digital Age. Bill Kovarik, Bloomsbury Academic 2011

The Information: A History, A Theory, A Flood. James Gleick, Vintage 2012